THE IDEA OF ORDER

HANS BARTH

THE IDEA OF ORDER

CONTRIBUTIONS TO A PHILOSOPHY

OF POLITICS

D. REIDEL PUBLISHING COMPANY

DORDRECHT - HOLLAND

DIE IDEE DER ORDNUNG

Beiträge zu einer politischen Philosophie

First published by Eugen Rentsch Verlag AG
Erlenbach-Zürich, Switzerland

Translated by Ernest W. Hankamer and William M. Newell

TABLE OF CONTENTS

TRANSLATORS' NOTE

It seems only fair to warn the reader that the style of this translation will occasionally seem somewhat rough and unpolished; this is true particularly of the first chapter of the present volume. Lack of smoothness is, of course, not desirable, but it is, in our opinion, preferable to alteration of meaning, particularly in a philosophical work, in which exactness is indispensable if the precision of the terminology is not to be impaired. We ask you to bear with us, because we think it worth your while.

One specific matter deserves separate mention. We have avoided footnotes wherever possible, at the cost of using several English words in a rather specialized, or perhaps better, Germanized meaning. Thus, the word *spiritual* is our rendering of *geistig*, which means *of the mind, of the intellect, of the spirit*, and implies a number of related nuances. Readers who have a command of German or French will probably recognize other translations of a similar nature.

Finally, a word of thanks to those friends and colleagues who have assisted us in our efforts. Miss Annette Kuhn, of Heidelberg, has rendered truly invaluable services throughout. Mr. Gustav Kemperdick, of Munich, has given us the benefit of his expert advice in the translation of the French passages in the book. And Miss Frauke Kelch, of Hamburg, has made many helpful suggestions and has been of great assistance in the arduous task of correcting and proofreading the text. Needless to say, for the shortcomings that remain we alone are responsible.

E. W. HANKAMER

W. M. NEWELL

Munich, Germany, March, 1960

INTRODUCTION

In these essays toward a political philosophy we shall be concerned with fundamentals. And because it is a question of fundamentals, they will, we imagine, be of interest to many readers. We should like to contribute to a clarification, historically and systematically, of some concepts with which every philosophy of society and the state has to deal. We shall admit historical considerations for the sake of insights into the systematic ones, and we trust that our inquiry into the systematic will help us to understand the historical. For we are moving in that circle exemplarily described by Johann Gustav Droysen in his *Vorlesungen über Enzyklopädie und Methodologie der Geschichte* (§ 37) when he writes: 'Undoubtedly we only understand completely that which is, when we recognize and make clear to ourselves how it came to be. But how it came to be, we recognize only if we investigate and understand, as exactly as possible, how it is. Our grasping that which came to be and comprehending its becoming is only one form and expression of our understanding of the present and existing. And this becoming and having come to be can be derived only by temporally conceiving and analysing the existing in order to understand it.' We must, therefore, center our attention on what may be called the structure and logic of social order. Three things appear necessarily to belong to a doctrine of communal and social organization: the problem of consensus and loyalty, the problem of sanctions in the broadest sense of the term, and the problem of authority and its hierarchy. Every doctrine of social order must deal with dynamic processes, with unavoidable and possible conflicts. Only by calling upon intellectual history can we present the immanent structural principles of order. And only if we succeed in asking history meaningful questions, starting from the logic of order and the necessary interplay of its essential elements, will history give us clarifying answers.

I

Some short mention must be made of an assumption with which we believe we must begin. A political philosophy must necessarily contain a doctrine of truth. Or to put it more precisely: we may under no circumstances fail to take into consideration that every political theory absolutely depends on a theory of truth whether it makes it explicit or not. As a basis for a program of action, it always conceals a theory of truth. In justifying any given type of state, to mention just one example, we must know of whom the recognition of truth in a social body may be expected, and under what conditions it may be possible. The problem of authority in social and political reality is inextricably tied up with the problem of knowledge. Conversely, whatever the doctrine of truth may be, it has certain inevitable and determinable consequences for political theory. Philosophical investigations concerning the possibility and range of true human knowledge directly affect the sphere of social life. In other words, the difference between an absolute and a relative theory of truth is not only a problem of philosophy; rather, this difference is of decisive, constitutive importance in establishing institutions which form the public will. Man has always justified unlimited coercion by rightly or wrongly assuming and monopolizing the possession of some absolute truth. And obviously all those political theories which prepare and foster revolutions, and subsequently justify them, are very closely associated with theories of truth.

We have said that these essays deal with fundamentals. It appears that mankind, whose already highly artificial life is determined by a universal, highly differentiated technical development and whose culture and civilization cannot keep pace with this rapid technical progress, can only be brought to a reconsideration of fundamentals by unusually strong inner or outer pressures. We are undoubtedly exposed to such pressures and thus beset by those questions which pertain to the conditions of communal order. Giambatista Vico's work concerning the one source and one end of law best explains what we mean. In the 51st chapter of *De uno universi iuris principio et fine uno liber unus,* published in 1720, he summarizes our argument.

For Vico, who is in the tradition of Roman law and Roman political philosophy, society is founded on truth. The basic demand that all action must be *bona fide,* that is, in good faith, and based on mutual trust, can be expressed as the commandment of living in and by the truth. The 'law of society' assumes two forms. This *lex societatis,* whose two imperatives are *ex bona fide agito* and *ex vero vivito,* constitutes for Vico natural law. Cicero maintains in *De officiis* (I, 7) that *fides,* that is, reliability and truthfulness in word and promise, is the basis of justice. But since truthfulness in word includes keeping one's word, Vico holds that Cicero should have held truth itself, the mother of faithfulness and all other virtues, to be the basis of justice. *Veritas dicti, veriloquium, veritas facti,* and *gestio rei sine dolo* (doing something without evil intent) – these constitute the essence of natural law for Vico, as they did, according to him, for Roman law. Of course, the assertion that truth is the basis of justice and thus of society does not make the real and inevitable problem of its recognition irrelevant. The commandment to live in and by the truth can only be fulfilled by remaining aware of precisely this problem of the knowledge of truth.

CHAPTER ONE

PHILOSOPHY AND POLITICS

I

It would not be surprising if our deliberate suggestion, indeed, our intentional insistence that there is a connection between the words philosophy and politics were to evoke suspicion and dissent. Philosophy and politics – this combination gives the impression that the hard-won and carefully nurtured separation of the academic and political platforms is threatened with extinction. This suspicion is based on the supposedly indisputable fact that, by origin and nature, philosophy is concerned with knowing, politics with acting. As Goethe said, the active man is always unscrupulous and recognizes no law other than that of success, whereas the philosopher admits of no law other than that of truth and consequently will not let himself be concerned with any practical results. The disregard of the vital laws of these two forms of human existence would lead to an ominous mixture out of which would be born the absurdity of a political philosophy or the nonsense of philosophical politics, and thus the beginning of the end of autonomous philosophy and purposeful politics.

To mention philosophy and politics in the same breath is to reassert philosophy's basic interest in politics and politics' fundamental concern with philosophy. Philosophy's interest in politics, that is, in the state and its activities in the broadest sense of these terms, is not difficult to understand, for it is nothing more than a manifestation of philosophy's perpetual desire to know what is. Philosophy and politics are thus related by the very fact that philosophy sees the state and political action as objects of knowledge. But what about politics' concern with philosophy? The answer to this question presupposes a definition of the concept of political action. Political action unfolds in the relationship between means and ends; it is meaningful action directed towards the attainment of certain goals. Granted that the goals of political action arise from the inherent needs of the social structure, in fact, even supposing that the self-assertion of society were *the* goal of political action, it would nonetheless remain true that this goal is but one among many possible goals of human life and that its realization must compete with that of others. But assuming a plurality of goals, who is to determine the goal of some concrete political action? Who is to coordinate various possible goals, fix their hierarchical order, or select some rather than others?

Indeed, political action cannot be described merely as purposeful or meaningful action. The conditions which owe their origin and constitution to human nature and activity are never content simply to exist and be as they are. The existence of the conditions of social life is never an end in itself, but strives beyond itself because it is in need of completion. It demands justification of its factuality, it seeks legitimation. Factuality requires philosophical foundation. Without this foundation it lacks the guarantee of stability. The defense of a merely factual, existing order has always been felt to be precarious. Only a well-founded order is an accepted and thus a binding order. This becomes clear when we consider the ultimate motive of political action. Political action is always an unfolding of power ranging from psychological influence to sanction by force. Its fundamental orientation is in the idea of the accumulation of power; it uses this power to realize certain goals and further to create and secure such institutions as serve to protect power. If we understand power, with Max Weber, as the opportunity of asserting one's will, the necessity of justifying the subjugation or elimination of another will becomes apparent. In society, the use of naked force is an extreme case. Usually, power rules, or at least tries to rule, as justified power. What we must remember is this: social order, even though it owes its origin and concrete form to struggles for power, always presupposes some

6

kind of justification and legitimation. The same holds true for political action. But who provides the required justification for political action? This question, too, we prefer to leave open for the moment. The history of Western philosophy supports the assertion that philosophy has always considered the state and political action two of the primary objects of knowledge. But this is no definition of philosophy; philosophy wants to do more and does more. It has always provided a philosophical justification for political action, and assumed the function of legitimating it. It laid claim to the realm of legislation in the sense that it determines what should be and legitimizes the means to be used. It justified that which is, or, by refusing to sanction that which is, exposed it to change. The philosophical foundation of political order and the legitimation of the use of power on the part of the state is the concern of those works of political philosophy connected with the illustrious names of Plato and Augustine, Thomas Aquinas and Nicolas of Cusa, Hobbes and Spinoza, Locke and Hume, Rousseau and Pestalozzi, Kant and Hegel, Marx, Comte and John Stuart Mill. Philosophy has an ideological function. That is its greatness and its danger.

But this description of the relationship between philosophy and politics is inadequate. Every social structure requires a minimum of cohesive forces. The body politic is fundamentally concerned with unity and solidarity, and expends no small part of its energies in integrating the individual forces within it. The legitimation of order plays an important rôle in unifying society, along with such factors as a common historical destiny, manners and customs, religion and language. The legitimating factors themselves come to be experienced as an integrating element of social unity. For political power aspires to a philosophical justification of its function; it is dependent upon legitimation. And every challenge of this legitimation of political action is interpreted as an attack on the community itself. But what does the possibility of such a challenge mean in terms of the function of philosophy within the social structure? What happens when philosophy attempts to replace the old order with a new one? We then have one philosophical justification against another, one legitimation opposed to another; but the accepted one is one of the unifying factors of the political community and thus equipped with the means to protect itself. The result is a conflict. The ideological function of philosophy has changed to a critical one.

2

We now raise the question whether there is a concept which can reveal the common structure of philosophy and politics. We believe this concept to be the idea of *Prozess*.* Philosophy and politics are agreed that they are a *Prozess,* that is, a process in the sense of a movement of thought and of life, and a trial in the sense of court proceedings. It may seem strange and unjustified to employ a legal concept in a philosophical and political context. Neither politics nor philosophy seem to have anything to do with the concept of *Prozess*. Nowhere is there such injustice as in politics; and what does philosophy's search for the truth have in common with a court trial? To allay this doubt, we need only point out that philosophy has always used images to clarify the meaning and purpose of its efforts. If one were to exclude, for example, the symbolism of light from the history of philosophy, one could not understand some of its most important achievements. Philosophy and philosophical mysticism make use of all degrees of the intensity and diffusion of light in order to express the otherwise inexpressible, from a mere spark to a shining sea of brightness in which there is no more distinguishing and therefore no more knowledge. But we can go a step further. Western culture conceives of man's nature in terms of *Prozess*. Western philosophy of history is based on the ideas of the kingdom of God and of the final judgement, ideas which permeate Western thinking in many forms, some of them unrecognizably transfigured, and give it its curious and

* Trans. note: The German word *Prozess* means both 'process' and 'court trial' and is here used in both senses.

8

impressive unity. According to the Old Testament, God, who sees all that is hidden, will judge all notions before His tribunal, and has placed our deepest secrets in the light of His countenance. The deepest secret is our heart, which, as Jeremiah says, is inscrutable and can only be fathomed by God, so that not man, but only God, is competent to judge it. And, finally, have not the two exemplary trials of Socrates and Jesus influenced philosophic and religious thinking decisively to the present day? One could argue that we are using evidence which stems primarily from the Old and New Testament and consequently does not apply to philosophy. Then let us turn to philosophy. Whoever tries to understand Kant's work will notice that he liked to characterize his achievement within the history of philosophy in terms of jurisprudence. Kant considered concepts and institutions from the realm of law to be the analogies best suited to explain his philosophy and its specific purpose. Kant conceives the definition of the limits of reason as a problem of the competence of reason. His philosophy rests on the insight that every philosophy builds on the ruins of another. In the lectures on logic, Kant said that no work has ever endured in its entirety. 'Therefore one cannot learn philosophy because it does not exist.' The critique of reason begins with the question why there are only ruins of philosophies, and no philosophy. And its task is to investigate what reason can accomplish, given its constitution. Kant is primarily concerned not with the *quaestio facti,* but with the *quaestio juris.* Neither the existence of, nor the need for, metaphysics can be denied. Confronted with nothing but contradictory metaphysical assertions, Kant examines their claims for the purpose of establishing a metaphysics in the form of a system of necessary and general statements which have their justification in the jurisdiction of reason itself. Reason is, in his own words, made the supreme court. Kant compares the various philosophical schools to parties, and the differences between systems are for him a matter for adjudication. Reason has the function of an 'appointed judge who compels the witnesses to answer questions which he puts to them', it must determine who is in the right

9

and keep the parties peaceful. In the preface to the first edition of the *Critique of Pure Reason*, Kant says that reason must 'assume the most difficult of its duties, that of self-knowledge'. For, he continues, it is called upon 'to establish a court of law which would secure reason's own just claims, but which would reject all unfounded pretensions not by arbitrary decree but by its eternal and unchanging laws'. Reason is accuser and accused, law and judge in one.

This tribunal is none other than the critique of pure reason. Reason not only claims a legislative function for the realm of moral action, but also is the authority which, by virtue of its self-knowledge, determines once and for all its own competence in the field of the scientific knowledge of nature and religion. The claim of reason to being a court of law means that the differences between religious creeds are resolved in one religion of reason, as well as that the rationality, that is, the legitimacy of the positive legal order is subject to the examination of this court. Kant's work is filled with the spirit, and motivated by the purpose, of arbitration, specifically with respect to the structure, stability and prosperity of the state. It is an unpardonable mistake to overlook the basic political intent of Kant's critical philosophy. Defining reason as a court of law has two consequences. The first concerns theology and the philosophical schools, the second the relationship between philosophy and the community. In its judicial capacity, reason can establish peace among religious creeds and settle the argument between philosophical scepticism and philosophical dogmatism. One can easily recognize the eminently political function of the tribunal of reason when one considers that religious, theological and philosophical differences can seriously threaten the unity of the community by leading to civil wars. 'At the beginning,' writes Kant, 'the rule of metaphysics, under the administration of the dogmatists, was despotic. However, because the administration still had a trace of the old barbarism in it, it gradually degenerated through inner wars into total anarchy, and the sceptics, a kind of nomads who despise the steady cultivation of the soil, from time to time dissolved the civil unity.' The political mission of reason consists in effectively combating despotism and anarchy, both of which stem from an unjustified and dangerous use of this very reason.

We find the idea that philosophy is a court trial in Hegel's thinking perhaps even more strongly than in Kant's, but much more heavily laden with theological and metaphysical presuppositions. Hegel sees life itself as *Prozess*. This means, primarily, that the spirit places outside of itself what it in itself is, comprehends this manifestation as a necessary product of its nature, and returns to itself through this comprehension. It is part of the nature of the spirit 'to bring forth duality and disunion, and to contend with their contradiction'. The spirit is, by definition, totality, not alone inner totality but also the realization of the inner with and in the outer. If it exists only one-sidedly, only in the one form, it becomes involved in the contradiction of being by definition the whole, but in its existence only one of the two sides. 'To go through this process of contradiction and its resolution is the higher prerogative of living beings.' But Hegel's definition of the spirit as 'eternal life' and thus 'progress' means not only that the spirit is a *Prozess* in the sense of meaningful motion, but also that this *Prozess* represents a court trial. Philosophy of the spirit attains complete realization in the philosophy of history. History is the self-manifestation of the spirit, in the sense that every form in which the spirit incarnates itself is destroyed and dissolved by the spirit itself through a new manifestation. This destruction is not only an annihilation, but also a preservation * in that the spirit retains and transfigures the truth of each form which it eliminates. Every distinct form of the spirit is, precisely because it is a distinct form, also a temporal one. The spirit could not come to rest in any one distinct form, for it wants to manifest itself in its totality; therefore it must dissolve * the distinctive, temporal forms since they contain only a part of the whole, not the whole itself. But this *Aufheben* is also a judging. The two-

---

* The German word is *Aufheben*, the double meaning of which (to abolish, and, to preserve) constitutes an integral part of Hegel's argument.

fold meaning of *Prozess* attaches itself to the concept of *Aufheben*. Life is movement. Life is creating life and annihilating life. But in transcending itself and destroying a form of its own creation, life has posited a higher right against a lesser one, and overcome a limited truth with a more comprehensive one. Every part of the totality of the spirit is, in its temporal unfolding, at once valid and invalid: it is valid in relationship to the part it has superseded because it brings the spirit one step closer to its goal of self-knowledge; it is invalid in relationship to the totality of the spirit since it is only a part and not the whole. And since history itself is the expression of the spirit in its totality, in the sense that its parts are realized in time, so is the history of the world a *Prozess,* that is, a movement of life as well as a court of law. But since the proper objects of history are the spirits of the peoples united in states, history is the *Prozess* in which the rights of various peoples compete with each other so that the factual outcome of the struggle is, at the same time, the realization of the spirit itself. In the relationship between states, says Hegel, 'there is no praetor who arbitrates: the only higher praetor is the universal and self-contained spirit, the world spirit'. 'The principles of the spirits of the peoples are, because of their particularity, limited; by nature of this particularity, and as existing entities, they have their objective reality and their self-awareness. Their fates and deeds in their relationship to one another are the visible dialectic of the finiteness of these spirits; out of this dialectic, the universal spirit, the world spirit, emerges unlimited. And as the supreme judge, it passes sentence, ultimate sentence, on the particular spirits before the tribunal of world history.' [1] And Hegel quotes Schiller's *Resignation:* 'Die Weltgeschichte ist das Weltgericht' (world history is the final judgement).

3

We have asserted that philosophy and politics are alike in that they conceive of themselves as a trial. Such a trial involves a judge and the law which is applied by the judge or interpreted by him when it is incomplete, as if he were the lawmaker and acting in his spirit. The parties appear before the judge with their dispute. A decision must be reached on their claims. The judicial process includes the possibility of appeal in case the parties are of the considered opinion that justice has not been done them. Now, it is possible, on the one hand, to conceive of an endless chain of courts; on the other hand, it is important, in order to safeguard legal rights, that controversies not be left pending but be settled. Therefore there must be a court whose decision cannot be appealed. There must be a final authority beyond which there can be no recourse, which settles disputes finally and bindingly.

We have maintained that an analogy can be established between this description of legal proceedings on the one hand, and philosophy and politics on the other, for example in the philosophical investigation of truth on the basis of the examination of the competency of reason. Similarly, politics settles all its conflicts by means of the fiction that they are legal cases. Even if they can invoke their right to freedom of conscience and the right of rebellion, heretics and rebels, in terms of the positive order valid at the time, are not murdered but liquidated through legal proceedings. Being inseparably joined with politics, philosophy, in its function of establishing political order, comes into conflict with politics as established action whenever it denies its sanction to a prevailing order and is prepared to grant its sanction to a new one. For what happens when the idea of justice denies an order its legitimacy? It becomes evident that even in such a case philosophy and politics are inseparably joined. We are confronted with the ominous question: who is the final authority in this instance? When the established order, complete with means of self-protection by use of force, stands opposed to an order newly established or held worthy of being established, who is to interpret the decisions of this authority? On the 25th of November, 1648, Oliver Cromwell answered a letter from his friend, Colonel Robin Hammond. Hammond expressed concern about Cromwell's leading his army against the Parliament and against the king. 'Hammond simply could not convince himself of the view held by his more radical friends in the Army, that the smaller party has the lawful right, if its cause is just, to impose its will on the larger. For him, Paul's declared principle of the divine origin of authority constitutes a rejection of this view; in this case, therefore, it forbade both active and passive resistance against Parliament. Thus it appeared to him to be tempting God if the Army were now to rebel against it.'[2] Cromwell wishes to remove these scruples of conscience and make them ineffectual. He writes: 'Authorities and powers are the ordinance of God. This or that species is of human institution, and limited, some with larger, others with stricter bands, each one according to its constitution. I do not therefore think the authorities may do anything, and yet such obedience (be) due, but all agree there are cases in which it is lawful to resist. If so, your ground fails, and so likewise the interference. Indeed, dear Robin, not to multiply words, the query is, whether ours be such a case? This ingenuously is the true question.' This question Cromwell of course answers in the affirmative. And the right to opposition is based on the appeal to conscience which has to answer to God alone. Cromwell asks Hammond to sound out his own heart on two or three points: 'First, whether *Salus Populi* be a sound position? Secondly, whether in the way in hand, really and before the Lord, before whom conscience must stand, this be provided for, or the whole fruit of the war like to be frustrated, and all most like to turn to what it was, and worse? And this, contrary to engagements, declarations, implicit covenants with those who ventured their lives upon those covenants and engagements, without whom perhaps, in equity, relaxation ought not to be? Thirdly, whether this Army be not a lawful power, called by God to oppose and fight against the King upon some stated grounds; and being in power to such ends, may not oppose one name of authority, for those ends, as well as another, the outward authority that called them, not by their power making the quarrel lawful, but it being so in itself? If so it may be acting will be justified *in foro humano.* – But truly these kinds of reasonings may be but fleshly, either with or against: only it is good to try what truth may be in them. And the Lord teach us.' Cromwell continues: 'My dear friend, let us look into providences; surely they mean somewhat. They hang so together; have been so constant, so clear and unclouded. Malice, swoln malice against God's people, now called Saints, to root out their name; and yet they, by providence, having arms, and therein blessed with defence and more... Dear Robin, beware of men, look up to the Lord. Let Him be free to speak and command in thy heart. Take heed of the things I fear thou hast reasoned thyself into, and thou shalt be able through Him, without consulting flesh and blood, to do valiantly for Him and for His people.'

Cromwell's argument is significant because it seems to contain all the elements which we have encountered in the analysis of our philosophical-political complex of problems. This reference to a letter by Cromwell does illuminate the nature of the problem in question, but risks the objection that the argument, by moving into the realms of religion and theology, abandons the realm of philosophy. This objection disregards the fact that our problem remains, even if we eliminate the factor of the human interpretation of the will and reason of God. For anyone who opposes the old order with a new one and thus considers opposition to the existing, traditional order justified, can only do this by formulating the idea of the just and acting accordingly. An appeal to the idea of the just implies making two claims: first, to the right of determining the idea of the just in the given instance, and second, to the right of determining who is to be the authority responsible for its realization. Apparently, the decisive point lies in the fact that in every case in which legitimate systems of political order oppose one another — and they always insist on being legitimate, when they come into conflict — an arbitrating court of appeal is called upon and becomes itself an object of the conflict. For the question is not only how the idea of the just is to be determined in a specific instance, but also who is qualified to be the final authority. Or, as Cromwell put it, it is the question, first, whether an existing violation of the welfare of the people justifies opposition, and second, who is to decide how the welfare of the people can more adequately be served. One cannot avoid this problem by appealing to the idea of the just, for the idea itself decides nothing. It is, indeed, the standard, the norm, invoked when making a decision. But the realization of the just, and the decision to look for a new realization, can be carried out only by an individual person. The personal element cannot be eliminated. And this is, in the last analysis, what Plato meant when he placed the power of the rational ruler above the power of the laws. Decision is a matter for the individual. The decision realizes the idea, and thus is authoritative while remaining personal.

In the second *Treatise on Government,* Locke defines the concept of the prerogative as the permission given the ruler by the people to undertake various actions according to his own free choice when the law is silent, and occasionally even contrary to the clear letter of the law, if such actions serve the public welfare. Locke's concept of the prerogative also includes the consent of the people, once the necessary measures have been taken. Again in the case of the prerogative the old question must be asked: who shall be the judge whether or not the right use is made of this power? Locke answers that there can be no judge on earth between a permanent executive power which is in possession of such a prerogative, and a legislature which is dependent on the will of the executive for being called into session; similarly, there can be no judge between the legislature and the people if the executive or the legislature, after coming to power, should intend or undertake the enslavement or ruin of the people. In this case, as in all others where there is no earthly judge, there is no recourse but to appeal for a decision from heaven. What is the decision of heaven? The right to meet force with force, the right to resist. But in whose hands rests the decision whether or not to make use of this right? Since the will of the people can only find articulation in the individuals that constitute it, the 'appeal to heaven' is left up to the individual person. If one does not accept this solution, the only possibility remaining is to settle the dispute between philosophy and the state

16

as Hobbes did. Hobbes employs theological concepts, which fact, however, makes no serious difference to the philosophical argument in question. Should there be differences concerning matters of faith, then, for the sake of public order and communal unity, final, authoritative and binding judgement may not be reserved for private reason and individual conscience but must be left to public reason. To be sure, Hobbes says, the private person is always free to believe what he wants to, for thought is free; but when his belief is given graphic or conceptual expression, private reason must bow to public reason. And what 'public reason' is, in the concrete case, is decided bindingly and authoritatively by God's governor on earth, that is, the state. It claims the right of final authority and thus is guilty of a usurpation which is not even permitted man, for whom the state is, after all, established.

One closing question remains to be considered. How should we conceive the relation of man to this final authority? There is no philosophical and no political problem which does not of necessity lead us back to the concept of the final authority, primarily because all conflicts – and we live in conflicts – demand a decision. The fact that man must conceive of a final authority does not make him this authority. He must accept his rôle as the interpreter of the final authority, and as such he shares its rank. But this rank necessarily remains precarious, because error, delusion and guilt can never be excluded. Man does have a definite relationship to a final authority just as he does to the idea of the unconditional. But the moment he tries to capture this thought, which he of necessity thinks, in image or concept, it loses its essence and becomes untrue. There is no guarantee that man can interpret the will of the final authority correctly and once and for all. And precisely because this is so, precisely because it is part of man's nature to exist within the tension between the conditional and the unconditional, he must safeguard his spiritual and political freedom, which determine and challenge each other, in order that the *Prozess* of life and thought remain an open one.

CHAPTER TWO

EDMUND BURKE
AND GERMAN POLITICAL PHILOSOPHY
IN THE AGE OF ROMANTICISM

I

English political philosophy reached undisputed, worldwide recognition three times in the 17th and 18th century, in the works of Thomas Hobbes, John Locke and Edmund Burke. The writings of these thinkers, who deserve the reputation of being statesmen of the first order, exerted an influence which was not restricted to the British Isles. Like mighty waves, the political insights and experiences, the great and vital principles of political order and leadership which Hobbes, Locke and Burke had made available to their compatriots, broke on the shores of the old and the new world. This influence has not ceased to the present day, although it was expressed in terms of a certain constellation of social forces in the British kingdom. The tremendous upheaval of the Western social structure which began – in Burke's words – like an earthquake in the age of the French Revolution has, to be sure, long since shaken and destroyed the social organization which forms the basis and supplies the standards of their thinking. There can be no question that Hobbes, Locke and Burke, in their views on the origin and meaning of the state, the nature of society, and the relationship of the individual to the state and to the social bonds in which alone he can really be said to become a man in the full sense of the word, achieved recognition for the material interests of certain social classes in a certain legal and political order. Their works contain an ideological foundation and justification of a certain political and social order resting upon the monarchy, the landed gentry and the propertied middle class. But is the only function of these writings that of an ideological justification? Are they merely the expression of an existing or desirable social constitution in which the play of opposing forces and ideas has culminated in a state of relative political stability? Why is it then that the after-effects of these works are to be felt with unparalleled force to the present day, although their political and social assumptions are by no means those of our age?

There is a limited number of problems which man in all ages has had to master and will have to solve. He must frequently reformulate his relationship to the state, to the family, to work, profession, property. And he must give a definite form to those feelings which he believes touch upon the secret of the origin and meaning of his and the world's existence. He is required – whether he wants to or not appears completely irrelevant – to bring these relationships into some kind of order. Human existence is defined by the inevitability of this demand. This demand is a compulsion, a necessity, but one which is directed at a free being. Man can respond to its challenge in one way or another, but in some way or other he must satisfy its claim on him. Given a measurable – because limited – number of 'natural' relationships in life, which demand a permanent, lawful order, one may surmise that the possibilities of solving the problems involved are also limited.

Hobbes, Locke and Burke represent such possibilities. One can make the individual radically and totally dependent on the state, as Hobbes did. The omnipotence of the state promises a solution of those eternal problems which determine the relationship of the individual to the state. The omnipotence of the state alone guarantees domestic peace. The state is the final authority in basic questions of faith, and its decisions must be accepted, at least outwardly, by the citizens within its domain. But one can also limit the function of the state to the protection of the citizens by arms and the law whereby the state assures men their 'natural rights' – above all, the right to life, liberty and estate. Natural law has undisputed precedence over that law which is merely the result of human contract. State and church are separated. The inevitable clashes of religious be-

liefs are allayed to the benefit of society through the idea of
toleration, since only God can know the human heart. This is
Locke's way. Finally, there is another conceivable possibility.
It consists, on the one hand, in taking the existing, historical
situation into account, consciously and completely, and, on
the other, in the attempt to determine the relationship of the
individual to the state in such a way that they are, from the
very beginning, conceived not as being in opposition to one
another but as representing a pre-established unity. That is
Burke's solution. It spans the tension between freedom and
restraint as the genuine poles with which every political philosophy has to deal. Since Burke never lost his sense for either
aspect, he could be claimed by opposing political ideologists
and philosophers; so the history of his profound and extensive
influence in the 18th and 19th centuries shows that he appeared
as the exemplary champion of political freedom to some, and
as the classical proponent of the subjugation of the individual
by the state to others. But since both of these interpretations
are unfounded, Burke had to submit to the reproach of inconsistency advanced not only by his contemporaries but also by
many readers of his works in the 19th century. It is no accident
that the validity of this reproach is denied, for good reasons,
by that statesman who determined the destiny of England in
her most difficult hour. Winston Churchill writes in his reflections concerning *Consistency in Politics*, included in the volume
Thoughts and Adventures : '[Burke's] *Thoughts on the Present Discon-
tents,* his writings and speeches on the conciliation of America,
form the main and lasting armoury of Liberal opinion throughout the English-speaking world. His *Letters on a Regicide Peace,*
and *Reflections on the French Revolution,* will continue to furnish
Conservatives for all time with the most formidable array of
opposing weapons. On the one hand he is revealed as a fore-
most apostle of Liberty, on the other as the redoubtable champion of Authority. But a charge of political inconsistency applied to this great life appears a mean and petty thing. History
easily discerns the reasons and forces which actuated him, and
the immense changes in the problems he was facing which

evoked from the same profound mind and sincere spirit these entirely contrary manifestations. His soul revolted against tyranny, whether it appeared in the aspect of a domineering Monarch and a corrupt Court and Parliamentary system, or whether, mouthing the watch-words of a non-existent liberty, it towered up against him in the dictation of a brutal mob and wicked sect. No one can read the Burke of Liberty and the Burke of Authority without feeling that here was the same man pursuing the same ends, seeking the same ideals of society and Government, and defending them from assaults, now from one extreme, now from the other. The same danger approached the same man from different directions and in different forms, and the same man turned to face it with incomparable weapons, drawn from the same armoury, used in a different quarter, but for the same purpose.'

2

To make apparent the influence of the English political philosophy on German political thought in the age of romanticism and of the wars of independence against French imperialism, we need only describe the effects of a single book.[1] This book was nothing but a work written *ad hoc* for a specific political situation and purpose. The *Reflections on the Revolution in France and on the proceedings in certain societies in London relative to that event in a letter intended to have been sent to a gentleman in Paris* are the work of that famous member of the House of Commons and celebrated orator, Edmund Burke. It is based on the observation that a considerable number of the nation's spiritual leaders, but also important members of his own party, the Whigs, viewed the revolutionary struggles in France and the ideas which stood behind them with sympathy. Particularly the comparison of the revolution of 1789 with the 'Glorious Revolution' of 1688 was widespread and popular in London. It appeared as though the events in France were a matter of the old established social classes demanding that the rights denied them by an absolute monarchy be returned to them. Burke's *Reflections*, which appeared in November, 1790, are the expression of vehement and brilliant dissent. In the realm of letters, together with Rivarol's critical articles in the *Journal politique et historique*, which were collected and published in book form as the *Tableau historique et politique de l'Assemblée constituante* in 1797, they begin the fight against the French Revolution on the basis of fundamental political and philosophical considerations. For this fight, they provided the intellectual arms with such thoroughness and precision that all the anti-revolutionists in England and France, in Germany and in Spain had only to avail themselves of this arsenal and employ it in their various campaigns. The only thing that was added later was the re-establishment of the idea of the theocratic state, which served as the basis for the entire complex of the political and spiritual restoration. But were the *Reflections* merely a political pamphlet concerned only with denouncing a political and social movement in a foreign land? Did they contain only a critique of the events in France and more particularly in its capital? Certainly, the fame of its author was secured by the fact that his prognostications were confirmed by the course of events; no one could fail to see later that the transition to the dictatorship of a successful general, accompanied by the elimination of all abstract human rights, had been predicted with great accuracy. But would this book have had such unprecedented success if it had restricted itself solely to the defense of the existing situation and to the guarded anticipations of the future? Admitted: it was a defense. For Burke could not very well imagine a better constitution than the one which England had given itself in its struggles against the absolutism of the Stuarts and which seemed to consist in a wise balance of monarchical, aristocratic and democratic institutions, in a 'mixed and tempered government' that would not admit of extreme solutions in any direction. But it is no less certain that Burke did not stop with mere defense. For in coming to terms with new political ideas and forms that threaten the traditional state of affairs, it has been shown repeatedly that mere defense of the *status quo* is denied decisive success. If this defense does not contain new and vigorous intellectual impulses and insights which make it possible to justify the maintenance of the existing order against the onslaught of revolutionary ideas through more profound insights into the historical and social context, it will ultimately remain ineffective. It is wrong to view Burke exclusively as a statesman and a political philosopher of conservatism. To be sure, his was a spirit of preservation. 'If I cannot reform with equity, I will not reform at all.' But: 'When the reason of old establishments is gone, it is absurd to preserve nothing but the burden of them.' And thus he, the defender of moderation – 'no excess is good' – sums up in the *Reflections* his attitude toward the problem of inertia and change in the political world in this way: 'A disposition to preserve, and an ability to improve, taken together, would be my standard of a Statesman. Every thing else is vulgar in conception, periculous in execution.'[2]

The *Reflections on the Revolution in France* owe their triumphal progress through the continent above all to the circumstance that they managed to oppose to the political and philosophical assumptions of the French Revolution – that is, to the rationalistic and individualistic natural rights doctrine of the 18th century – a conception of the state and of social groups which was capable of convincing and even stirring Burke's contemporaries. New in this work was the recognition of the dignity of history, of tradition and of time, the evocation of the power of the heart on which the social structures are essentially founded, and the insight into the fundamental condition of man as a political and social being. This was the message of the *Reflections;* in this new conception of the nature of the state rests the secret of their effectiveness. But the mere opposition to revolution alone would not have raised Burke to a political philosopher of the first order. His importance lies rather in his insight into the structure of human societies. It is this fact that is expressed in Novalis' notable aphorism: 'Many anti-revolutionary books have been written for the Revolution. But Burke has written a revolutionary book against the Revolution.'[3]

This book was revolutionary because it brought new ideas, of which men until then had had only a vague presentiment, into the bright light of consciousness. But it cannot be denied that in France, and particularly in Germany, the way had been well prepared for a favorable reception of this book.

3

A survey of the influence of Burke's thinking in Germany can be made in one or two ways. One possibility is to take an inventory of all the evidence which points to direct or indirect contact with Burke's ideas. The first observation then would be that the kingdom of Hannover – at that time in political union with England – was the first cell in which Burke was well known and revered. The Hannoverian officials and political writers, Ernst Brandes and August Rehberg, were in touch with Burke even before 1790.[4] Particularly the confidential secretary of the chancellory, Rehberg, a friend of Baron von Stein from his youth, was indebted to Burke for important insights and strong support in his fight against the Revolution. His *Untersuchungen über die Französische Revolution* in two volumes, appeared in 1793. Stein himself often admitted to having been deeply and lastingly influenced by Burke. Along with Montesquieu, Justus Möser and Herder, Burke plays a decisive rôle in the development of Stein's ideas on the state and on reform.[5] Nothing is more indicative of Stein's character and views than his praise of Burke. 'This great, experienced and noble statesman defended with vigor and transporting eloquence the cause of civil and religious freedom in his immortal work *Reflections on the Revolution in France* against the metapolitical innovators who were laying France waste.'[6] The cause of civil and religious freedom – it was this that Stein aspired to for Germany as well. Since Stein's criticism of 18th century philosophy is based on a clearly articulated moral criterion, he must have felt strong bonds with a position which anchored political order and civil liberties in firm moral views and religious principles. He found both in Burke, who writes in the *Reflections:* 'All other nations have begun the fabric of a new government, or the reformation of an old, by establishing originally, or by enforcing with greater exactness, some rites or other of religion. All other

24

people have laid the foundations of civil freedom in severer manners, and a system of a more austere and masculine morality.' Stein's history of the period preceding the revolution and of the first decade of the revolution itself, written in exile, deals not only with the political and economic aspects of the subject; rather, it is concerned with an extensive critical analysis of the political and religious philosophy of the Enlightenment, which shows that Stein – whose views on ethics and history necessarily led to an emphasis of these points – appreciated Burke's opinions as welcome allies in the front against the common enemy. In addition they shared many principles concerning the institutional structure of the state. The idea of local self-government which educates the citizen to take an active and responsible part in public affairs; the idea of the responsibility of ministers to the parliament; an open aristocracy, defended so vigorously by Burke, which lends stability to the leadership of the state through ownership of land; the idea of freedom, not as a rational right of man but as a system of privileges distributed according to classes; the right of the people to resistance against unjustified tyranny as *ultima ratio;* and finally, Burke's foundation of the state on God's will, and his sense for the right and dignity of the historical tradition, the glory of the past, particularly of the chivalrous and Christian Middle Ages – these were the characteristics of the *Reflections* which appealed to Stein, and confirmed or brought to full expression his own views.

Stein's later colleague, who was asked by the Baron to enter the Prussian government, was Berthold Georg Niebuhr, the historian of Rome, a Dane by birth, and a German by choice. As a politician and as a man of letters, he, too, credited Burke with the advancement and confirmation of his own political aims. In the foreword to the second edition of his *Römische Geschichte* (1827) he says: 'There are no principles of political judgement which are not to be found in Montesquieu or Burke.' Niebuhr's political articles from the years 1814 and 1815, and above all his lectures on *Die Geschichte des Zeitalters der Revolution* which he held at the University of Bonn in 1829 and which were published posthumously, clearly show the influence of the 'profound thinker Burke'.[7] Niebuhr, too, is most impressed by Burke's ideas on the political structure of the state. They are essentially the same as those which attracted Stein to the English constitution and to its champion, Burke. Niebuhr found a splendid confirmation of these ideas in the history of the Roman republic, which was his great passion. The necessity of an open aristocracy which renewed itself by the admission to its ranks of vigorous and capable citizens and which, secure through its material independence, assumed the responsible leadership of the state in the interest of the general public; the proportional participation of all classes of working people and property owners in the affairs of the state and the formation of the public will; the political primacy of landownership over ownership of mobile goods; the protection of personal freedom and integrity – these were the ideas for whose rightness and proven strength Niebuhr found an example in the history of the Roman republic, ideas which had been realized in the English constitution and praised by Burke. His work is shot through with references to his own time. Niebuhr made the events in Rome understandable by comparing and explaining them in terms of events in modern history. For him, the first centuries of the Roman republic, up to the legal code of Licinius Stolo and Licinius Sextius, which brought the political equality of the plebeians with the patricians, represent the classical example of the rise of the people. 'The Romans of the good days of the republic,' he says in the introduction to his lectures at the University of Berlin, 'are the natural object of our admiration.'[8] Niebuhr's *Römische Geschichte* has not unjustly been called 'a historico-political textbook in the grand style',[9] because this historian, like Burke, was dominated by the idea of the right constitution. In modern times he saw England as the positive, France as the negative example of the idea. One is justified in saying that both Niebuhr and Burke are Platonists – the one, insofar as he speaks of the state as a 'divine idea' of which the real historical state represents 'an imperfect approximation of the eternal divine rule', the other, insofar as he

26

seeks in English history the idea of the English state, for him the idea of the state in general.

Whoever speaks of Niebuhr must think of Savigny. These two men, whose lifework centered on Rome and its laws, were, through personal liking and common professional interests, good friends from 1810 on. The question should be asked whether the founder of the historical school of law is not indebted to Burke as well as to Herder for the discovery of the historical principle. Friedrich Karl von Savigny's letters contain no mention of the English thinker. One would have to clarify whether any of Burke's thoughts are indirectly expressed in the famous program of the historical school, *Vom Beruf unserer Zeit für Gesetzgebung und Rechtswissenschaft* (1814), and particularly in the introductory contribution to the *Zeitschrift für geschichtliche Rechtswissenschaft* (1815). In view of the genuine and comprehensive culture of the leading representatives of the period, in view of the ubiquity of each individual mind and the intensive exchange of thoughts and impressions which was the vital element of these high-minded men – we need only think of Niebuhr's journals, of Savigny's letters, of the letters of the two Schlegels, and many more – we can assume that Savigny knew of Burke at least by hearsay. An indirect connection between Savigny and Burke is given in Rehberg's book *Über den Code Napoléon* (1814) to which the program of the historical school of law explicitly refers. Rehberg, thoroughly acquainted with Burke, shows that the law develops slowly by adapting itself to geographical and temporal conditions, and appears as the essence of accumulated tradition at every given point in time in the history of a nation. The Code Napoléon, although it claimed to be the codification of pure rational law, did not, according to Rehberg, cut itself off from traditional French law and custom. These are thoughts which could well be reconciled with Burke's insights. For they betray the same aversion to, or better, the same hate of the unhistorical, abstract principles of rational, intellectual law which is clearly discernible in *The Reflections*. Further, they reveal the sense for the traditional, the habitual, the geographically and temporally conditioned and singular which will not submit to a generalized rule, the sense for time, whose might creates right, and for what Burke calls prescription, which seems to him the surest safeguard for property and the state as the protector of property. But Rehberg's argument is also in agreement with Savigny's teachings, which has led to the conjecture that Savigny received 'direct inspiration' from Rehberg in the formation of his basic ideas.[10] In this connection, an elegant passage from the article with which Savigny launched the *Zeitschrift für geschichtliche Rechtswissenschaft* deserves attention. It reads: 'According to the others (the historical school) there is no completely single and separate human existence; rather, that which can be seen as single is seen, from another side, part of a higher whole. Thus must the individual man necessarily be seen simultaneously as a member of a family, a people, and a state – and every age of a people as the continuation and development of all previous ages. But if this is so, then every age does not bring forth its world, arbitrarily and for itself; it does so in an insoluble communion with the entire past.'[11] The recognition that man can truly be man only as member of a family, of a state, of the human race is one of those favorite notions of Burke upon which his fame is founded. Who had praised more emphatically than he the 'wisdom of the species'? To whom would 'reference to antiquity' have appeared a principle not only of superior political leadership but also of prudent lawgiving according to the demands of circumstance? Could not Savigny, just as well as Burke, have written that the science of law is 'the collected reason of the ages, combining the principles of original justice with the infinite variety of human concerns'?[12] Had not Burke, to everyone's enormous relief at being delivered from the natural-rights doctrine of the social contract, termed the state a community whose goals could be reached only through the labor of generations and is thus a partnership not only of the living but one of those who are living, those who are dead, and those who are to be born?[13] In this community, Burke says, necessity reigns – a necessity which is not chosen, but chooses, a necessity which admits of no discussion and is above all debate. This life of the dead inspires respect and awe for the past. This awe for that which has been and continues to be felt is also the basis of the responsibility of the living for those yet to come. For the coming generations are included in the life and considerations of the living ones. 'The great mysterious corporation of the human race,' Burke therefore says at one point, 'at one time, is never old, or middleaged, or young, but in a condition of unchangeable constancy, moves on through the varied tenour of perpetual decay, fall, renovation, and progression.'[14]

The comparison of Burke's thought with Savigny's cannot be taken as definite proof that Savigny literally thought of Burke while he was occupied with formulating the fruitful basic ideas of the historical school of law. Nevertheless there is an undeniable resemblance in their way of thinking.

In the classical German philosophy of the period of the French Revolution and the wars of liberation there are no traces of Burke's spirit to be found. Neither Fichte nor Hegel enter into a discussion with him.[15] But we must remember that Wilhelm von Humboldt was deeply impressed by the Gentz translation of the *Reflections* and their philosophical and political insights. It is not impossible that his acquaintance with this 'masterpiece of political thought and eloquence' persuaded Humboldt to postpone 'indefinitely', as he puts it in a letter to Schiller from the 18th of January, 1793, the publication of the *Ideen zu einem Versuch, die Gränzen der Wirksamkeit des Staates zu bestimmen* in book form. Burke sees the relationship between the state and the individual quite positively. Where the German thinks of limitation, the Englishman speaks of mutual permeation, so that Humboldt was forced to realize that the central intention of his *Ideen* ran contrary to an observation in the *Reflections,* to wit, 'that man can only prosper as a citizen'.[16]

It is worthy of mention that the philosopher of law and specialist in criminal law, Paul Anselm von Feuerbach, in his early teaching and writing years 'a genuine representative of early idealistic liberalism', had read, and agreed with, Burke.[17] For the legal philosophers Friedrich Julius Stahl [18] and Johann

Caspar Bluntschli,[19] recognition and acceptance of Burke's principles had become a matter of course within the framework of intellectual history.

In addition to the evidence which for the most part, or at least to a great extent, recapitulates the after-effects of Burke's practical political ideas, we find evidence of another kind, in which Burke's epoch-making views concerning the nature of the state and of human society have found expression or predominate. Friedrich Gentz, Kantian and erstwhile adherent to revolutionary ideas, published his brilliant but deliberately slanted translation of the *Reflections* in 1793. The book was enthusiastically received by Novalis, Burke's 'first disciple' in Germany. Its basic message helped to form what is usually called, with some exaggeration, the political philosophy of Friedrich von Hardenberg.[20] But Burke's real herald in Germany was Adam Müller. It is one of the quirks of history that Burke, the powerful, original, incorruptible, courageous and productive thinker that he was, should find a propagator in this vain, unsteady, basically syncretistic even though linguistically talented and influential man. Niebuhr referred to him as the 'notorious' Adam Müller, a 'thoroughly bad person'.[21] Wilhelm Grimm mentioned the 'deceitful appearance' which he knew how to spread in his writings, and Savigny calls him 'a strange mixture' and says that he could not get himself to trust him. 'His exceptional talent hangs on his shoulders like a coat, it does not live within him, just as his writings do not come from within him.' 'He is,' Savigny remarks, 'the most striking example of the strength and weakness of our time.'[22]

Burke's untiring disciple in Germany was Adam Müller, a protégé of Gentz. Müller understood his own thoughts as 'hopeful children (or better, grandchildren)' of the Burkean spirit. Burke is, for him, the great renovator, indeed, the founder of modern political science. Müller speaks of him emphatically, in the foreword of his brilliant youthful work on *Die Lehre vom Gegensatz* (1804), as the man 'to whom Great Britain and perhaps Europe owes its deliverance'. He is, we read in Müller's book *Über Friedrich II* (1810), 'the last prophet to have come into this disenchanted world'. In the *Vorlesungen über die deutsche Wissenschaft und Literatur,* Müller testifies to Burke's importance for him personally as well as for Germany. One can reconstruct the worth and meaning of this expressive document only by realizing that Adam Müller, without himself being a creative thinker, did give political philosophy of the romantic period its proper form. Müller writes: 'The most important epoch in the history of German political science was the introduction of Edmund Burke into Germany, this greatest, most profound, most powerful, most human and most bellicose statesman of all times and all peoples. He raised all the hopes of those few who recognized this German mind for what he was (I prefer to call him German because of the spiritual kinship with our fatherland which I discovered in him, without forgetting that he expressed and grasped the whole world, and that he belongs more intimately to his own beloved fatherland); he allayed all their fears with his eloquence, inspite of his undeniably melancholy temperament. Here in Germany, his works have been translated, understood and incorporated in their full compass into German science; we live, write and educate in his spirit, whereas abroad he goes unheard, and his own fatherland only half understands him, and honors him only as a brilliant speaker, party leader and patriot. I say with pride, he belongs more to us than to the British; my own ideas concerning the state boast of being immature, but hopeful children (or better, grandchildren) of his spirit. He is recognized in Germany as being the most effective and successful mediator between freedom and the law, between the separation and the unity of power and labor, between the middle-class and the aristocracy; and thus, no matter how useful his deeds may have been for Great Britain, it has been Germany's privilege to sing his praises: may future writings, may life itself be a worthy continuation of this praise!'[23]

4

We have said that it is possible to describe Burke's influence in Germany in two ways. One of these we have presented rather hurriedly. The other promises a better – because systematic – survey.

We shall restrict ourselves to a few basic questions, since, by limiting the questions, we can expect more precise and comprehensive answers. Which political ideas are associated with Burke's name in Germany? And which political principles were, in the period of the wars of liberation, confirmed or fostered by his work, or deemed desirable for the reconstruction of the German states and the German empire?

If we remember the deeds and writings of those who appeal to Burke or are at least indirectly connected with his work, we have no difficulty in observing four things:

1. Burke's immediate influence lies in his critique of the French Revolution and of the philosophy which helped prepare the Revolution and determine its course. He placed particular emphasis on the observation that the preparation of the revolution lay predominantly in the hands of a 'new description of man'. He called them, with a distinct undertone of contempt, ridicule and hate, 'political men of letters', and obviously meant that social group which present-day sociology refers to as the intelligentia. This intelligentia is made up of men who are neither directly connected with the political life of the people nor really familiar with affairs of state. They have no political responsibility. But they act as critics of existing conditions. As critics of that which is, the 'political men of letters' compare the prevailing order in the state with one they believe should be realized because it alone would correspond to the nature of man and would not only promise but guarantee him salvation. The guiding principles of this order are firmly established, for the fixed points of orientation are determined by human reason which in turn appeals to the laws of nature. Some of these 'political men of letters' construct a paradisic original state of man to which they attach paradigmatic significance. Others pride themselves on rational anticipations of the future. The 'political men of letters' are the born adherents to, and defenders of, a theoretically justified despotism. For since they believe themselves to be in possession of the principles of moral-

32

ity and justice which they consider to be exclusively definitive and authoritative for the establishment of the state, they tend to consider an omnipotent government desirable and justified because, due to its unlimited, rationally founded absolute power, it is capable of translating the legal and political principles from the realm of the ideal to that of the real. Abstract rationalism, which sees man in himself isolated from the manifold conditions of cultural and civilized life and from the hierarchical order within organized society, this abstract rationalism, which understands man's nature as being primarily defined by 'an enlightened self-interest', reduces social structure to a mechanism. The idea of the absolute equality of men transforms the totality of the citizens into 'one homogeneous mass'. The apostles of equality, antagonistic toward the church and destructive of religious ties, reduce men, as Burke once said, 'to loose counters', which need only be counted, not weighed. The aspect of quantity predominates over the aspect of quality. The principle of the essential and original individuality of the living spirit is sacrificed to the principle of abstract equality. The transformation of the hierarchically structured society into a uniform mass of relatively isolated and undifferentiated concentrations of power which are linked together by the mechanical and calculable pressure and counterpressure of their self-interests leads of necessity to the establishment of a rational despotism. 'In the groves of their academy' (of the mechanistic philosophers) – we read in the *Reflections on the Revolution in France* – 'and at the end of every vista you see nothing but the gallows'. Burke was convinced that a victorious general would assume power in France; Rivarol, when asked in 1790 how the Revolution would end, answered, 'We shall have a happy soldier.' Burke's critique of the autocratic dogmatism and absolutism of the rationalistic political philosophy of the late 18th century anticipates the arguments which were to be expressed in the 19th century against the exorbitant faith in the natural sciences and the unconscious metaphysical presuppositions which characterize the positivism of Comte and Marx.

33

2. Burke then appears as an advocate of the organic theory of the state. This opinion is prevalent to the present day.[24] Under the influence of the *Reflections*, Novalis and Adam Müller developed the idea that the state is an organism. For Novalis, the state was a 'macroanthropos'. Adam Müller makes the distinction between a 'mechanical political science'. 'which rests on the principle of progress and the mechanical acceleration of forces, that is, on neutral talent' on the one hand, and, on the other, a 'living' and 'organic' political science, which has as its point of departure the 'recognition of the interrelation' of the sexes, that is, the 'nature of the family'. Edmund Burke is the 'founder' of organic political science. In this sense he is the forerunner of the political philosophy of German romanticism. There can be no doubt that Burke rejected the contract theory of the origin of the state and of government. Of course, Hume had *de facto* anticipated him on this point. In his *Essays*, Hume still speaks, to be sure, of an 'original contract' which he supposed to be the true basis of the state, but he traces the real establishment of the state back to power. 'We have obligations to mankind at large,' says Burke, 'which are not in consequence of any special voluntary pact. They arise from the relation of man to man, and the relation of man to God, which relations are not matters of pact. On the contrary, the force of all pacts which we enter into with any particular person or number of persons, amongst mankind, depends upon these prior obligations.'[25] These moral obligations are the expression of the divine order of the world, which is in no way subject to historical change. But the renunciation of the doctrine of the contract as the foundation of state and society does not as such imply the acceptance of the organic theory. Nevertheless, the German romantics were not entirely unjustified in maintaining that Burke's thought contained at least intimations of this doctrine; they could point to such expressions as the 'great mysterious incorporation of the human race', and the 'permanent body', with which he was wont to characterize the individual states. Burke had furthermore called upon the power of emotion, the strength of instinct and the might of traditional and proven

34

prejudice to help understand political order and social life. He initiated a feud with all those men of the 18th century – Voltaire, Helvétius and Holbach – who expected to bring mankind permanent happiness through the fight against prejudice. In the last analysis, the primary unit and the real foundation of the state was for Burke the family, in which man's proper virtues, devotion and faithfulness, piety and prudence, and his essential qualities of authority and freedom can develop. 'We begin our public affections in our families. No cool relation is a good citizen.'[26] Burke gives the state a soul. He makes it personal, he fills it with the values and contents of the individual soul. He wants to make it worthy of devotion and of the possible sacrifice of one's life. 'To make us love our country, our country ought to be lovely.'[27]

And finally, not only the romantics, but also such statesmen of the national uprising as Stein and Niebuhr considered Burke their star witness because he had restored the religious and moral foundations of the state to their proper place. 'Nothing is more certain, than that our manners, our civilization, and all the good things which are connected with manners and with civilization, have, in this European world of ours, depended for ages upon two principles, and were indeed the result of both combined; I mean the spirit of a gentleman and the spirit of Religion.'[28]

3. Burke is further considered the discoverer of the principle that man and social groups are to be understood as historical entities. It was Karl Hillebrand, the noted German essayist, 'the last humane German who knew how to write', as Nietzsche put it, who called Burke a 'colleague of Herder', 'more than a colleague, for he was for England and political theory exactly what Herder was for Germany and literary theory: the herald of the historical principle, who gave the signal for the attack against the rationalism and mechanism of the 18th century'.[29] Heinrich von Sybel described the basic trait of Burke's character admirably when he sees it as the instinct 'of giving himself up to things, of penetrating into the wealth of life, and of beginning his own mental activity only after being sated with

35

an abundance of observations'.[30] This is reverence toward that which is. But it alone would hardly suffice to make Burke a discoverer of the historical world and the specifically historical way of thinking and observing. For the respect of the past would only justify the defense of the *status quo*. *Status quo* is purely static. But history is not only the permanent, but also the changing, which, while changing, retains its identity. In order to establish truly historical thinking, other assumptions are required. We must have a sense for the constant change of human things and institutions. The insight into 'the great law of change' brought Burke close to the truly historical. The nature of many a political or philosophical theory becomes clear when we consider the views against which it was directed. Burke stood in opposition to the rationalism of the 18th century. He did not believe that the basic principles for the establishment of states could be derived from timeless reason. Was there such reason? Was it not rather characteristic of a wiser reason to adapt itself to changing political and spiritual situations and find suitable responses to new circumstances? It is an undeniable fact that man is always born into the community of the state and the people. His perception is minimal compared to the collected experience of past generations. 'The species is wise and when time is given to it, as a species it always acts right.'

The 'reference to antiquity' requires legitimation. For the traditional political institutions and customs are not venerable and valuable simply because they are historical, because they have existed and have been accepted for a long time. Their acceptance rests rather on the fact that they represent the reason of earlier generations. That is the meaning of Burke's assertion that the species is wise. The historical view of man and of the forms of social life does not, for Burke, under any circumstances mean renouncing the basic principles of moral order. 'The great law of change' had to be reconciled with the 'principles of original justice'. Burke would have insisted, as Herder did in his consideration of Shaftesbury's ethic, that there can never be 'a plurality of reasons within the human species' and that 'several highest principles of morality' are not 'even thinkable'. Not a trace of the relativism of value and truth, which resulted from the radical historization of thought in the latter part of the 19th century, is to be found in Burke's speeches and writings. For him, only abstract and general reason is fatal because, compared with concrete reason which deals with real, given situations, it is inferior precisely because of its abstractness and exerts a destructive influence on the concrete political and social reality to which it is applied. Burke's discovery of the historical principle and his insight into the changeability of things human rests on the basis of an unshakeable moral and religious order which comes from God, the 'great Master, Author and Founder of society'.

4. Finally, Burke is a passionate and influential champion of the English constitution, a system of political principles and institutions which challenged France and Germany, if not to imitation, at least to attentive consideration. In any event it had the character of a prototype in which vast political experience had been consolidated, so that it was very much worth studying if one wanted to determine the principles of one's own state constitution. Burke did indeed think highly of his country's constitution. 'Our political system is placed in a just correspondence with the order of the world.'[31] In the famous sixth chapter of the eleventh book of his *Spirit of the Laws,* Montesquieu had made a sizeable contribution to this image of the English constitution, which, as the historians have long since agreed, in no way corresponded to the facts. The widely circulated book by the Genevan De Lolme, *De la constitution de l'Angleterre* (1771), pointed in the same direction, and attributed to the English political system a character which was unequalled on the continent and thus exemplary. The institutional ideas of the English constitution, as they were understood and described by Montesquieu and Burke, were capable of making a significant impression on German politics in the age of the wars of liberation, which was at the same time an age of reflection on the German situation as a whole, because, among other things, they led of necessity to a kind of self-encounter.

For Montesquieu had asserted, appealing to the 11th book of Tacitus' *Germania,* that the English had adopted their free political constitution from the Germans. 'This beautiful system had been found in the woods.'

5

Burke's popularity in Germany, more particularly the popularity of his political ideas, was fostered through the respect which the constitution of his country enjoyed on the continent. That Burke's writings, above all in Germany, were felt to be not only the proclamation of a rigorous conservatism but also a call for re-establishing conditions which were long since a thing of the past, must be considered a tragic mistake. Conservatism and restoration are by no means the same thing. Furthermore, one must take into account the nature of the conditions which are to be preserved. The political and social order which Burke wanted to maintain in England was progressive in comparison to German conditions. Popular representation comparable to that represented by the House of Commons, the institution of responsible ministers, the hard-won freedom of the press, the right of petition – these institutions and many more were unknown to the predominantly absolutist German states and to their loyal subjects. Sociologically speaking, Burke represented the propertied and politically active middle-class. Such a social class, equipped with such political rights as Burke championed in England, did not exist in Germany, or did so only in embryonic form. Thus, although Burke's work appeared to be a justification of existing conditions for such romantic minds as Adam Müller or Friedrich Schlegel, this conservatism had a completely different meaning when applied to England and to Germany. Indeed, the full weight of a remark which Marx makes in his *Kritik der Hegelschen Rechtsphilosophie* applies here: 'German history rejoices in a movement which no people under the historical sun has ever experienced or will ever imitate. We have shared in the modern restoration without having shared in the previous revolution.'

It is not all the same, which political institutions are the object of the reverent desire for preservation. Burke's conservatism is transformed by the German romantic political philosophers into the desire to preserve and re-establish the feudal order of the Middle Ages and into the glorification of the idea of a universal Christian empire with a distinctly theocratic organization. His political principles and insights, based indirectly on two revolutions (those of 1649 and 1688) and on the liberal doctrines of Locke and Blackstone, were misused for the justification of the maintenance of a political and social constitution which could not adapt itself to the social conditions which were in fact beginning to emerge in Germany. Stein's efforts at political reform and education remained piece-work; when the promises which the Prussian king had made to his people under the threat of military collapse were not kept after the victory over Napoleon, and the reaction set in, Stein had to recognize that he was again being forced into the opposition, which weighed all the more heavily upon him because of his irreconcilable rejection of the liberal and democratic ideas which were stirring on all sides. Adam Müller and Gentz, as well as Novalis, had placed themselves in the service of restorative and reactionary ideas; their enthusiasm for Burke was gradually supplemented and supplanted by the veneration of the Catholic political doctrines, above all of Bonald and Joseph de Maistre, who pleaded for a theocratic restoration. Theocratic ideas, however, were foreign to Burke. To be sure, he called God the 'great Master, Author and Founder of society'.[32] But this means that society, in order to endure, is bound to fulfil certain conditions inherent in the nature of things.

This false image of Burke, which resulted from the union of German romanticism with the historical school, is itself a confirmation of Burke's ideas. Historicism, as soon as it saw itself as a philosophical *Weltanschauung* and method, assigns Burke's works a high place among its forebears. The justice done Burke consists in applying to him the methods of perception which he helped to develop. The 'reference to antiquity', for Burke the primary principle of life, and his vehement criticism of the belief in an abstract, timeless reason which was supposed to yield generally valid and inviolable norms for forming a political order, constitute the triumphs which earned him the title of a pioneer of the historical approach and of political conservatism. His thinking cleared the path for the conception of political and social institutions as organically developed and growing structures. In the course of time, state and law, religion and morality, art and science form a unique association. For time is the medium of change, it is the assumption on which moral striving is based, it alone makes possible the realization of social goals. Time creates law. In this light we understand the importance Burke assigned to prescription in political life. One recognizes the old natural-right formulations Burke used, but senses that they no longer have their original meaning. Burke represents the age in which the transition takes place from unhistorical, individualistic, natural-rights thinking to historical, organic and collectivist thinking. He is not yet free of what he is about to reject. The slag of traditional rationalism clings to his brilliant insights into the nature of history and the historical world. His belief in the exemplary nature of the British constitution is rationalistic and 'enlightened'; for had he been aware of the full implications of the historical principle, he would not have failed to notice that every people arrives at the political organization proper to it and only to it on the basis of its individual spiritual and political assumptions. This is the not unjustified argument of modern historical criticism in placing the work of one great father of historical thinking into the larger context of its full development.[33]

6

Now, there would be no objections if Burke's writings did not occasion doubts which resist this interpretation at every step along the way. Or should the reason for the apparent discrepancies lie in Burke's having – to use a metaphor – poured new wine into old bottles, in having expressed his discovery of the historical conception of man and of all social structures at least partially through inadequate means – in short, in having used rationalistic, natural-right terminology to express thoughts which had developed toward an organic doctrine of society? This solution would perhaps be commendable if there were reason to assume that Burke's thinking can in fact be characterized by the discrepancy which exists between the old rationalism and the new, organic historicism. But just as Burke makes no distinction between pre-revolutionary and post-revolutionary political doctrines, so one can find no sign that he ever changed his political views. If we consider that, from the standpoint of the history of American political thought, Burke is celebrated as the 'greatest theoretician of the American Revolution', and that he is at the same time honored as 'the great theorist of British conservatism', we realize how absurd it is to split Burke's work into two contradictory parts.[34] The fight against the Revolution in France did not mean a betrayal of the political ideals which had made him one of the most brilliant spokesmen for the Whigs. His genius as a statesman proved itself precisely in forseeing, in spite of the promises of the Revolution, the perversion of the system of abstract political freedoms into the absolute power of the state and the autocracy which was to destroy these freedoms.

In closing, we shall turn our attention to a larger question, the clarification of which we have good reason to believe will bring us a step further in understanding Burke's political philosophy and philosophical anthropology.

At this point, two questions must be raised. Historical thinking and the conception that the state is an organism independent of individual wills requires the use of metaphors which are, for the most part, taken from the realm of living nature. The state as 'macroanthropos',[35] the state as an organic, 'ever-moving and living whole',[36] 'its silent, inner forces', 'the organic connection' of the law with the consciousness of the people,[37] society as 'the sum-total of organic life, from which the individual parts derive their function'[38] – these are some of the figures of speech which, in promising to convey knowledge, are intended to be more than figures of speech. Are

these attempts, we must now ask, suited for the task of understanding human societies? And can we – the second question –
really call Burke a forerunner of the romantic idea of the social
organism? That he has been understood as such remains un-
contested, as does the fact that he gave occasion to this interpretation.

Nevertheless, it is, to say the least, strange that the historical
school and the organic doctrine of the state arose at a time in
which *de facto* the victorious advance of the thoroughly rational, bureaucratic and centralized state on the continent
could no longer be battled. It was the triumphal march of a
conception of the state which, as the romantics had very clearly understood, had been prepared by Frederick II and had been
given exemplary importance for future times by the despotic
and imperialistic military state of France during the Revolution and the imperial autocracy. That this French state, too,
had roots which reach far back into the history of French
absolutism, has long since been pointed out by historians. The
general leveling of society under the throne, the systematic
exclusion of the aristocracy from responsible positions in the
administration and in the political leadership of the nation,
the decline of the landed gentry, the centralization of the administration in Paris – all these processes, which de Tocqueville had seen, resemble a rational, technically perfected and
highly manoeuverable machine more closely than they do a
living and growing organism. If the political institutions, in
which man's social life unfolds, develop gradually and organically, how does it happen that men turn to rational construc-
tions to regulate their affairs? [39] Romantic and organic thinking
cannot answer this question, unless it invokes a religious interpretation of history which links Protestantism with the falling
away from the one true faith of the Catholic church in the
Middle Ages. This is the path taken by Novalis, Adam Müller
and Friedrich Schlegel. But this is merely putting off the
question, for we should now have to ask, how it was possible
for the European peoples to effect a schism of the church and
thus depart from the divine order of worldly affairs. To be

sure, Novalis and Adam Müller rejected the state as a machine particularly as manifested in the Prussian kingdom under Frederick II; they contrasted it with their ideal of an organism hierarchically ordered according to estates which they likened to a marriage. But whence comes the transition of the state from an original, living and growing organism to something which clearly appears as a machine, as a mechanical, rational and abritrary work of art, or at least as an artifact? And how can a state, conceived as a machine, revert to a living and growing organism? How must man and society be constituted to make possible such a 'development'?

This question is not an idle one. We shall attempt to answer it by calling on Burke.

We must keep in mind from the outset that Burke never speaks merely as an observer, but always as a statesman and politician as well. What this implies is obvious. It means that he knows from long experience that men, concrete, thinking men driven by desires and interests and ruled by heterogeneous prejudices, are the factual substratum of all social institutions and of the state. Of course there are natural social relationships into which man is born: the family, the social class, the race and the state. But these associations are made up of men; they have no organic life of themselves, as the romantics believed. This applies particularly to the state: it has a separate existence and its own laws, but both are realized in such individuals as enforce observance of its laws and accept these as their own.

In order to clarify this last socio-political question, we must refer back to an early theoretical work of Burke's, to the *Appeal from the New to the Old Whig* (1791), and to his first *Letter on a Regicide Peace* (1796).

In 1756, Burke had published a treatise in the form of a letter, entitled *A Vindication of Natural Society or, a View of the Miseries and Evils arising to Mankind from every species of artificial Society*. The author signed as a deceased nobleman and man of letters. It was a satire, a polemic, directed at Bolingbroke, whose collected works had appeared in 1754, some years after his death. Burke imitated the brilliant, much admired and supposedly inimitable style of Bolingbroke so well that his satire was taken for a genuine work of Bolingbroke. Bolingbroke made the countless religions, dogmas, churches and sects responsible for the misfortunes of mankind. The remedy seemed to him to consist in the renunciation of these 'artificial' products of the human mind and the return to the general, natural and rational religion with which man is originally endowed. Now what does Burke do? He transposes Bolingbroke's line of reasoning to the state and to society, and shows, eloquently, ironically and yet in such a fashion that the bitter seriousness of his polemic comes through clearly, that all wars, distress and sorrow have their origin in 'artificial' societies. Full of derision, he glorifies the return to the original state of the noble savages who are not depraved by civilization. But what is behind this satire, which made Burke famous overnight as soon as it became known that he was the author? There is, first, Burke's life-long and heartfelt struggle against rationalism which, in Bolingbroke's thinking, appears as an original rational state of nature. Further, we find a defense of the 'artificial' society, for which Burke fought to the end of his days; he defends the idea that the social groups and structures in which men live are of his own creation. The first *Letter on a Regicide Peace* summarizes Burke's socio-philosophical views once more. In it, he firmly and expressly rejects the application by analogy to the social structure of those metaphors which are taken from the realm of nature. 'Commonwealths are not physical but moral essences. They are artificial combinations, and, in their proximate efficient cause, the arbitrary productions of human mind.'[40] It appears as though we are dealing here with an insurmountable contradiction of all the ideas so powerfully and movingly formulated in the *Reflections*. This impression is erroneous. This becomes apparent if we recall the philosophical anthropology upon which Burke's doctrine of the state and of society is based. It is present in his writings only in fragmentary form; Burke never incorporated it into a system. Whoever tries to understand Burke as a perfectly consistent philosophical systematician (as a philosophical systematician who avoids all contradictions) is sure to fail. Nevertheless one must study his view of man for it yields – so it seems to me – the key to the understanding of his political and social philosophy and his conception of the process of history. Burke's anthropology culminates in the concepts of freedom and reason. In the *Reflections*, Burke writes that it is man's 'prerogative' 'to be in a great degree a creature of his own making'.[41] Man is, apart from his physical constitution and from his relationship to the conditions imposed on him by nature, what he makes of himself. This applies not only to his individual life but above all to the structure of history and society. Burke declares: 'In the state of rude nature there is no such thing as a people. A number of men in themselves have no collective capacity. The idea of a people is the idea of corporation. It is wholly artificial.'[42]

The second 'natural' attribute of man is his reason: 'Man is by nature reasonable.' 'And he never is perfectly in his natural state, but when he is placed where reason may be best cultivated, and most predominates.' Burke's philosophical anthropology is summarized in the concise sentence: 'Art is man's nature.'[43] Man's nature is art because it is raised above the constraints and necessities of nature through freedom and reason. Art is the nature of man; that means that man forms himself into what he is and should be. He is 'a creature of his own making'. Now, 'artificial' does not, of course, mean arbitrary, abstract or rationalistic; Burke has also no intention of excluding from his anthropology the power of feeling, the intensity of instinct, or anything else that happens without reflection.[44] On the contrary, he is their champion. But this does not prevent his insisting that man's essence is fundamentally defined not merely in terms of nature. Many of the moral assumptions of Burke's doctrine of state and society are contained – some of them word for word – in Adam Ferguson's important *Essay on the History of civil Society,* published in 1767. In the first chapter, dedicated to the description of the state of nature, we read: 'We speak of art as distinguished from nature; but art itself is natural to man. He is in some measure the artificer of his own frame, as well as of his fortune, and is destined, from the first age of his being, to invent and contrive... He would be always improving on his subject, and he carries this intention wherever he moves, through the streets of the populous city, or the wilds of the forest. While he appears equally fitted to every condition, he is upon this account unable to settle in any.'

The conclusion appears unavoidable that there can be no transition from these anthropological views to an organic doctrine of the state. But it would also be wrong to interpret Burke as a representative of enlightened rationalism. We must ask and answer only one question, to wit, whether Burke's political and sociological views contain real insights. The notion of history as a supposed 'organic development', and the idea that the state and other social structures are organisms, only conceal the real facts, above all the fact that a social group, which indubitably has its own laws, preserves, expresses and renews itself only according to the moral forces and ideas, the industry and insight of those men who *de facto* constitute it. If one conceives of the state and social structures as organisms, one gives the impression that they have a 'life' independent of the factual behavior of individuals. To be sure, the state is a community of the dead, the living and those who will come after us, but it is so only insofar as the responsibility to our tradition, and the responsibility toward future generations who will till this soil and speak this language, remains alive and strong in the living generation. States are only what the succession of generations makes of them in each instance. 'The resource of the state,' says Burke in the second *Letter on Regicide Peace* – supporting this view – 'depends upon opinion and good-will of individuals.'[45]

When Burke asserts that art, that is, the possibility of intentional and considered action, constitutes man's nature, he does not mean that the structure of society depends on man's arbitrary desire. He says explicitly at one point: 'When we marry, the choice is voluntary, but the duties are not the matter of choice. They are dictated by the nature of the situation.'[46] This argument permits of application to other social institutions –

46

in fact, it invites such application. In order for social groups to exist, certain conditions which are inherent in the nature of things must be fulfilled. Their fulfillment is always contingent on man's free decision. Herein lies, in the last analysis, the possibility of their success or failure. If man wants them to endure and prosper he must give heed to the conditions necessary to their existence. Although Burke does not say more than this, he has said a great deal. For he has placed the responsibility for the state and for every human community in the freedom of the individual.

Here we have reached the source of the strength, determination and integrity of Burke's thinking: in an ethos of freedom whose law and limit lies in the 'moral constitution of the heart'. 'It is better to cherish virtue and humanity by leaving much to free will, even with some loss to the object, than to attempt to make men mere machines and instruments of a political benevolence. The world on the whole will gain by liberty without which virtue cannot exist.'[47]

CHAPTER THREE

ANTOINE DE RIVAROL
AND THE FRENCH REVOLUTION

I

In the year 1716 or 1717, an Italian nobleman arrived in Nimes. He was on his way home from Spain, where he had served under the banner of Philip V. He did not continue his journey to Italy, remaining instead for unknown reasons in Nimes. This officer, who apparently had neither parents nor possessions at home, was called Antoine-Roch Rivarol. He was born on August 16th, 1685, in Vinsali near Novara. In Nimes he married a commoner, Jeanne Bonnet, the daughter of a tailor. The marriage was blessed with five children. One of them, born in 1727, was named Jean. He settled in Bagnols and also married a commoner, Catherine Avon, in 1752. From the birth papers of his children we learn that he was a 'silk maker', then an innkeeper, and finally an official, to wit, a 'customs collector'. During the Revolution he helped supply the army in the eastern Pyrenees. Long after his famous son, an unwavering supporter of the monarchy, had evaded the pressure of the Revolution by emigrating, and was working against the republicans in power from abroad, Jean was made responsible for raising the standard of health and for the general improvement of the communities of the canton. He tried his hand at poetry, knew Latin, and was sufficiently fluent in the language of his fathers to translate some of the songs of the *Gerusalemme liberata* into French. On June 26th, 1753, nine months to the day after the marriage of his parents, Antoine, the first of sixteen children, saw the light of day.[1] He was precocious, of above average intelligence and endowed with an exceptional gift for language. Lioult de Chênedollé, a friend of his Hamburg days, to whom we are indebted for some important biographical information concerning Rivarol, remarks that Germaine de Staël 'did not have a more elegant, quick, brilliant or varied command of words than Rivarol'. His eloquence completely enraptured his friends. 'In his company there was no thought of eating, the senses were all ear, the heart was in ecstasy, the spirit was in raptures.' In twelve months Antoine mastered material for which three years are usually necessary. When he lacked the funds for lodgings at the academy and was in danger of having to break off his education, he explained his situation to the Bishop of Cavaillon. Impressed by the intellectual capabilities of the young man, the Bishop assumed the costs of his training. His intellectual talents were matched by his striking appearance. Rivarol was big and handsome. 'There goes the handsome abbé from the Sainte-Garde seminary' whispered the ladies to each other when Rivarol and his colleagues strolled along the walls of Avignon. The best portrait we have of Rivarol was painted by Melchior Jacob Wyrsch, an artist from Unterwald, who spent many years in Besançon. It was painted in 1784, when Rivarol's position in society and in the intellectual life of Paris had become firmly established. A high, handsomely arched forehead rises above firm eyebrows. The eyes, directed clearly and examiningly at the viewer, complete the impression of self-confident superiority. The well-formed, slightly arched nose betrays in the powerful formation of the nostrils, genuine sensibility. Full, sharply drawn lips hint at the tendency towards maliciousness and sensuality, so that, although the bright intellectuality which dominates the eyes and forehead is not disturbed, his more human traits – physical and spiritual – are evident.

In 1777, after Rivarol had received a humanistic and strongly theological education at various institutions, he came to Paris. His rise in France's capital can only be described as triumphant. The two founders and publishers of the encyclopedia, d'Alembert and Diderot, were very much taken with the young man. He impressed both Buffon and Voltaire, with whom he became acquainted in 1778 through d'Alembert. The *Mercure de France* wanted him to become a contributor; publishers pressed him to write for them. In the salons he revealed the gifts of his mind and – as 'the best dressed man of his time' – the charm of his appearance. 'Men offered him their purses, and the women their hearts.' Two circumstances cast a shadow over his life: his parentage was open to slander and ridicule, although there was no doubt of his noble blood on his father's side. And he himself was undisciplined and lazy. In the year 1797, the story goes, his publisher Fauche had him locked into his house in Hamm near Hamburg so that he would work. He could not leave the house until he had given the hired guards a few pages of manuscript. Rivarol would not have been a shrewd judge of men if he had not known his own weaknesses. 'To have done nothing is a great advantage, but one must not misuse it.' And in a letter to the king of Prussia, Frederick II, he confesses:

Moi, qui, toujours bercé des mains de la paresse
Et par la volupté de bonne heure amolli,
Ne dois faire qu'un pas de la mort à l'oubli.

His command of the enchanting play of conversation was effortless, his wit inexhaustible, his power of observation discriminating, and his feeling for words unerring. He depended upon the immediate success of conversation. Society appealed to him. He easily surmounted the obstacles which confronted him, and derived the greatest satisfaction from transforming indifferent listeners to enthusiastic ones. But his work did not come easily, and its effects were only felt very gradually. He wrote very few larger works: the *Discours sur l'Universalité de la langue française*, published in 1784, which brought him the prize of the Berlin academy, the esteem of Frederick II, and a secret pension from Louis XVI; and the *Discours préliminaire du nouveau Dictionnaire de la langue française*, of which the first and only part appeared in 1797 under the title *De l'Homme de ses Facultés intellectuelles et de ses Idées premières et fondamentales*. He had planned a *Théorie du corps politique*, but never got beyond a brief and trenchant critique of the concept of popular sovereignty. A discussion of the French Revolution followed in a series of articles published in the *Journal politique national,* which had been founded by the Abbé Sabatier des Castres. In these articles, which have been collected as the *Tableau de la Révolution,* Rivarol subjected the events from the summer of 1789 until the fall of 1790 to a running analysis and commentary. If we add that Rivarol translated Dante's *Inferno* into prose, that he published a *Petit Almanach de nos Grand' Hommes* – a sort of collection of freaks in contemporary literature, which made him some enemies and caused much laughter –, that in 1788 he answered Necker's book, *De l'importance des opinions religieuses,* in two letters concerning religion and morals, and that he wrote several poems and a few essays on aesthetics, we have enumerated what remains of his production as a writer.[2] His notebooks and diaries, which contain remarks and comments on himself, his contemporaries and history, are partially included in the collection of *Maximes et Pensées* and of *Pensées inédites,* published in 1836. On the *Maximes et Pensées* rests his fame to the present day, with the result that he is considered one of the most brilliant of the French moralists in the line beginning with La Bruyère and La Rochefoucauld, including Vauvenargues and Chamfort, and extending to Joubert and the Prince of Ligne. Neither his knowledge of men nor his education kept him from making the great mistake of his life. In 1779 or 1780 he met Louise Mather Flint, the daughter of a Scotch refugee family which had followed James II into exile to France. Louise, who later managed to eke out a living by translating, did not hesitate to compare her wit with that of Madame de Sévigné and her beauty to that of Madame de Maintenon. The marriage and the ensuing bitter disappointment were almost simultaneous. Their son, Raphael, born in 1780 and raised by Rivarol's sister, served as officer in the army of the king of Denmark and died on the Russian side in the winter campaign of Napoleon's armies which marked the beginning of the collapse of the French hegemony in Europe. Rivarol's separation from his wife followed inevitably and almost immediately. Rivarol lived with the charmingly pretty and perversely capricious Manette.

When he left France in order to escape the threatening pressure of the growing radicalism, she bravely shared the trials of his emigration which was marked by the tension between hope and despair. Sulpice de la Platière, one of Rivarol's first contemporary biographers, reports that on the eve of his trip to Brussels, he said to Manette: 'My dear, if you want to be independent, stay in Paris; if you want to remain Manette, you must follow me. Manette agreed, travelled around the world, saw princes by the grace of God captivated by her charms, was virtuous although pretty, listened to Rivarol's verse and prose, did the honors at more than one banquet, was universally loved, shared his good and his bad fortune, in short, Manette was the guardian angel of his sensitive and difficult nature.'[3]

As much as one could praise her beauty, so little did one value her intelligence. 'One day, when she was ill, and mentioned to Rivarol that she was uneasy as to what would become of her in the next world, he said to her, "Leave it to me, I'll give you a letter of recommendation to Molière's maid-servant".'[4]

She belonged to his life, even if he knew: 'Cats do not caress us, they only nestle against us,' and she will be called to mind when one reads Rivarol's *Pensées* and his poems, one of which is addressed to Manette:

> Ah! Conservez-moi bien tous ces jolis zéros
> Dont votre tête se compose,
> Si jamais quelqu'un vous instruit,
> Tout mon bonheur sera détruit
> Sans que vous gagniez grand'chose.
> Ayez toujours pour moi du goût comme un bon fruit
> Et l'esprit comme une rose.

In 1792 began Rivarol's life of emigration, the misery of which has been incomparably described by Friedrich Gentz in his translation of the *Considérations sur la Révolution française* by Mallet du Pan. At first, Rivarol stayed in Brussels, where news from France flowed in abundance and the hopes for the succes of the counter-revolutionary movement were high because the complaints about the unbearable conditions in France seemed to admit of no other expectations. The social customs which had been cultivated and enjoyed in Paris were renewed. In the fall of 1794, the French armies nearing the Netherlands drove Rivarol on to London. There he met Burke, to whom we owe the first work against the Revolution not in the French language – the *Reflections on the Revolution in France*, of 1790 – which became the fundamental work of conservatism in England, France and North America and of political romanticism in Germany. Burke held Rivarol in great esteem. Nobody who compares Burke's *Reflections* with Rivarol's articles in the *Journal politique national* can fail to notice how far the two thinkers agree in their judgement concerning the Revolution and in their accurate prognoses for France and Europe. That Burke assumes a dominant rôle in the history of political philosophy, whereas Rivarol barely appears in it – Paul Janet, in his *Philosophie de la Révolution française* (1875), does not even mention him – stems from the fact that Burke's work contains a theory of the body politic, whereas such a theory is only hinted at in Rivarol's work. In the Lettre de M. Burke sur les Affaires de France et des Pays-Bas, written in 1791 to Rivarol's brother Claude-François, we read: 'I saw your brother's admirable annals too late to make use of them; someday they will rank with those of Tacitus. I conceive there is a resemblance in our way of thinking although this may appear to you as presumptious as it is sincere. If I had seen these annals before writing on the same subject, I should have enriched my efforts with many quotations from this brilliant work before daring to express the thoughts which we have in common in my own way.'[5]

In the spring of 1795, Rivarol settled down in Hamm, near Hamburg. Throughout the hard years of the emigration he insisted on maintaining his independence. In 1796, the young Louis Philippe of Orléans was to be induced to a gesture of obeisance toward Louis XVIII in order to reduce the tensions in the royalist camp. Rivarol was among those persons who were expected to exert their influence in this matter. But he refused to compromise although the expectations of a generous reward on the part of the interested parties were considerable. In 1800, the hope arose in Paris that he would be called to head the Bibliothèque nationale. The only condition was that he would have to gain Bonaparte's favor. But Rivarol mistrusted this first consul. The defender of the principle of legitimacy could not make peace with the usurper. His judgement is prophetic, if we consider that Rivarol died in 1801. 'Louis XIV made the nation proud and irritated kings; Bonaparte mystifies the one and humiliates the others. It would be curious if he would one day decorate the kings, create princes and ally himself with some old dynasty. One can expect everything from a great and ambitious man, and the kings of Europe are such that he can expect anything from them. Legitimacy is in peril, and that leads to great and new calamities.'[6]

The diaries of the last days in Hamburg are dismal. 'Since nature has nothing more to offer me and society even less, I only want air and water, silence and seclusion, four things without taste and beyond reproach.' 'Of twenty persons who talk about us, nineteen say bad things, and the twentieth says what he has to say badly.'

To a friend he wrote: 'My friend, one must collect one's store of troubles in this mean world. I have, I think, amply filled mine.'

In September, 1800, Rivarol moved to Berlin. Once more his talents were in demand. His lustre was undimmed. Berlin was seething. Revolutionary diplomacy was struggling against the old powers. There was the court, whose queen, 'who is very French', granted Rivarol her favor; 'she very much likes what one is wont to call my mind'. There was the salon of Frau von Krüdener, whose favor Rivarol forfeited by a bon mot. There were the salons of the French nobility. There was the palace of the much loved and admired Princess Dolgorowski, whose exotic beauty was unenviously and hymnically described by Madame Vigée-Lebrun.[7] Rivarol charmed her and was captivated by her. The final play of his mind and his senses began ... and died away. On the 4th of April, 1801, Rivarol felt ill. In his modest dwelling Unter den Linden his close friends gathered. Pneumonia set in. Failing to realize the seriousness of his condition, Rivarol said: 'We shall breathe the good air of Languedoc for six months, then we shall betake ourselves to Paris, and you will see that no one on earth is easier to live with.' He became delirious. In a moment of lucidity, he 'gave some instructions pertaining to his personal toilet and the care of his apartment, on Friday the tenth, the eve of his death'. On the 11th of April, blessed with the sacraments, he died in the arms of a friend.

2

Rivarol could not complain about lack of recognition. But he was denied success in the one field in which he sought it. A few weeks before his death, on the 21st of February, 1801, he wrote to the banker David Cappodoce Pereira: 'One is feasted, caressed, applauded, quoted, but receives no other favors.' If, as André Le Bretons so convincingly does, we substitute for 'no favors' the expression 'little esteem', or 'little influence', we recognize the reason for his secret disappointment. This confession shows that Rivarol was not content with being what, according to Paul Bourget, had brought him his undisputed fame: 'the prince of French conversation, the frivolous and prophetic adventurer, His Impertinence, Count Rivarol.'[8] Rivarol shared this disappointment with many others who had set themselves the same task of fighting the French Revolution. With all the signs of resignation, Mallet du Pan, for example, declares in the foreword to his *Considérations sur la Revolution française* (1793): 'Appearing in print, without serving any purpose, arguing, without convincing anyone, presenting facts that are forgotten tomorrow – that is all that one gains in these times by appearing on the scene.'

To be sure, it would be oversimplifying this complaint of ineffectiveness to see it as nothing more than the expression of an impotent aristocracy, whose goal is the re-establishment of pre-revolutionary conditions. It is equally unsatisfactory to associate this discontent solely with the confusion and disorganization of the French emigration and the inner disunity of the

55

counter-revolutionary forces. At a time in which the Revolution had long since ceased to be restricted to France alone, and had – as Mallet du Pan said – become 'cosmopolitan', at a time, in other words, in which 'every resident of Europe' was personally concerned 'with the last and decisive struggle which civilization had to survive',[9] it had to become unmistakably clear that the concept of counter-revolution only simulated a spiritual and political unity of purpose. Behind the unity of words were hidden the most heterogeneous ideas and interests which could not be reduced to a common denominator. The threatened European powers understood very well that the French wars had the goal 'of consolidating the French Revolution and transforming it into a general revolution of human society, of leaving no throne unturned, of permitting no constitution which did not rest on the maxims of unlimited, armed and legislating democracy, of abolishing all differences of class and of plundering all property owners... of incorporating conquered lands into their territory and introducing revolutionary regimes there, and of supporting the war by plundering and sustaining the plundering by war'.[10] These nations could, according to international law, consider themselves justified in taking measures against revolutionary France. One could, for this purpose, appeal to Emer de Vattel's *Le Droit des Gens ou Principe de la loi naturelle* (1758). It was Edmund Burke who, in his efforts to unify the political position of France's opponents, recalled Vattel's doctrines in order to use them as the ideological foundation of a counter-revolutionary political theory. Vattel, an adherent of the philosophy of Leibniz and Wolff, had maintained the right of all peoples, in view of their freedom and independence, to govern themselves as they saw fit. This principle excluded the interference in the internal affairs of other peoples (Book II, Chapter IV, Paragraph 54). However, if they met with 'a restless and malevolent nation, always prepared to injure others, to violate their borders, and to incite domestic disturbances', then the wronged and threatened nations undoubtedly had the right to join forces and punish the agitator, and make him incapable of harming other states (Book II, Chapter IV, Paragraph 53). Vattel admits that no nation is called upon to judge another. But when a nation disregards the rights of the remaining states and infringes upon them at every opportunity, 'constantly and as a matter of principle', and openly admits 'to wanting to undermine the foundations of justice', it is a duty as well as a right to take steps to eliminate the evil in the name of justice and for the welfare of mankind (Book II, Chapter V, Paragraph 70). Burke, who excerpted Vattel's international law for his own purposes, had referred back to these views.[11] But even granting the assumption that there is an authorization in international law for a war against revolutionary France as an act of legitimate self-defense, it did not assure, by any means, the co-ordination of the political will of the European nations. The sense of being threatened did not have to be equally strong in all countries, and the trust in the forces of resistance which opposed the revolutionary ideas, could also change from state to state. Furthermore, nobody could fail to realize that the policies of the various powers were by no means solely determined by the relationship to France.

To understand the complaint of ineffectiveness in the contemporary political sphere, we must realize that the answer to the question, how the Revolution could be halted and counteracted, assumes the answers to two other questions: the question of the causes and the question of the nature of the Revolution. Only if one knows, or at least thinks one knows, why the Revolution came to be and what its real significance is, can one meaningfully set about to determine how it should be combatted with the greatest likelihood of success. The choice of means is contingent upon the answers to the questions. Obviously, these questions and answers are not concerned exclusively with political order. For political order is always a variable quantity which depends on the constitution, structure and tendency of mental and spiritual forces and on the economic conditions of life upon which it is based. The insight into the causes and nature of the Revolution, therefore, can only be gained under the condition that one takes into account religious, historical, political, philosophical and ultimately anthropological considerations. The best way to understand the individual peculiarities of Rivarol's discussion of the Revolution is to compare them with other contemporary views. We should like to make a contribution to this comparison. But we must be permitted one prior remark concerning the purpose of our stressing the meaning of contemporary views on the Revolution. The immediate witnesses of the Revolution in France made observations which are of the greatest relevance in understanding phenomena which are reappearing in the 20th century. The monarchists and the adherents of the tradition need not have been frightened only by the purely political upheaval and the radical republicanism of the Revolution. Nor need the outbreak of inhumanity alone have been the sole cause of the horror which shamed and repulsed many an early partisan of the Revolution. Is it not conceivable that the events of the Revolution revealed something to its contemporaries which alarmed them but which they could hardly express adequately with the verbal and ideological means at their disposal? Is it not possible that the early critics of the Revolution could intuitively see events and correlations which were not generally seen and soon forgotten, and did not reveal their full significance until the 20th century? The fact that Tocqueville's work *L'Ancien Régime et la Révolution* continues to be valued highly for its insights into the nature of the Revolution is due largely to the circumstance that Tocqueville, in describing the Revolution's more important aspects, depended almost exclusively on this early phase of its philosophical analysis. The memoirs and letters of Jacques Mallet du Pan, which appeared five years before the *ancien régime,* had lasting influence on Tocqueville. And how much Tocqueville has in common with Rivarol in the characterization and judgement of the Revolution is quite apparent.

Many opponents of the Revolution gained the impression very early that they were dealing with a political and intellectual event that had to be distinguished from all other revolutions in history. 'We must guard against the comparison of this revolution with any other revolution of ancient or modern his-

tory.'[12] It had in common with a political revolution what
Mallet du Pan called the 'displacement of power'. Whenever
political power changes hands, we are faced with a revolution.
Revolution is a change of the type of government, and comes
about of necessity 'when the old government no longer has the
strength to protect the body politic from attack or when it lacks
the courage to protect itself'.[13] But it also occurs if, in a given
state, the legal order, which yields the standards for the distribution of power, no longer corresponds to the actual social
and economic conditions. Then the revolution is an adaptation
of the political order to the real distribution of power. But the
French Revolution differed from a political revolution, from
the mere alteration of the constitution of the state, on two ac-
counts. It was not, as earlier revolutions were, an event which
was limited to a single people. To the contrary, it made a
claim, on principle, to universality. And further, it had an
undeniable similarity to the occidental religious reformations.
On the other hand, it differed fundamentally from the religious revolutions because of its obviously unchristian character. Ethics and logic, Rivarol remarks, had furnished the
philosophers who prepared the Revolution nothing but 'objections to the political order, to religious ideas and to the laws
of property'; 'they aspired to nothing less than a reconstruction
of everything by means of a revolt against everything, and forgetting that they themselves are of this world, they demolished
its foundations'.[14] To its contemporaries, the Revolution appeared as a new religion. It is an 'insurrection against all principles' which is founded on a 'philosophical and national religion'.[15] The difficulty, of course, consists in the fact that it is
a religion without religion, in the sense in which religion is
understood in the Western tradition. The central observation
lies in the fact that revolutionary theory and practice has undeniable similarity to the forms of religious and church life.
As early as 1791, Burke wrote in his *Thoughts on French Affairs*
that the Revolution in France was not concerned with eliminating local abuses or adopting the political order to changed
conditions. 'The present Revolution in France seems to me to

59

be quite of another character and description, and to bear little resemblance or analogy to any of those which have been brought about in Europe, upon principles merely political. It is a revolution of doctrine and theoretic dogma. It has a much greater resemblance to those changes which have been made upon religious grounds, in which a spirit of proselytism makes an essential part.'[16] Burke goes on to remind the reader of the Reformation, which he considers the last revolution of dogma and theory in Europe. Mallet du Pan expresses himself upon the same lines. 'The revolutionary doctrine... is for all its partisans a veritable religion.' These partisans of the Revolution are compared to a sect which 'is in touch with all the adherents of the modern philosophy in Europe'. If we want to describe the practices of the Revolution and the ideological influences to which they are related, we arrive almost of necessity at concepts which are borrowed from the realm of religious life: the Revolution proselytizes, propagandizes and catechizes. 'The revolutionary system is applicable to all nations; it is based on philosophical maxims proper to all climes and the enemies of all governments. Its authors... have poisoned republics as well as monarchies with their preachings. We have seen, and still see, its emissaries catechize the people of neutral states, Genevans, Swiss and Swedes, exactly like those of belligerent powers... The fanaticism of irreligion, of equality and of propagandism is just as strong and a thousand times more odious in its methods than religious fanaticism ever was.'[17] Burke, who did not doubt that the pre-revolutionary philosophy had 'something like a regular plan for the destruction of the Christian religion' speaks, by way of analogy to the church fathers, of the 'atheistical fathers with a bigotry of their own'.[18] Mallet du Pan and Burke also made a comparison between the Revolution and Islam. Burke, in his first *Letter on a Regicide Peace*, declares: 'It is with an armed doctrine that we are at war,' and thus invokes the image of a holy war.[19] The Revolution, writes Mallet du Pan in 1794, 'develops and spreads like Islam, by word and sword: in the one hand they hold the sabre, and in the other the rights of man. One of the principal motives behind the founders' decision to enter into a war was the hope of accelerating the advance of the revolutionary religion by conquest and by the corruption of peoples and soldiers. The convention and the club of Jacobins had organized their proselytizing missions at home and abroad like the Jesuits had organized theirs in America and in China'.[20] But also the relationship of the revolutionaries to their doctrine can best be characterized by the use of religious language. As early as 1789, Mallet du Pan points out: 'When attacking all abuses, we must denounce one in particular which, more than any other, menaces personal freedom and security. For some time now, a class of writers has regarded all its opinions as dogmas, its decisions as oracles, its pronouncements as official reports. If one adopts other ideas, what am I saying, if one raises a doubt or proposes a modification, an angry and despotic voice denounces, reviles and slanders everything which resists it; the slightest opposition to its doctrine becomes an attack on natural right. Having escaped the sword of censorship, we succumb to the assaults of intolerance... In our day, public opinion expresses its judgements through the sword and the rope. Believe or die – that is the anathema pronounced by the fanatics; they pronounce it in the name of liberty. But without the support of law, where is this liberty?... one seeks the public interest and the truth honestly but in vain; so many corrupted pens have profaned these sacred words that one must either profane them like the others, or risk rejection or persecution.'[21]

In order to understand how the political theory and practice of the Revolution could assume the characteristics of a religious belief, we must remember that 18th century philosophy had spared no effort to enthrone reason as an absolute. Once given an absolute, theoretical reason, an absolute practical reason which need brook no contradiction could not fail to be derived from it. It was a true idea of the Enlightenment that man is much less determined in his behaviour by things and events themselves than by his opinions about things and events. From this assertion it logically follows that there was such a thing as an enlightenment in the knowledge of things and their interrelation and that in this way – that is, through the perceptions of reason – the yoke of mere political opinion and religious prejudice could be shaken off. Letting oneself be determined by things and events meant accepting the principles of things and the laws of events as the measure of all behavior. Since reason is the organ of cognition, it was possible to speak of reason as the determining faculty. Such was the content of the posthumously published work of Helvétius, *De l'Homme, de ses Facultés intellectuelles et de son Education,* in which he credits education with unlimited power for improving the human condition. 'Education is capable of everything.'[22] It can do anything for two reasons: first, because, as Rousseau had taught, man is in himself good and has been corrupted solely by the conditions of society and culture, so that the changing of the conditions of life according to valid principles must of necessity bring man his salvation; and second, because human reason is capable of recognizing these principles. The same views, expanded into a philosophy of history, we find again in Condorcet's thought, which identifies human progress with the progress of rational and scientific knowledge of nature and of man. After many struggles, truth has finally come into its own, 'in submitting all opinions to our reason, that is to employ, in arriving at truth, the only instrument which has been given us for recognition'.[23] A special class of men develops which is less concerned with recognizing the truth than with disseminating it and with persecuting all prejudice.[24] These men constitute an intellectual society which sets itself the task of destroying political and religious prejudices. With the spread of enlightenment, of rational truth, this society will gradually merge with the body of the people. The 'new doctrine', which dealt the last and decisive blow against the complex of religious and political prejudices in which the interests of a single class or of two groups, the nobility and the clergy, but never of the people as a whole were represented, is the 'doctrine of the unlimited perfectibility of the human species';[25] this doctrine is inseparably bound to the 'triumph of reason', that is, to the gradual development of reason, which development is the basis of perfectibility. Philosophy could rest on 'the firm foundation which the sciences had prepared for it',[26] and it could be predicted that a great political revolution would 'unfailingly' occur: 'Either the people itself must realize the principles of reason and nature which philosophy had succeeded in endearing to it, or the governments must hasten to anticipate the people, and chart their course towards its opinions.'[27] The process, by which science becomes the unconditionally reliable guarantor of human salvation, finds expression in Condorcet's thinking. 'The only basis of belief in the natural sciences is the idea that the general laws which govern the phenomena of the universe are necessary and constant.'[28] The constancy and universality of these laws, whose application to man and to the development of his intellectual capacities can be assumed, permit the prediction of events with 'almost absolute certainty'. Since both nature and man are subject to the same laws, it is not an 'illusory enterprise' to maintain the possibility 'of tracing with some probability the pattern of the future destiny of the human species'.[29] Condorcet does not hesitate, then, to conceive of the future condition of man – the universal political order – as the necessary result of a process regulated by laws: the elimination of inequality among all peoples, the progress of equality within every people and the real perfection of man.[30] The analysis of the progress of the human mind in history and the development of human capabilities justify the belief 'that nature has placed no boundary to our hopes'.[31] Since it is beyond question that 'all errors in politics and ethics are based on philosophical errors, which in turn are tied up with errors in physics', it is only a matter of determining the laws of a universal, all-inclusive and generally valid political order through the scientific knowledge of nature and the application of its principles and methods to all realms of life.[32] The result is an absolutism of reason which makes the claim of being steward and herald of all truth. When, therefore, the theoreticians of the revolution proclaim their doctrines as dogma, justify and demand unconditional belief, issue their decisions like oracles and damn their opponents, they do so on the grounds of a faith in science which makes the discovered law of nature appear as the law of political life. A promise of salvation for man and a pointing of the way to this salvation, both based on the rational recognition of the laws of nature, constitute what the counter-revolutionaries have called the 'philosophical religion'. This was no religion in the traditional sense, but in its appearance exhibited many of the characteristics identified with religion and the church. It is no wonder that this phenomenon was something new to its contemporaries, something felt to be not only disturbing but also dangerous. It meant a break with the entire spiritual tradition. It was the 'revolt against everything' of which Rivarol had spoken. It was 'the open disorder' of many parts of Europe, 'the general earthquake in the political world' which Burke had diagnosed in the *Reflections on the Revolution in France*.[33] This philosophical religion promised to put the social and political order for all men on a new basis which, having been derived from reason and the laws of nature, would not be subject to doubt: 'the reconstruction of everything through the revolt against everything'. It is easy to see that this conception has been prototypal from Saint-Simon and Comte's 'positive catechism', up to the idea of technocracy and cybernetics in the 20th century.

In this connection, another insight must be mentioned which points far into the future. Burke noticed that the wars of the Revolution were fought in a new way, even if one disregards that mercenary troops were replaced by a national army. They have the characteristics of a civil war. 'It is a dreadful truth that cannot be concealed, in ability, in dexterity, in the distinctness of their views, the Jacobins are our superiors. They saw the thing right from the very beginning. Whatever were the first motives to the war among politicians, they saw that in its spirit, and for its objects, it was a *civil war*, and as such they pursued it. It was a war between the partisans of the ancient, civil, moral, and political order of Europe against a sect of fanatical and ambitious atheists which means to change them all. It is not France extending a foreign empire over other nations: it is a sect aiming at universal empire, and beginning with the conquest of France.'[34] The war was the *ultima ratio regum*. It was the means of enforcing one's claim and forcing one's will on the opponent. The right to decide whether or not a war was just was considered an integral part of the sovereignty of the state. There could be – strictly speaking – no unjust war, because the decision concerning the justification of an armed conflict rested not with a supra-national court but with the sovereign state. Indeed, sovereignty expressed itself in the right to decide whether an armed conflict should take place or not. The revolutionary wars can be understood as civil wars only if a number of ideological assumptions are made. A war is civil when one party makes a claim which it insists the other party, as a whole or in part, recognize. A civil war presupposes that national unity, that is, sovereignty, is no longer an ultimately valid fact of spiritual and political reality. One must rather proceed from a spiritual unity which binds many or all states and peoples. The revolutionary wars can be described as civil wars only if they are fought within a unified structure. But the revolutionary doctrine presupposes precisely such a structure. It is by no means concerned only with the freedom and equality of the French people, but lives from the conviction that its claim is universal, cosmopolitical. Privileged and non-privileged classes stood opposed to each other not only in France but everywhere. The revolutionary doctrine assumed the opposition of classes, which extended beyond political borders and constituted a supra-national unity. It is easy to see that this self-interpretation of revolutionary doctrine could be an ideological justification of a thoroughly national desire for power. However, this does not mean that this interpretation could not meet with approval and acknowledgement outside of France. Thus Burke was justified in saying that the armed doctrine with which England was at war 'has, by its essence, a faction of opinion, and of interest, and of enthusiasm, in every country'.[35] The revolutionary doctrine does not accept the vertical separation of sovereign states and substitutes for it a horizontal division which runs through all the European states. Under these conditions, the war appears as a struggle for the unity asserted

by the revolutionary doctrine which only malicious and ig-
norant rulers fail to recognize along with those who profit un-
deservedly from the established order. The Revolution, however, appeals directly to the people. It counts on the tension
which exists between the rulers and the ruled. It does everything to increase this tension. The revolutionary war becomes
a war of liberation, which has the true interests and the salvation of the people at heart. For the war promised as its goal a
political order of freedom and equality which is the only proper
expression of the true will of all peoples.

Burke, the Irish Protestant, and Mallet du Pan, the Calvinist
from Geneva, could obviously not assert that the anti-religious
philosophy of the Revolution was directly descended from the
Reformation. It remained for the French theocrats to see the
Reformation and the Revolution as a single, continuous process, and interpret the Revolution as the consummation of the
Reformation. For Louis Gabriel de Bonald and Joseph de
Maistre, the Enlightenment of the 18th century, as embodied
by the encyclopedists, meant the enthronement of reason
which one trusted to produce the principles of morality, law
and political order in a generally binding and valid form without appealing to any divine revelation. In the eyes of both
these traditionalists, the default, or, in the words of Bonald, the
crime of the Enlightenment and the Revolution, which only
continued in its arrogant interpretation of history what Luther's
and Calvin's Reformation had begun, lay in the assertion of
the 'religious and political sovereignty of man'. This sovereignty meant that man is the final authority in all questions of
political order and law, of morality and religion, beyond which
there is no appeal to a higher authority. Human reason is the
measure as well as the foundation of political and religious life.
Bonald consequently, in his *Essai analytique sur les lois naturelles
de l'ordre social*, sharply contrasts the anthropology of the Enlightenment with religious anthropology. The former knows no
check for reason except reason itself; the latter sees 'in a divine
law a law above that of reason'. Assuming that reason is its own
law, Bonald concludes 'that it is impossible to rescue reason

66

once it has erred'. 'Because what is irreformable is necessarily infallible, since nothing can make it perceive that it has erred, the same philosophers have been trained to maintain the natural integrity of human reason and the infallibility of the people, and thus arrived at these two principles, the one religious, the other political, literally advanced and resolutely maintained by the religious reformers of the 18th century and by the legislators of ours.'[36] The religious principle of the Reformation and the political principle of the Revolution reveal a complete 'parallelism'. It is expressed by the notions, first, that 'human reason needs no visible authority in order to regulate religious belief', and, second, that 'man's authority needs no justification to validate his political acts'.

De Bonald and de Maistre expected salvation from 'the fight unto death between Christianity and philosophy' through the restoration of religion and the Roman Catholic Church. [37] Rivarol found himself, in this respect, in an ambiguous situation. He was, on the one hand, convinced that religion is an indispensable basis for political and social order; on the other hand, one does not gain the impression that he was himself a truly religious person. That he knew and revered Pascal proves only his predominantly intellectual mind. To be sure, he was justifiably furious about Necker, who had said, in his book *De l'Importance des Opinions religieuses:* 'The more the burden of taxes keeps the people in a state of prostration and misery, the more indispensable it is to give them a religious education.' Voltaire's fight against religion also did not by any means find his approval. In the *Discours préliminaire* he remarks that Voltaire boasted 'very proudly', 'I have delivered you from a ferocious beast.'[38] Rivarol also noted an incident which had occured in Voltaire's house in 1778. After Voltaire had intoned his habitual refrain, 'crush the infamy', and praised his fellow combatants in the fight against religion, he seemed to expect to be congratulated for having made the attack even more successfully than all the others. Rivarol countered: 'Intelligence is required not to attack religions, but to support and maintain them, because all the epigrams about Jesus Christ are good. And as for courage, a philosopher needs no more than, and sometimes not as much as, an apostle.'[39] The position in which Rivarol found himself with respect to the Revolution and its preparation through the philosophy of the 18th century is marked by a strange ambivalence. He was certain that the Revolution was a realization of a philosophy. Doctrines concerning the state, based on the law of reason, and demands founded on these political views, constitute the meaning of the Revolution. This philosophy can be termed rationalism. For it assumes not only that man is a being endowed with reason, but also that this reason represents the force in the economy of human powers which must be granted the deepest and most far-reaching effect. The fact that men are all endowed with one common reason leads to the assertion of the equality of men and to the acknowledgment of a universal political order. This rationalism is for Rivarol the first, hardest and biggest stumbling-block. Nothing became more completely and utterly questionable through the course of the Revolution than this rationalism. The Revolution was an outbreak of passions. Dark, chaotic, anti-rational forces came to light which drove the leaders of the Revolution out of their responsible positions and degraded them to mere puppets of the masses. It is no accident, then, that contemporary observers unanimously confirm Joseph de Maistre's observation in his *Considérations sur la France* of 1797: 'It has been remarked, with good reason, that the French Revolution led men more than men led it... The same scoundrels who seem to lead the Revolution, actually appear in it as mere tools, and as soon as they pretend to dominate it, they fall ignominiously.'[40] Rivarol detected, in all the revolutionary events, the early manifestation of a force which flatly contradicted all theories of a rationalistic anthropology. His notebooks contain an entry which strikingly illuminates Rivarol's opposition to the views on which, according to him, the Revolution is based. He writes: 'The great metaphysician Sieyès... perverted all the principles of metaphysics when he posed his mad axiom of universal reason, the mistress of the world; he has entirely overlooked the theory of the passions and the effects of ignorance.'[41] Rivarol considers a theory of the passions indispensable. Or better, he abandons the view of man as being determined by reason and posits a non-rational and anti-rational *libido dominandi* which proceeds from the passions. And now it should be possible to explain why we spoke of the ambivalence which characterizes Rivarol's attitude towards the Revolution and its philosophy. For a confusing question arises. How can a man, who, like Rivarol, is an intellectual and a political writer, that is, a thinker and observer diagnosing and prognosticating events, influence men and their decisions (which is, after all, what he intended to do by writing) if he, in contrast to the philosophy of the Enlightenment, assumes that man is basically determined by the passions and blind will, not by reason? The answer, oddly enough, is through clear and distinct ideas. This answer is not as strange as it appears. In his unusually instructive but little known prospectus to the new dictionary of the French language, he argues that the 'social man' is of primary importance and that, in view of the ramification of human knowledge and the increasing division of labor, man has only one binding force remaining at his disposal: the universality of language. But this presupposes a system of well defined concepts. No one blames the stones for the flaws in the house. Since the dictionary of a language is the 'measure of truth', it must be protected from bad definitions, from which errors – 'sources of disputes, of misfortune' – arise. Rivarol remains, in this sense, deeply indebted to the Enlightenment. It is not a question 'of attacking the indestructible power of the passions, but of channeling this power', 'not of submitting to its frightening rule but of rendering it less arbitrary and more gentle. But, given this total and fatal subjugation of man to the passions, there is nothing except the mediating power of ideas which can deliver him from despotism'.[42] His philosophical program was 'to speak to the whole man, which has always been too much neglected in metaphysics'.[43] The philosophy which Rivarol attacked was guilty precisely of not bearing the 'whole man' in mind; rather it preferred to see one part as the whole, thereby preventing, through such dangerous one-sidedness, the formation of a sound theory of the body politic. The ambiguity of Rivarol's concepts, and the essentially 'enlightened' elements of his thinking could hardly be more clearly illustrated than in his fragment concerning popular sovereignty. 'These delirious people must be told: your new ideas will be destroyed by reason, your furious passions must yield to your own interests, your wishes will be contradicted by necessity, your efforts and your illusions will be annihilated by the eternal and inalterable nature of things. Moreover, if Europe should one day see fit to put an end to the French Revolution by force of arms, then every man with a trace of humanity should combat it with the maxims of reason: for, although force kills, it does not persuade, it suppresses, but it does not enlighten.'[44] A dedicated believer in the Enlightenment could not have put it better.

Rivarol fought against the Revolution while at the same time recognizing that it had been prepared long in advance. 'One is forced, in reading history, to admit that our kings, toward the end of increasing their power, spent their lives encroaching on the privileges of the nobility and the clergy, so that the people and the national assembly, in crushing the clergy, the nobility and the magistrature in the current revolution is only completing the work of the kings.'[45] 'The kings incited the people to help them against the nobles, until the nobles, themselves corrupted or out of fear of the kings, came to terms with them against the people. If the kings had not been ruined in turn, nothing could have resisted them; but the disorder of their finances forced them, as it did the old nobles, to come to an understanding with the people.'[46] The kings of France had contributed to the destruction of the inequality which had characterized the feudal order. Feudal Europe was divided into countless sovereignties.[47] 'Our kings, in excessively curtailing the privileges of the religious orders and the nobility, prepared the soil, or better, the manure for the revolutionary equality which was so favorable for the usurpers who succeeded the people.'[48] Rivarol was of the opinion that France must be given a constitution. But it should be a constitution which would correspond to the historical tradition of the state – a monarchy. He always remained a passionate royalist because he was convinced that every state needs a supreme head capable of decisive action; at the same time he pointed out, with a lack of prejudice which does him honor, that the king and the court were incapable of real action, and that the nobility were divided among themselves. 'The nobles, who, in the eyes of the people, were in the wrong because they had privileges, were soon to be in the wrong because of being nobles. These heirs of the old conquerors of the realm were incapable of the discipline and unity necessary for the common defense, whereas in the third estate all was strength and harmony. The middle class performed splendidly, the little people were courageous, so that, in this great revolution, the victors, as odious as they are, have merited their success, and the vanquished their misfortune.'[49]

Along with the monarchical principle, Rivarol considered the aristocratic one to be of decisive importance. On this point he is in agreement with Burke and de Maistre, both of whom emphasize the necessity of an elite for the political community.[50] Regardless of a nation's choice, it must, Rivarol says, entrust itself to someone: 'But as soon as a people has chosen guides or leaders, they constitute an aristocracy no matter what they are called.' Even a monarchy appears to him 'a revivification of the aristocracy'.[51] His insight into the necessity of an elite – 'There is no such thing as a pure despotism on earth; all governments are more or less aristocratic'[52] – makes him an opponent of democracy in the sense of the social contract. There is no such thing as a pure democracy on earth. For 'there is no people simple enough in its customs and small enough in number constantly to govern itself'. Rivarol distinguishes in every nation the sovereign, who is the source of all power, the government, and the state which is the object – 'le sujet' –of government and administration. The will of the sovereign consists in a single principle: 'to maintain itself through good laws'.[53] Whereas the state – the totality of the subjects – and the sovereign are two 'simple beings', government is made up of the legislative, executive and judicial power. Rivarol admits of a purely factual sovereignty, determined by power, founded on justice and therefore true – in other words, of popular sovereignty, which is nothing but the embodiment of vital strength and force. 'But, might is not right.' Then, there is a sovereignty of the body politic, 'which consists in those who know and who possess', and which requires a king and a senate, 'in order that there be justice, strength and unity in power'.[54] Sovereignty, therefore, lies in the union of education and property. It is clear that Rivarol avoids the question as to what should be done when the sovereignty of the body politic is misused. Under the impression of the ideological uprisings against the traditional spiritual order and of the insurrection of the masses, the interest of all the counter-revolutionists was concentrated on the problem of how order could be achieved and all possible sources of disorder eliminated in the political community. The sovereignty of the body politic becomes the means of eliminating all conflicts. Just as Rousseau had asserted that the general will is, by definition, always right and always directed toward the common good, so Rivarol maintains that the 'sovereignty of the body politic' can never do wrong. 'Moreover, sovereignty cannot be culpable.'[55] Rivarol proceeds just like de Bonald and de Maistre, for example, who tend to infer from the necessity of sovereignty for the state, the rightness and justice of its decisions. That this conclusion is unjustified need hardly be mentioned. It is also not justified by Rivarol's fear that 'the principle of popular sovereignty sows the seeds of endless revolutions'.[56]

When a nation rules itself, it is state and sovereign in one. Such a constitution is called a democracy. For Rivarol, however, it is a historically proven fact that when a people exercises all three powers itself, democracy turns into anarchy. But history also proves 'that if the three powers are united in the hands of a senate or a single man, aristocratic or monarchic despotism is the result'.[57] The exemplary constitution appeared to Rivarol to have been realized in England. Since every force in nature, like every human will, is despotic, the constitution must accomplish the feat of making the absolute rule of a single force impossible.

Rivarol recognized how quickly the struggle began between the king and the assembly to win over the army, and how detrimental it was for the royal cause that the army was no longer completely reliable. 'The defection of the army is not one of the causes of the revolution: it is the revolution itself.'[58] As early as 1789 he saw that the idea of equality would remain no mere concept of a political right, but that it must necessarily bring with it the demand for economic equality.[59] The dogma of popular sovereignty had the same effect. And finally Rivarol predicted the coming of a usurper, although, at the time, everyone was still rejoicing over the declaration of human and civil rights. 'I was asked in 1790 what the outcome of the revolution would be, and I gave this simple answer: Either the king will have an army, or the army will have a king. And I added, we shall have some happy soldier, for revolutions always end by the sabre.'[60] Thus he followed Bonaparte's rise with great interest. 'Europe should be prepared for great upheavals with this ambitious consul governing France.' Three powers must unite against him, Russia, Austria and Prussia; England will be the financier. 'Spain can only take care of itself; Italy is nothing, and Poland is approaching its end. In a century, when Russia has a hundred million inhabitants, it will itself become Europe. The northern hordes will destroy the Roman empire – that is a natural tendency.'[61]

The *Discours préliminaire du Nouveau Dictionnaire de la langue française* is dedicated to the 'whole man'. A theory of the passions and of the will is therefore required, along with a theory of the understanding and of language. Its central thesis is 'every force in nature is despotic, like every human will'.[62] Rivarol's position in the history of French philosophy must be seen in the light of Condillac's and Maine de Biran's work. The *Discours* was meant to be an 'image of man' and must therefore include human ills. For this reason, the second major section of the *Discours préliminaire* is a critical analysis of the philosophy of the 18th century, which Rivarol views as 'one of the greatest plagues ever to strike mankind'.[63] The pathology of modern man consists in his substituting philosophy for reli-

gion, of making philosophy into religion. This new religion no
longer has its goal in the next world, 'but restricts its realm to
this life'. It has identified the 'spirit of independence' with the
'despotism of its own decisions'.[64] 'Whereas the old philosophers
sought the highest good, the new ones only looked for the
greatest power.'[65] The new philosophy produced a fanaticism
like the one which religion had once inspired. It misunder-
stands the nature of man and of the body politic by becoming
fanatical, creating a system of dogmas and declaring its decisions
to be infallible, with the result that political struggles of necessity assumed the character of religious struggles. Political
questions were treated as if they directly affected the ultimate
salvation of the soul. Political affairs assume the aspect of the
absolute. The great error of the philosophers of the 18th century lies in the belief 'that knowledge and power would never
separate and that artillery and printing-presses would always
be in the same hands. Experience disappointed them cruelly:
from the day that the philosopher Robespierre assumed power,
he suppressed the sciences'.[66] The new philosophy believed in
'the miracle of a sudden clarity in all minds and a spread of
the enlightenment among all peoples'. But it is wrong to identify
freedom, equality, happiness and enlightenment. Knowledge
does not have the slightest tendency to become universal. 'It
is . . . certain that science becomes vulgar to the degree in
which it increases; it is the progress of concentration and not the
spread of enlightenment which ought to be the object of good
minds, for, in spite of all the efforts of a philosophical century,
the most civilized empires will always be as close to barbarism
as the most polished steel is to rust.'[67] For Rivarol, the new
philosophy is only destructive and demoralizing. 'The radical
vice of philosophy is that it cannot speak to the heart. But the
mind is only one side of man, the heart is all of him.'[68] The
Discours préliminaire closes with an unparalleled vision of terror.
Sainte-Beuve assigned this masterpiece its proper place when
he wrote in 1851: 'It is in this last section that one finds por-
trayals of the Revolution and of the Terror from the point of
view of morality which occasionally recall the spirit, the pen,

and, if I may venture to say so, the verve of a Joseph de Maistre.'[69]

The *Discours préliminaire* contains a radical rejection of the philosophy of the 18th century, which believed in the possibility of creating a social and political order with abstract principles. Under the influence of the Revolution, Rivarol became aware of the anti-rational and chaotic forces of the soul. As cause is related to effect, so is dogmatic and fanatical rationalism related to the rule of terror,[70] which, according to Robespierre's famous words, is 'the despotism of liberty against tyranny'.[71] But Rivarol was honest and perceptive enough not to close his eyes to the mistakes and inner instability of those who were to become the victims of the Revolution. 'When chaos is presented on our stages, the boxes resound with applause, but the author of the piece does not conclude from his success that one could not carry chaos, murder and nothingness into the world quickly enough.'[72] He opposed the absolutism of abstract reason and freedom with the truth, 'that public authority has the weight not of a yoke but of a shield'.[73] The apostles of human equality reaped his most bitter scorn. One could call Rivarol a moderate, critical follower of the Enlightenment because he considers the radical adherence to any principle to be fatally one-sided, and because he considers man to be in a very precarious situation – he is born 'capable of becoming just or unjust, above all to be one and the other, and in general, to be only tolerably good and tolerably bad'.[74] 'Man is born judge, but he is not born just in the moral sense.'[75] Whoever knows that man's judgements are relative will not expose him to the dangers of a moral or political system which considers itself absolute. One cannot number Rivarol among the Catholic theocrats and apologists of a political and ecclesiastical restoration who honored de Bonald and de Maistre as their most important spokesmen. For they would never have approved of his avowal 'that there is no false religion on earth, in the sense that every religion is a true religion, just as every poem is a true poem'.[76] His prescription for good rule is characterized by distrust of men and resignation in the face of historical experience. 'A government would be perfect, if it could bring as much reason to bear on force as force on reason.'[77]

CHAPTER FOUR

DE LAMENNAIS' POLITICAL AND SOCIAL PHILOSOPHY

I

Félicité Robert de Lamennais was born on June 19th, 1782, in Saint-Malo. After having received an excellent education, he took the first vows under the influence of his brother Jean, and in 1816, not without serious inner struggles, decided to become a priest. Napoleon's return from exile on Elba induced Lamennais to go to England, which he did not leave until the first empire had finally collapsed. In France, Lamennais grew to be a productive, brilliant and extremely influential writer. In the course of his career he developed from a defender of an extreme ultramontanism and monarchism into a religiously oriented social revolutionist who suffered the consequences of the consistency and daring of his political demands for the fourth estate and for his reinterpretation of the Christian teachings in the form of an irreconcilable breach with the Roman church. He became a feared and deeply honored champion of republicanism, who openly disavowed his traditionalist and monarchist past without, however, abandoning the religious foundation of his political and social philosophy. Filled with a real love for the working people, he fought against the 'censitory monarchy' in order to bully it into granting the general and unlimited right to vote and the right of free political association. He became a member of the chamber, remained true to his democratic convictions when Napoleon carried out his *coup d'état* and paved the way for the transition to the empire. Lamennais died on February 27th, 1854, without having been reconciled with the church. In order to prevent the Parisians from participating at his funeral, the authorities ordered his coffin to be brought to the Père-Lachaise in the early morning. Nevertheless, the populace left their places of work as the little funeral train moved through the workers' quarters to pay the last respects to the deceased, and the police were obliged to restore order by force.[1]

Overnight, Lamennais became a figure of whom not only France but all of Europe spoke in tones of the highest respect. The work which earned him the title of the 'greatest genius of our time' is the *Essai sur l'Indifférence en matière de Religion*, the first volume of which was published in 1817. Chateaubriand, who had initiated in 1802, with his *Génie du Christianisme*, a romantic and emotional rebirth of the Christian religion and brought about a stormy suppression of the belief in reason which had characterized the late 18th century, wrote the author that his talent had given his work immortality. And Lamartine declared: 'It is magnificent, thought like de Maistre, written like Rousseau.' What was the nature of this book so enthusiastically received by its contemporaries and so deeply indebted to the works of Bonald, Pascal and Bossuet? Lamennais distinguishes three forms of religious indifference: there are those who consider religion a political institution and do not consider it necessary for a people; then there are those who hold all existing religions to be questionable and recognize only natural religion as being undoubtedly true; and finally there are those who accept a revealed religion while at the same time expressly permitting the rejection of some revealed truths and the retention, as fundamental, of others. The problem which occupied Lamennais is that of the truth and unity of religious knowledge. If the Holy Scripture is the only criterion of faith, and Jesus has left no living authority for the interpretation of the Bible, then every individual is forced to undertake this interpretation for himself. Lamennais thus examines the same problem Rousseau had dealt with in the *Lettres écrites de la Montagne*. But for Lamennais the unity of morality is lost through the multiplicity of religions. 'But will morality escape the shipwreck of all truths?' No, for '[there are] as many moralities as there are symbols. It will therefore be necessary to tolerate all moralities just as one tolerates all symbols'. 'As soon as one rejects all living authority, the rule of morality becomes just as uncertain as the rule of faith.' The second volume of the *Essai* appeared in 1820. Lamennais describes the purpose of the work as follows: 'One must push man to the edge of nothingness to make him recoil before himself; one must make him see that he can not prove his own existence as he would have God's existence proved to him; one must destroy all his beliefs, even the most indomitable ones, and place his reason before the alternative of living by faith, or perishing in a void.' Like the founders of French traditionalism, like Louis-Gabriel de Bonald and Joseph de Maistre, Lamennais, too, was convinced that the state and society could neither come to be nor continue to be without religion. For this insight, anti-revolutionary traditionalism was by no means indebted to Christian teachings or to the fathers of the church. It considered this insight much more the heritage of Greek and Roman philosophy. Lamennais, in his *De la religion considérée dans ses rapports avec l'ordre politique et civil*, published in 1825, formulates this crucial doctrine at the beginning of the first chapter. Religion is the source of law, it is its foundation and support; it is the regulative principle of the states which are constructed according to the nature or the will of God. Religion is 'the foundation of social organization'. From this assertion follows the 'intimate union of religious and political laws in the constitution of every polity'. The basic dependence of the state on religion means the undermining of religion results in the destruction of society. 'Suffice it to say that whenever the influence of religion became weaker in the state and in the family – ... all the bonds which united men were suddenly dissolved.' Whenever religion begins to disintegrate, social bonds are loosened. 'Religion, banished by the philosophical systems, disappeared from the previously living society, and nothing but a cadaver remains.' Unity among men is not founded on similar interests; 'the only true unity which can and does exist is the unity among minds. Therefore society and all its essential laws are of a spiritual or religious nature, and the perfection of society depends on the perfection of the spiritual or religious order.' But if political order depends on religious order, then all political and social life must be ultimately and unqualifiedly interested in the unity and immutability of religious knowledge.

It is obvious that this insight, which was valid for the Greek and Roman world, was equally applicable to those peoples who had been converted to Christianity. In fact, this ancient knowledge necessarily became more profoundly significant in the Christian era. For was not the Christian religion *the* religion? Had not God revealed himself once and for all in Jesus, and was not the church which had been founded in Christ the only true protector and interpreter of this divine self-manifestation? But if these questions are answered in the affirmative, it necessarily follows that the Christian religion represents the unity and immutable foundation of all states. Now, traditionalism obviously could not deny two tremendous and momentous events of Western history: the Reformation and the Revolution. It could not deny them, if for no other reason than that it conceived of itself essentially as the counter-movement not only against the Revolution and the philosophy of the Enlightenment which had prepared it, but also against the principles of the Reformation. The Reformation meant the destruction of the religious unity of the West through the rise of a new religious principle. And the Revolution brought with it the destruction of the traditional social order. It would have been strange if traditionalism had not made some kind of connection between these two events which shook the religious and political structure of the Christian world to its foundations. Traditionalism had only to apply its principle in order to assert that the relationship of the Reformation and the Revolution was that of cause and effect. If religion is the basis of the state, every political revolution must depend on a change in religion. The upheaval of the political and social order which the Revolution brought about was thus in the last analysis only the expression of the religious principle which had put the Reformation in the place of the Catholic church. 'The revolution, begun in the church, always and of necessity invades the state, which in turn consummates it in the church.' This is the assertion from which Lamennais proceeds: the French Revolution unfolds in the field of political and social order only those principles which the Reformation had produced in the field of religion. 'Long before our revolution, the alleged reform of the sixteenth century had shaken the political system of Europe. Wherever it was carried through, despotism or anarchy immediately developed.' This interpretation of history goes back to Bossuet. The archbishop of Meaux, the powerful antagonist of the great Fénelon, was a brilliant and productive writer and preacher. He placed his pompous style in the service of French absolutism and the Roman church; with polemic passion and forceful logic, he fought for the religious unity of the French state and against the principles of the Reformation. The *Politique tirée de l'Ecriture Sainte* and the *Histoire des variations des églises protestantes* bear eloquent witness to his sense of national power and to the universal mission of the Catholic church. Bossuet had, in his funeral oration for the Queen of England, launched an attack on the Reformation. Henriette-Marie was the daughter of Henry IV and Maria de Medici. Born in 1609, she married Charles I of England in 1625; in 1649, in the course of the Puritan revolution, Charles was beheaded. Henriette-Marie outlived her husband by twenty years. On November 16, 1669, Bossuet held a funeral oration for her in which, with a view to the religious and political revolution in England, he formulated the religious principle of the Reformation and its necessary consequences for the state and society. The Reformation meant, for Bossuet, the opposition to all authority. 'Something violent began stirring in men's hearts: it was a secret distaste for everything which had authority, and an incessant yearning for innovation, once the first example had been given.' This aversion to authority must have a reason: it consists in each individual's making himself the judge of his own faith. The principle of the Reformation, then, is freedom of conscience, or, as Lamennais was to say later, the autonomy and sovereignty of man in all matters which concern his relationship to God and to His revelation.

'Everyone,' Bossuet declares, 'has made himself a tribunal in which he has appointed himself the arbiter of his belief, and yet it appears that the innovators had wanted to restrain the mind by confining it within the limits of the Holy Scripture; as this could only happen under the condition that every believer would become the interpreter of the Scripture and would believe that the Holy Ghost would explain it to him, there was hardly anyone who did not believe himself justified by this doctrine to worship his phantasies, consecrate his errors, and call whatever occured to him God. Since then, it has become clear, freedom being no longer restricted, that the sects would multiply infinitely, that obstinacy would become invincible, and that, while some would not cease to dispute and proclaim their ravings to be inspirations, others, weary of all these mad visions and no longer able to recognize the majesty of religion torn by so many sects, would finally seek a deadly repose and a total independence in indifference to religion, or in atheism.' With the loss of the unity of faith, however, the unity of the state and of society is also lost. If the determining of divine law is left to man's discretion, then the law of the state, which is founded on God's law, must also be left to man's autonomous judgement. A stable order is thereby sacrificed in favor of a dynamic and changing one. Bossuet's work not only anticipates the traditionalist positions in the fight against the Reformation and the Revolution, but also supplies the slogan which was to rally its forces in the attack against the evils caused by the Reformation. This was the call for a 'return to unity', or, as it was put in the first years of the 19th century, a restoration. This return meant the restoration of the unity of faith through the submission to the authority of the Roman church. 'In fact, it is apparent that, since the separation from and the revolt against the authority of the church has been the source of all evils, their remedy will never be found except in the return to unity and in the ancient submission.'

Lamennais fought the Reformation and the Revolution. 'The French Revolution... was nothing but a rigorously exact application of the ultimate consequences of Protestantism which... itself, in turn, brought forth the philosophy of the eighteenth century.' The philosophy of the Enlightenment was 'a daughter of heresy'. This heresy was the Reformation. Reformation and revolution are rebellion and defection. The Reformation as a rebellion within the religious order destroys divine authority; the Revolution as a rebellion within the political order destroys worldly authority. The Reformation destroys religious unity and 'in destroying religious unity, Protestantism destroys political unity as well'. Now, since the Reformation indubitably represents the unfolding of a religious principle, and since the Revolution by no means seeks to replace the traditional order by chaos but rather by a new political order which is considered a more just one than the old, the question must be answered how Lamennais reaches the conclusion that both movements, the religious one of the 16th century and the political one of the 18th century, are to be seen as movements toward radical and total destruction. The fact that Lamennais does not hesitate to denounce the principles of the Reformation and the Revolution as the cause of the destruction arises from his conviction that the Reformation enthroned religious atheism, and that the Revolution is based on political atheism.

2

Before we turn to the foundation of this exorbitant accusation, we must touch on a socio-philosophical question which concerns the problem of the unity of the social structure. Lamennais rejects the view that the unity of a social body is guaranteed by economic interests and that the state owes its formation to the desire for satisfying material needs. Playing on a famous remark by Burke, he says: 'A bazaar is not a city.' But if desires and interests do not unite men into communities, where can the principle of agreement be found? What unites men are principles of belief. Only in the realm of the human spirit can the unifying forces be found. 'Is it not always in the spiritual order, and in it alone, that the principle of unity is to be found?' The question implies an affirmative answer. But there is also no more powerful and more dangerous cause of disunity than the diversity of beliefs. This is particularly true of European peoples. 'Among those peoples spiritualized by Christianity... beliefs formed... the basis of human life and social life, binding men and nations together. The recognition that the constitutive principle of unity in society is a spiritual one does not, however, exhaust the definition of the social structure. The 'principle of unity' must be formulated by an authority in a manner binding for all parts of society. Furthermore, the possibility must exist for realizing the contents of the principle of unity even against the will of some individuals, if necessary. There must be a force which ensures unity. 'That which, in reality, constitutes society, is power.' This highest power Lamennais calls sovereignty. In addition to these two factors which characterize every society there is a third determinant: the traditionalist principle that the religious order is the foundation of every political order. This principle can also be somewhat differently formulated: political and social authority is based on intellectual and religious authority. If a social structure is dependent on the unity of belief, and if it arises and endures because of such religious unity, then it is obvious that the immutability of the principle ensures the indestructability of the social structure. Indeed, the protection of society rests on the immutability of the religious principle. But what is less mutable than the truth? 'Truth does not change... it remains for all times and for all places.' 'It is destined to spread by nature and to unite all peoples in its unity.' And in what else could truth be founded than in the divine testimony which the Godhead granted men in an act of inconceivable love and undeserved grace, in religious truth, on which authority and sovereignty are founded and which determines religious and political order? We must now concentrate on two questions: what is religious truth, and how does it come to be? The answers are concise: religious truth is the Christian message as it is understood by the Roman church; and religious truth comes to be through revelation. It is of decisive importance to understand that Jesus not only founded a religion but also created a society. The moment Jesus began to fulfil his mission in public, he founded 'a true society' – the church. Since Jesus had created a social body, he must also have revealed the principles on which the order of this body is based; that is, the characteristics which are peculiar to a society must also be characteristics of the church. We know these characteristics: they consist in the unity of faith and in a higher authority which is capable of guaranteeing this unity. Revelation constitutes the unity of the church. And the guarantor of the unity is the teaching office which Jesus instituted. In this office, the authority and sovereignty of the church finds its expression. 'The entire edifice of Christianity... must rest, in view of its institution through Jesus Christ, on the doctrine of a divine, infallible authority.' 'Jesus established the monarchical organization of the church ...the pope is its sovereign.' Lamennais makes the assertion, as bold as it is untenable, that the Christian religion and the monarchical form of the state correspond to each other. 'Christianity had created true monarchy... democracy in a large nation invariably destroys Christianity, because a supreme and unchanging authority in the religious order is incompatible with a constantly changing authority in the political order. Christianity stabilizes and preserves, democracy changes and destroys.' The religious truth of Christianity is the foundation of a universal community in which all the peoples of the earth are gathered together under a divine law. That means that religious authority, whose visible expression is the pope, is the final, incontrovertible authority not only in all questions of faith but also of social and political order within and between states. 'The church undoubtedly has rights in this world, because God himself has rights, since Jesus said: All power is given unto me in heaven and on earth (Matt. XXVIII, 18). But the church claims no dominion other than spiritual dominion.' Since revealing the true religion, Jesus also created the lasting and true foundation of the social order. 'Jesus Christ... gave religious society its public status, its marvelous external organization, which unites all families into one family ruled within the order of salvation by the authority

85

of a spiritual minister who in turn is governed by a single sovereign. Consequently, the interpretation and defense of divine law, which is at the same time the basic political law, should not be left to the people but rather to the spiritual minister and to his sovereign to whom God himself entrusted this office. Power is protected against the subjects, and the subjects against power by the sovereign of the universal religious society, the supreme defender of justice.'

Having tried to indicate the basic characteristics of Lamennais' political and religious philosophy, we can return to the question with which we started. What is the nature of the Reformation and, since the Reformation is the religious and political condition of the Revolution, what are the principles of the Revolution?

If we want to understand the intensity and concern with which this question was examined by the most important representatives of the anti-revolutionary generation, we must remember that the French traditionalists' sense of life bears the unmistakable imprint of an unprecedented upheaval. The Revolution did not stop after the third estate had assumed power. The wars which France had to fight against the forces of European traditionalism had helped to lead to a radicalization of the Revolution which resulted in a state a national emergency; the warring revolutionary factions believed that the situation could only be mastered through terror and despotism. A wave of persecution and misfortune inundated the nation; merely in order to gain peace and security, it threw itself into the arms of the autocrat Bonaparte who promised to satisfy the primitive desire for order at the cost of the freedoms aspired to by the Revolution. The series of wars was not interrupted. After the brilliant victories came defeat. Small wonder that a feeling of insecurity was widespread. 'General instability' is the expression Lamennais uses to describe the situation and the prevailing attitude toward it. The destruction of order, the collapse of society – these were the facts which had occasioned truly apocalyptic feelings among the thinkers of French conservatism. The intransigent philosophy of the 18th century had developed a critique of religion which attacked the church and the body of dogma. What had been understood and protected as the foundation of society had to submit to the judgement of sovereign reason. For the Enlightenment, church and religion were no binding elements, but rather institutions which only endangered peace by giving occasion to the persecution of religious minorities and to religious wars, and furthermore sanctioned the material interests of certain social classes in the state. The counter-revolution, therefore, had two aims: it attempted, as far as possible, to counteract the political upheaval, and it tried to show that the ideological assumptions on which the Revolution was based were in irreconcilable contradiction to the truth. But, although the anti-revolutionaries were certain that the political and philosophical rationalism of the 18th century could not stand up against the political and religious principles of traditionalism, they lacked, oddly enough, the confidence that that which they had held to be true would, in view of the political and religious shambles, be realized in a new political and spiritual order. This tormenting doubt, which even their faith in the one, indivisible and eternal truth could not remove, corresponded to the dark and melancholy mood which sought relief from an inevitable fate in the retreat to apocalyptic expectations. The alternative of returning to the divine order of wordly and spiritual things or of persisting in the revolt against this order weighs like a curse on mankind. The presentiment that the historical process cannot be reversed did not, to be sure, lessen the expenditure of intellectual means called upon to give uncompromising battle to the Reformation and the Revolution, but it did dampen the expectations of victory. If one reads carefully, if one ignores the extravagances and injustices of the traditionalist attack, and if one disregards the untenable view that there can never be such a thing as a restoration in history, one cannot fail to get the impression that these thinkers themselves sensed that they were fighting for a lost cause and that the dams which they had built would shortly be swamped by the political and social currents released by the Revolution. The last volume of Chateaubriand's

Mémoires d'outre-tomb represents an impressive proof of this point, and Lamennais confirms it. For his separation from the Roman church was at least partially due to his recognizing, as a priest, that the church would not be in a position, as a result of its excessively close ties to the existing social and economic distribution of power, to master the labor movement and the political demands which would arise from it. Important representatives of traditionalism were torn between a consuming longing for the traditional order and the oppressive recognition of the hopelessness and futility of their desires. Out of this tension an apocalyptic attitude toward life arose which made the mistake of equating the dissolution of a particular social order and its ideology with the dissolution of all human society. Traditionalism not only lived in the hope of a restoration of the original order; it was also tortured by the terrible question whether such a restoration was still possible. Traditionalism, which struggled to preserve the Catholic and monarchist tradition, took the possibility into account that the restoration of the true faith and the true law of the state would fail, and that the collapse of the European social order and destruction of the religious convictions on which this order is based represent an irrevocable event in the history of mankind. At the end of his book, *De la religion considérée dans ses rapports avec l'ordre politique et civil*, this ambivalent mood, a mixture of gloomy despair and jubilant confidence, finds brilliant expression: 'If governments blindly persist in destroying themselves, if they are determined to perish, the church will certainly lament this fact, but it will not falter in deciding which rôle to assume: it will withdraw from the activity of human society, tighten the bonds of its unity, sustain in its breast the courageous exercise of its divine authority... fear nothing from man, expect nothing from him, await with repose and patience what God will decide for the world. If it is His plan that it be reborn, then this will come to pass. Following terrible disorders, violent upheavals and evils the likes of which the world has never known before, mankind, exhausted by suffering, will look toward heaven. It will plead to be saved, and out of the scattered ruins of the old society the church will form a new one similar to the first in all that is of a fundamental nature, but differing in that which changes in accordance with the time... But if this should be the end and the world be condemned, then the church, instead of gathering up the ruins, these bones of peoples, and giving them new life, will pass over them and rise to the realm which has been promised it, while singing the hymn of eternity.'

3

Let us now turn once more to the question concerning the nature of the Reformation and the Revolution, to which two answers will be necessary according to the traditionalist doctrine that the religious order is the foundation of the political order. In religious terms, Protestantism is 'the act of independence of human reason'. The reformers – this is the gist of the charge – substitute for the authority of the church the subjective authority of their conscience and their reason. 'Everyone must search with his own reason, without ever deferring to the authority of another. True Christianity has been distorted since its [Protestantism's] inception.' The 'fallible judgement' of subjective reason displaces the 'infallible judgement' of the church. 'When a Protestant believes, it is never for the fundamental reason that God has revealed the truth which is the object of his belief, but rather because his reason deems this object to be a real truth.' The entire structure of Christendom, its dogmas, its rites, its morality, had for fifteen centuries rested on the teachings of an infallible divine authority instituted by Jesus himself. 'For this divine authority, Protestantism substitutes the private judgement of each individual.' The nature of Protestantism consists in its asserting the 'sovereignty of the individual reason'. This sovereignty is also called 'freedom of conscience'. If Protestantism sees itself as the principle of the independence of reason in matters of religion, religion can be nothing but 'free opinion, a human thought, which changes or can change incessantly and from which there would never ensue any responsibility'. Protestantism is the religion of freedom. It grants each individual the right to make the final decision as to what, religiously speaking, is truth. Together with this authority a second is given: the subjective decision concerning what each individual recognizes as his moral duty. 'Everyone must make his own morality just as everyone must make his own belief.' The Protestant religion of freedom thus means the negation of an unchanging divine law independent of space and time. It leads of necessity to moral relativism.

By focusing our attention on the morality which can be deduced from the religious principle of Protestantism, we have entered the realm of politics. What are the consequences of the religious principle of Protestantism for the social and political order? First it should be noted that the sovereignty of human reason brings the element of continuous change into social relationships. Protestantism is by nature and from its very origin the principle of permanent revolution. 'Through an inevitable extension of the principle which makes every man the final judge of the truth, we are condemned to refashion religion, morality... society, everything, even human reason and man himself.' Lamennais asks whether there is any hope of ever eliminating this evil. 'Can freedom of thought, weary of destruction, devoid of any principle but freedom itself, erect a new edifice on these immense ruins?' Lamennais' answer could only be negative. For transposing the religious principle of Protestantism to the state and society means revolutionizing political order. But Lamennais' decisive step is his equating of revolution with destruction. Protestantism, religiously speaking, is rebellion against the church hierarchy and against papal authority, whose decisions in doctrinal matters are infallible. Protestantism revolutionizes religious order. This revolutionizing is nothing more than the attempt to destroy the Catholic church and religious order in general. 'The first act of anyone who breaks with the church is to disavow this necessary authority and to substitute his own in its stead, the authority of his own reason, and from then on, no matter what his efforts to gain a firm footing on the declivity of doubt, the irresistible consequences of the principle which he himself has established drag him to depths of the abyss.' Politically speaking, Protestantism means popular sovereignty. But since, as a rule at least, sovereignty cannot be put into practice by a whole people, that body is sovereign which represents the nation. By declaring itself sovereign, the state or the people frees the social groups within the political order from the laws of religious order. Political sovereignty implies the independence from religious authority. Through this declaration of independence, the social groups dissolve the bonds of universal divine law and arrogate the arbitrary right to decide what they wish to recognize as binding law. But, according to Lamennais, if the one, unchanging divine law no longer represents the norm for action, they have no choice but to make subjective material interests the means of orienting action. And just as the interests of individuals in social groups do not unite but divide, so do the interests of peoples and states. The principle of unity which was given in divine law is replaced, the moment states declare themselves sovereign, by a plurality of principles whose unity consists only in the fiction of a national interest as the guiding principle of political action. This means that the Reformation destroys the Christian unity of the West by granting sovereignty to the state and to individual reason. It destroys the claim of divine law to obedience and proclaims a plurality of contradictory and warring national interests. Lamennais describes the consequences of the Reformation as follows: 'Sovereignty deprived of spiritual power, the supreme defender of justice and of the rights of mankind, deprived even of all doctrine and all responsibility, since it alone created all responsibilities and all doctrines, has had no other rule of conduct, no other principle of government than interest; that is to say that every people is in a natural state of war with all the others, and the sovereign, for the same reason, in a natural state of war with the subjects, so that consequently there could only be short truces among the people, and no less short truces between the subjects and the sovereign. On the other hand, Protestantism utterly destroys the religious as well as the political society since it cannot prescribe the belief in any positive dogma, and since it forces man to form his faith according to his own light. For a religious society can no more be established by saying, let us agree that everyone believe everything which appears to us to be true, than a political society can by saying, let us agree that everyone do what appears to us to be good, and the one is a necessary consequence of the other. Whoever is free to believe what he wishes, is free to do what he wishes, and the judgement which determines faith also determines action. Thus, more general responsibility or, in other words, more society is established than that society, whose laws are written in the civil and penal code, has the force to guarantee and the power to sanction.'

Every order, whether religious or political, requires a norm to which it can adhere. And every order depends on an interpreter of this norm, who determines finally and authoritatively the meaning and scope of the norm. In the unified and hierarchical structure of the Christian West, the universal divine law had been revealed through faith, and mankind had, in the infallible teachings of the church, the sovereign and final authority which interpreted and applied the law. Both, the law and the authority, were challenged by the Reformation. For this reason, it deserves to be called not only a revolution but *the* destruction of religious and political order. But since no society can do without a norm and a final authority which interprets this norm, Protestantism must search for a new norm and must create a new authority. Both the individual states and the community of states are faced with this necessity. Now, if political sovereignty is absolute, that is, if the state considers and declares itself independent of religious authority and sovereignty, then it holds itself to be neither subject to nor bound by the universal law. The law which the sovereign state substitutes for the universal law is interest, which, in order to insure respect, requires force because it no longer has any moral justification. For the view that individual reason and the individual state are sovereign implies, of course, a break with the universal order. But an order ultimately founded on force and without moral legitimation is a despotic order. Thus Lamennais says: 'There is no judge, no mediator between power and the subjects; since they collide on all points in which their interests differ, they are continually at war with one another. In order not to be overthrown, power becomes oppressive; oppression hastens revolt, which soon brings greater oppression. Society vacillates ceaselessly between the tyranny of one and the tyranny of all, between despotism and anarchy.'

Given this forceful image of the Reformation as Lamennais saw it, we must now attempt to formulate the ultimate nature of Protestantism. Lamennais sums up his accusation in a single concept: 'It is the atheistic principle which constitutes Protestantism.' Religious and political atheism has been the foundation of law for the European peoples since Luther and Machiavelli. Equally atheistic is, for Lamennais, the doctrine of popular sovereignty, 'since in virtue of this sovereignty, the people, or the parliament which represents it, has the right to change and modify the national religion when it pleases. Reason, law and justice are nothing but what the people or the power which represents them wishes it to be'. If politics is separated from religion, it can only by defined as 'force governed by interest'. The result of religious and political atheism, which for Lamennais constitute the nature of the Reformation and the Revolution is this: 'a political system which, by substituting force for right, deprives the weak and even the strong of all security and plunges nations into a permanent state of war, must lead either to a dismemberment of Europe into a multitude of little sovereignties constantly occupied with destroying one another, or to a vast despotism, should one of them succeed in firmly establishing its supremacy.' Given these facts, there can no longer be such a thing as a principle of stability. General insecurity spreads. 'The reign of force was proclaimed.' Under its sway the world has suffered since the days of the Reformation.

Contemporary Protestantism must decisively reject Lamennais' characterization of the Reformation and of its political expression, the Revolution. For it sees the work of the reformers neither as a declaration of independence on the part of individual reason, nor as the glorification of freedom of conscience. But although Lamennais' description of the Reformation is the embittered testimony of a monarchistic and ultramontane clergyman, it was undoubtedly based on the way contemporary Protestantism saw itself, as far as the liberation of reason and conscience from the compulsion of the church was concerned. Charles de Villers, in his *Essai sur l'esprit et l'influence de la réformation de Luther* (1804), had seen and praised the Reformation as an act of liberation.

4

Lamennais' work, as we have seen it till now, may be called an exemplary system of political and religious traditionalism and ultramontanism. It was reserved for Lamennais himself to overthrow this system which he had made so effective. In the process, he came into conflict with the pope, a conflict which led to his leaving the Catholic church.

What were the convictions which led to the break with Rome? Lamennais gave up the idea that the structure of political order must correspond to the structure of religious order. In the religious realm, the hierarchical organization of the church, culminating in a sovereign monarch at its head, corresponded, in the political realm, to the absolute monarchy, whose legal rights and sovereignty were limited solely by the authority of religion. In his work *Des progrès de la révolution et de la guerre contra l'église*, published in 1828, Lamennais began to attack the 'monarchical idolatry which had spread throughout the *ancien régime*'. He challenged the church to separate its cause from that of the kings. In 1830, Lamennais, together with some like-minded friends, began to publish a paper called *Avenir*. Its program was revolutionary. The defender of monarchy became a champion of republicanism. There is, Lamennais now announced, no divine right of kings. 'Power is nothing but the agent delegated by collectivity in the administrative order.'

94

This doctrine of popular sovereignty is no longer an error, for it expresses the inherent right of the family, the province and the nation to look after their individual and common affairs themselves. Lamennais demands freedom of conscience, which must result in the separation of church and state, freedom of instruction, freedom of the press and freedom of political association. In 1831, *Avenir* suspended publication. In 1832, Pope Gregory XVI issued the encyclical *Mirari vos* which condemned the views propagated by Lamennais and his friends. In 1834, Lamennais published his powerful, deeply mystical and passionately written book *Paroles d'un croyant*, which the pope in the same year condemned as a 'work of the devil himself'. Lamennais' success was unparalleled. In no time, 100,000 copies were sold. Transports of enthusiasm clashed with cries of condemnation. The book was called 'the gospel of insurrection' and 'the Marseillaise of Christianity'; 'it is Babeuf proclaimed by the prophet Ezekiel.' What had happened? How had Lamennais fallen out with the church? The answer can be expressed in one sentence: the social movement, the fight for the political rights of the masses, the efforts to improve the economic conditions of the fourth estate had assumed paramount importance in Lamennais' thinking. This new orientation is coupled with a new conception of the meaning of the Christian message. Christianity, Lamennais says in his *Affaires de Rome,* far from being hostile toward the social revolution taking place in our midst, is, to the contrary, its author and primary cause. Christianity becomes the principle of social and political revolution. Christianity is no longer a 'force of preservation' but one of revolution. A new historical principle takes the place of the dialectic between the falling away from the true political and religious order and the restoration of this order. The idea of restoration is replaced by the idea of progress. The principles of the Revolution are the principles of Christianity. What the Revolution strives for is nothing else than the realization of the Christian promise. The goal of man is infinite perfection. The biblical summons, 'be ye therefore perfect, even as your Father which is in heaven is perfect', converts the history of mankind into a unified process, whose meaning consists in approaching this ultimately unattainable goal. The challenge to perfection founds and justifies the idea of progress. The law of progress is the first Christian law; it commands unceasing activity that man may increase steadily in goodness and truth. To increase in truth means to develop insight, to increase in goodness means to develop the power to love. Insight and love have a common enemy, force, under whose rule there can be no progress. Two commandments arise from the general Christian commandment of love, which contain the duties of men toward their fellowmen: do not do unto another what you do not want him to do unto you, and do unto everyone what you want him to do unto you. The first commandment holds everyone within the bounds of law, preventing the infringement of the rights of others and therefore determining justice. The second commandment realizes the good through mutual communication and brings about the merging of individuals, thus protecting and maintaining justice. It unites men through voluntary self-surrender and constitutes the nature of compassion, which, being pure love, is eternal and inexhaustible life itself. Lamennais distinguishes two ways in which the Christian principle can be realized. Up to then, it had guided and determined the individual life. Now it had begun to appear in a 'more perfect form', 'embodying itself in social institutions'. The 'mighty principle, which is constantly fermenting in the womb of all society', is, if we separate the permanent meaning from temporal and spatial interpretation, Christianity itself. 'What the people want, what they demand with tireless persistence, with never-cooling ardor, is the overthrow of the rule of force in order to put the rule of reason and justice in its place. The first principle of the Christian community is the genuine recognition and realization in society of equality which is inseparably coupled with freedom, the necessary condition and essential form of which, in the state, is the institution of elections. What else do the people demand? The improvement of the lot of the suffering everywhere and of the laws protecting labor, resulting in a more just distribution of the general wealth, so that henceforth a few can no longer exert an exclusive influence to their advantage in the management of the general interest. The good which the heavenly father gave all his children must become available to them, and the brotherhood of man must cease to be a ridiculous and meaningless phrase.'

What happened when Lamennais declared the Christian principle, which for him was identical with the content of religion as a whole, to be the real revolutionary principle of the social movement of the 19th century? Lamennais had, with great consistency, interpreted the trinity of the revolution – liberty, equality, fraternity – in Christian terms, had liberated it from its original limitation as the core of the political demands of the third estate, and had made it applicable to a comprehensive political and economic reform-program of the fourth estate for the benefit of all the people. The revolutionary trinity became the true content of the Christian message. Mankind's task is the realization of the gospel. 'In partnership with God in the eternal authorship of His work, we have, like Him, a world to create.' 'Since they participate in one and the same nature, all men are equal before God, and thus brothers... endowed with the same rights, subject to the same duties. Equality, fraternity and therefore liberty: this was ...the summation of the doctrine of the gospel, the formula... which men thenceforth were to realize in unending labors, the final goal of which was to mold mankind into perfect unity.' 'In the distant future, one glimpses the happy era in which the world will be one city ruled by the same law, the law of justice and charity, of equality and fraternity, a future religion of the entire human race which will greet Christ as its supreme and final lawgiver.' The people have the task 'of establishing brotherhood on earth', 'of forming the universal family, of constructing the city of God'. Christianity is 'the true principle of the future development of mankind', just as it was the principle of its previous development. It is 'the perfect expression of the laws of mankind'. It is the only true religion because it is 'the unchanging law and living, driving force' which unites created beings with

97

one another by uniting them with their creator. The political, economic and moral demands of the modern proletariat are proclaimed in the basic ideas of Christianity. This is, in short, the content of Lamennais' writings following his break with the Roman church. The realization of the Christian message means the establishment of the original dignity of man and the abolishment of modern slavery. The realization of Christianity brings about the rule of the laws of justice and of love. It is the truly revolutionary element in the history of mankind. It contains the religious and moral justification of all social revolutions for the good of the people; it indicates the goal of all historical movement. It alone reveals the meaning of history.

Lamennais developed his religiously founded social and political program primarily in three works: *Le livre du peuple* appeared in 1837, *De l'esclavage moderne* in 1839, and *Du passé et de l'avenir du peuple* in 1841. These writings are among the most influential and important documents of a Christian social movement in the 19th century. Lamennais tried to reconcile the ideas of the French Revolution with those of Christianity.[2] In doing so, he presented a Christian justification of Rousseau, and confronted French Catholicism with problems which, in the long run, could not be avoided. For the struggle with the ideas of 1789 could not take the form of mere rejection, particularly because the traditionalist conceptions of the political philosophy and the philosophy of history could not master the social problems inherent in the rise of the fourth estate by appealing to the idea of the restoration of the traditional religious and political order. It is obvious that Lamennais' interpretation of the Christian message as a social and revolutionary principle necessarily implied abandoning the traditional doctrine of the identity of the structure of religious and political order. To be sure, one principle Lamennais never relinquished. The problem of a comprehensive social reform always remained for him an ultimately moral and religious problem. The improvement of the material conditions of life does not guarantee the perfection of man. Rather, the struggle to improve the external circumstances of the masses can only be successful if it is founded on a rigorous morality of the working classes. That is an idea which has always played a great part in the history of social thought in France. For Proudhon, as for his greatest pupil Georges Sorel, the solution of the modern social problem was an eminently moral problem, which presupposes the moral improvement of the people because only a moral people can lead the fight for its material improvement in such a way that all the worthwhile goals are not lost in the chaos of general lawlessness and the use of force. 'Either one wills what the majority of the people wills, and thus submits to its great and irresistible power, or one wills what the majority of the people does not will, and then force assumes tyrannical intent. One still only succeeds in creating two essentially inseparable conditions: complete devotion, indifferent to the common cause, [and] a profound sense of justice for its own sake.'

After Lamennais' break with the Roman church and with the political doctrine of traditionalism, he no longer saw the meaning of history in the restoration of the Catholic religion and the monarchical form of government. Its meaning lies rather in the founding of the city of God on earth. God's kingdom on earth means the 'realization of liberty, founded on the equality of nature'. It means 'the extinction of the proletariat'. Combining these two factors, one can say: the realization of freedom means the end of the proletariat. In order to understand what is meant by the realization of freedom and the elimination of the proletariat, we must know what freedom means and what the specific conditions of life for the proletariat are. We can come close to the answer if we remember that, for Lamennais, the problem of the people lies 'in recapturing the dignity of man,' that is, in 'the free exercise of the inalienable sovereignty of man and of the people'. History is, therefore, a process in which man becomes what he really is. History is a recapturing of a quality which man has lost. One cannot help seeing the strong resemblance between this view and those developed a few years later by Marx. History is the loss and regaining of an essential quality of man. The loss of this quality

99

characterizes the proletarian conditions of life. The removal of these conditions means the regaining of this quality. But what determines the conditions of the people's life? The people, Lamennais answers, live from their work alone. 'By people we understand the proletariat, that is to say, those who, since they possess nothing, live only from their work.' The people are a tool, are 'simple, exploitable material'. They are not, like the slaves in antiquity, 'property, that can be sold'; they are legally free, but their freedom remains a fiction, for they are forced to work under conditions which they do not themselves determine but which are imposed on them from outside, by means of the laws of the labor market and the rules made by those who have the political power in their hands. The situation of the people of his time Lamennais calls modern slavery. It is characterized by the fact that man has nothing but his capacity for work which he must sell in accordance with the law of supply and demand, that he is unable, under the prevailing economic circumstances, to acquire property, which is the indispensable prerequisite for genuine freedom, and that has no political rights which enable him to take an active part in the formation of the public will. We must remember that the struggle of the fourth estate for the right of association for economic and political purposes had just begun in the thirties and forties of the 19th century. The existing political and economic conditions result, according to Lamennais, in the dehumanization of man. They make it impossible for man to be what he can and ought to be. 'The first duty is to be and to remain man, the duty to repel slavery which drags him below the level of the brutes.' What, then, is the nature of modern slavery, which results in the dehumanization of man? 'The essence of this slavery is, in effect, the destruction of the human personality, that is to say of the liberty or of the natural sovereignty of man, which makes him a moral being, responsible for his acts, and capable of virtue. Reduced to the level of an animal or below that of an animal, in ceasing to be a personal being, he is excluded from humanity and consequently from all right as well as all duty. No longer knowing what to call him, because one no longer knows how to define him, he is called a thing, *res*; this is what has become of God's most noble creature.' The condition of modern slavery dehumanizes man by degrading him to the level of an object. It consists of factors which refuse to let man be man. It subjects him to a code which deprives him of his original and essential qualities. It robs him of the possibility of being a free, and therefore moral being. The economic and political order of modern slavery destroys the basic constitution of man; it is the 'complete negation of the personality'. It perpetuates the violation of man as made in God's image. It is radical disorder as opposed to the order of the Creator, Who placed man in the condition of equality and freedom.

The law of history is, for Lamennais, the law of progress. Progress is the progress of personality and freedom. 'The law of progress, deduced from history, could be defined thus: the evolution of mankind in liberty, by the simultaneous development of intelligence and love.' The meaning of history consists in the abolition of modern slavery. 'The Christian right to equality and freedom' is to be realized in the political order. To the question, how this goal can be reached, Lamennais has this answer: economic, legal and moral conditions must be created which permit man to be what he is – a free, responsible personality. The moral conditions consist in the recognition of the original rights and duties of man. Lamennais never tires of pointing out the necessary connection of right and duty. The French Revolution had begun with a declaration of human rights; Lamennais added a proclamation of human duties, in the knowledge that, although rights are indispensable for the unfolding of the human personality, they must be supplemented by a bond of agreement, which only love can establish, if a community is to exist and prosper. Duty can only be based on religion, that is, on the will of God. 'The totality of duties which is the source of life forms what we call religion.' All we call sacrifice, devotion and love is an expression of basic religious emotions. But no society can endure without sacrifice and love. Therefore religion is and remains the foundation of society.

It is the truly unifying force which is qualified to master and channel the natural, egoistic tendencies of man. 'To deny religion is to deny duty.' – In addition to this religious and moral condition for the abolition of modern slavery, those external conditions are required which make human freedom possible. Lamennais summarizes them as follows: 'The political conditions for participating in the government, in the administration of communal affairs, and the material conditions for ownership.'

The goal of history, therefore, is reached when, first, the masses, who live from the work of their hands, are not denied the rights of citizens. Man is free only if he obeys laws which he has given himself. The participation in the formation of the public will guarantees man his freedom. For by 'participating in the government' man determines his own course, that is, realizes his freedom. The goal of history is reached when, second, the material conditions of freedom are given. They consist, in a word, in property. Only the possession of material goods makes man his own master, only property makes him free. In the future, property must depend on labor, not labor on property. It is a question, therefore, of freeing labor from the restraints which the existing social order imposes on it. Lamennais distinguishes three kinds of obstacles: legal, spiritual and material. 'The law... does not permit the workers freely to discuss their interests with the buyers of labor. The law relegates them to a veritable condition of servitude.' 'Work is composed of two elements: physical strength and the intelligence which directs it... But the worker lacks instruction and in this respect he is still in fact in a condition of servitude. He will be freed from this condition through the introduction of a comprehensive, gratuitous educational program, which must include general and professional instruction.' 'The worker... will not be the master of himself and of his work if the materials necessary for his work, the instruments which make it possible, and finally, capital are not directly accessible to him.'

With this we have presented the main points of the program of social reform which Lamennais had drawn up. But how was this program to be realized? Through the formation of labor corporations, through political association. 'Everyone... deprived in his isolation of the means of establishing and sustaining real competition between capital and labor, is completely at the mercy of the avarice of those who... exploit everything.' How can you, Lamennais calls out to the people, abolish this 'deadly dependence'? 'By uniting, by forming associations', in other words, by the political organization of the workers for the purpose of attaining their original rights. But this purpose can only be realized on a religious and moral basis. 'No association is possible, none can prosper if it is not based on mutual trust, on probity, on the moral conduct of its members, as well as on wise economy. Injustice and bad faith, sloth and intemperance undo it immediately.' Because the political demands of the proletariat, which Lamennais identifies with the people, are morally and religiously justified demands, the objection raised against them by their opponents – namely, that the people only want to assume power at the expense of the ruling class – can be refuted. 'It is not with disorder that one remedies disorder.' Therefore, 'proclaim duty at the same time as right'.

It remains for us to turn our attention to a problem which, although it has become the major problem of the 20th century, deeply concerned and affected thoughtful men in the first half of the 19th century. We are referring to the problem of the political, economic and spiritual omnipotence of the state. Lamennais saw a development on the horizon which was to threaten the very thing that was closest to his heart. His work after 1830 was primarily concerned with the idea of freedom. History itself was for him a process directed toward the establishment of universal human freedom. Freedom he understood as the liberation of men from nature by means of the scientific knowledge of nature, and as their deliverance from the bondage of the economic conditions of the existing social order through the universal right to vote and the political organization of the workers. Lamennais was possessed by the idea that freedom – moral, responsible freedom making possible a truly human life – presupposes property. 'In order that liberty be individual,

– and liberty is individual or it is not liberty – property in accordance with its essence, must be individual also.' Therefore the liberation from the existing order of political and economic conditions culminates in the demand that all citizens must be able to acquire property by labor. Lamennais saw a serious threat to the development toward this goal in the socialist and communist movement, which had also begun to crystallize in the thirties of the 19th century. This movement had also taken over an idea from the revolutionary ideals of 1789: the idea of equality, although understood not as equality of rights, but, for Mably and Babeuf, as an equality of economic conditions. Socialism and communism are movements whose intention, Lamennais notes, is also to abolish proletarian living conditions. Socialism and communism also set themselves the goal of a social order in which man could enjoy a maximum of freedom. But how was this goal to be realized? In both cases, for the communists and for Lamennais, the crux of the solution lies in the question of the significance and meaning of property. However, it must always be kept in mind that the question of property should not be an end in itself, but merely a means to an end, for the real end remains the establishment of human freedom. We can best understand Lamennais' criticism of socialism if we remember what he considered to be the dangers threatening the creation of individual property. Personal property is confronted by two different obstacles: 'Its formation can be prevented either by the excessive accumulation of individual property itself which, by concentrating property in the hands of some few, leaves nothing which can be the property of others, or by an extreme degree of this same abuse, which concentrates all property in the hands of the state.' Lamennais had met the first obstacle to individual property with the demand for the right of all people to participate in the formation of the public will. That meant that democracy became the guarantor of individual property. Lamennais met the second obstacle with equal vigor. For what solution does socialism offer to the question of property? 'The absolute concentration of property in the hands of the state is the means they propose for abolishing the proletariat and setting it free.' In the socialist system the state becomes the only property owner, and it is assumed that it will also be the incorruptible guarantor of equitable distribution of the national property and of the whole production of goods. But what is the state? Lamennais' answer is indicative of his well trained, concrete political thinking. If one makes the state the sole property owner, and expects it to act in strict accordance with the law of justice, one overlooks that the will which passes as the will of the state is always and of necessity the will of those who have the political power in their hands at the moment. Now, is there any guarantee that those in possession of power use this power justly simply because they possess it? This is the decisive question. Lamennais recognized it and did not evade it. 'Are we really to believe that human beings in possession of such power, power over everything, people and things, would only use it in accordance with justice, forgetting themselves in order to consider only the general welfare? That, since they are more powerful than any sovereign of the most enslaved people has ever been, their power would be a safeguard against the abuse of their power? That they would never turn it to their advantage, would never clutch it in their hands and perpetuate it in their race? That, once masters, they would consent in their turn to become slaves?' All these questions, which are the really vital questions of social existence, must be answered in the negative. The experience of history and the insight into the nature of the human soul combine in the recognition that maximum power is no guarantee against the misuse of this power. The individual must retain the possibility of exerting his influence; this means that he must have part in political and economic freedom, which in turn means that, since freedom is guaranteed through personal property, individual property must be recognized.

The second objection which Lamennais raises against a communistic system of order concerns the practical realization of the demand for equality. According to what principle should the total proceeds of the people's labor be distributed? There are two possibilities. Either everyone receives the same amount, or everyone receives an amount which corresponds to his ability and his achievement. The first principle of distribution denies the natural inequality of man. Man would then attempt to create the absolute equality which nature did not grant him, that is, natural inequality would be compromised if not destroyed. But since society is not in a position to alter natural facts and gain control over them, it must assume power over individuals the moment they leave the realm of nature and enter the realm of social influences. This moment is the moment of birth. 'Since they are unable to alter the basic conditions of organization and development, the work of the partisans of absolute equality begins the instant man is born, the instant the child leaves the mother's womb. The state then seizes it in order to place it in conditions of intellectual, moral and physical development which are the same for all, and which shield it from all influences other than the state's, thus determining the doctrines which are to be taught exclusively, the notions of Truth and Good, of religion, right, duty and science. It is the absolute master of spiritual as well as organic being. Intelligence and conscience, everything depends on the state, everything is subordinate to it. No more family, no more fatherhood, consequently no more marriage. A male, a female, children which the state manipulates, with which it does what it wishes, morally as well as physically, a servitude so universal and so profound that nothing escapes it, that it penetrates even into the soul.'

That means that the attempt to abolish the proletarian conditions of life and thus the proletariat itself, that is, modern slavery, turns into the exact opposite. For, contrary to the natural inequality of men with respect to their physical, psychological and mental constitution, an absolute equality is created which is impossible without intensifying and increasing the power of the state to a maximum. 'Among those in the service of this goal of rigorous, absolute equality, the most consistent settle on the use of force, on despotism, on dictatorship in one form or another in order to establish and maintain it.' Freedom is sacrificed for equality, and thus the goal of the whole social and political endeavor is abandoned. Man does not become what he was intended to be, his own master; he assumes the rôle of the functionary who acts and reacts without initiative or responsibility as prescribed by the omnipotent state. 'For being directly charged with providing for all social needs, whatever kind they may be, executive power must exercise sovereign authority in each of its commands.' The criticism Lamennais levels against communism is not directed against its goal but against the unsuitable means proposed for its realization. Lamennais' argument is based on a principle deeply rooted in his ethical and religious convictions: the principle that a political and economic goal cannot be indifferent to the means by which it is to be realized.

CHAPTER FIVE

AUGUSTE COMTE AND JOSEPH DE MAISTRE: THE SYSTEM OF POSITIVISM AS THEOCRACY

I

Any investigation into the realm of the history of political ideas and political philosophy should, from the very outset, state the assumptions from which it proceeds. For such an investigation is confronted with two tasks, the one predominantly historical, the other predominantly systematic, and particularly the latter is contingent on understanding the political, social and philosophical views and convictions with which the investigator begins his work. It is, of course, obvious that in order to facilitate a contemporary self-appraisal, the history of political ideas clarifies relationships between thinkers, points out and delimits influences, indicates re- or misinterpretations of traditional or rediscovered ideas, measures their effects and traces them up to the present. But the results of these historical efforts unquestionably leave much to be desired. They merely reveal connections and transitions. But a complex of political ideas is always representative of the structure and nature of an historical social body. Whoever studies the history of political ideas will seek to discover as well what the structure of the social body is, how the play of forces within it functions, and with which means it attempts to master the difficulties it encounters. He wants to understand its constitution, which is determined much less by a set of laws than by spiritual forces. But can this be accomplished? It has been asserted that it is not only pointless, but, in fact, wrong to compare the political philosophy of Plato with that of Hobbes, for the 'state' with which both philosophical systems are concerned can under no circumstances be considered to be the same thing. Supposedly the Platonic polity is a theory concerning one thing, the *Leviathan* of Hobbes a theory concerning something else.[1] But aren't we justified in asking whether a minimum of facts underlying the experiences, opinions, demands and counsels of Plato and Hobbes cannot be reduced to a common denominator? Even if we take the fact of historical change into account and are of the opinion that the unity of the concept of the state by no means guarantees the unity of the object denoted, we can hardly doubt that the strange, dynamic complex of sanctions and institutions which we usually call 'state' is in fact characterized by its relationship, on the one hand, to the concept of order and its justification in the idea of justice, and, on the other hand, to the possibility of achieving and maintaining this order. We could therefore assume that, in spite of the undeniable change of the formations which have been called states in the course of history, a minimum of functions has remained constant. In the state, there must be a more or less ordered system for forming the public will by which it can adapt and adjust itself to the changing political environment and the varying domestic circumstances. There must be an authority which puts into practice and applies the more or less accepted order through judicial verdict and interpretation. There must be a unity of opinion expressed in customs and mores, in religious commandments and prohibitions and in moral convictions, which form an effective, because reliable, body of sanctions without which no social structure can endure. As a rule, there are also institutions designed to train the oncoming generations to assume responsibility for this body of sanctions and to grow up to accept the fixed expectations which the community has developed into norms. And finally, there is the question of the means by which the unity indispensable to society may be achieved. We have assumed that we are justified in speaking of a constancy of functions and a constancy of the structure of social and political organizations. This assumption underlies our consideration of two such outstanding and influential political philosophers of the 19th century as Auguste Comte and Joseph de Maistre, in the expectation that we shall not only become acquainted with certain relationships within the history of thought, but shall also gain insights into the organizational structure of the social body itself.

2

From the very beginning, Comte's philosophical work makes the two-fold claim of striving to be scientific and political at one and the same time. 'My works,' writes the founder of positivism to his friend and teacher Valat on September 28, 1819, 'are and will be of two kinds, scientific and political.' Science is his aim because the salvation of man depends on it. 'I should attach very little importance to scientific work if I did not perpetually think of its usefulness for the human species... I have a pronounced aversion to scientific work whose direct or indirect utility is not clearly apparent to me; and in the second place, I assure you that in spite of all the philanthropy, I should be a great deal less enthusiastic about my political work if it did not provide vigorous exercise for my mind, in short, if it were not difficult.'

Positivism as philosophy is the quintessence of recognized laws which connect isolated phenomena with one another. As the science of society, as sociology, it is the essence of those laws governing the statics and dynamics of the social organism. Positivism as politics consists in the application of the laws of the social organism to the sum-total of social conditions. Positivism as religion means the establishment of an ultimate spiritual authority. This authority, first, realizes the scientifically justified system of education which alone can guarantee human happiness. Second, as Comte puts it in the preface to the *Catéchisme positiviste* with his characteristic and excessive sense of mission, it is responsible, 'in the name of the past and the future', for assuming the 'general direction of terrestial affairs', 'in order to bring about true moral, intellectual and material providence, by irrevocably excluding all the divers slaves of God, Catholics, Protestants and Deists, since they are behind the times and cause unrest'.

A philosophy which is not only intent on founding a school but also confesses to the goal of winning a following which is to include all of mankind in the future, is naturally interested in clearly determining its own origins. The system of positivism necessarily includes a genealogical tree as a consequence of the positive principle that knowledge of the past is required for knowledge of the present, which in turn makes possible the conceptual anticipation of the future. Auguste Comte did not neglect to fulfil these expectations, although it must be pointed out that he tried arbitrarily to do violence to the historical prerequisites for self-appraisal by excluding his immediate and extremely important predecessor Saint-Simon. Positivism's family tree is traced in the *Catéchisme positiviste*. Six immediate forerunners – Hume and Kant in philosophy, Condorcet and Maistre in politics, Bichat and Gall in the 'sciences' – connect Comte with Bacon, Descartes and Leibniz. These 'three systematic fathers of the true modern philosophy' point back to the Middle Ages, the intellectual structure of which is exemplified in Thomas Aquinas, Roger Bacon and Dante. At the beginning of positivistic philosophy stands 'the eternal prince of true thinkers', the 'incomparable Aristotle'.[2] That Plato is not even mentioned is extremely odd in view of the original intention of positivism to be philosophy *and* politics.

It is our object to discuss the relationship of Comte to Joseph de Maistre. This famous, highly controversial political philosopher of the counter-revolution is a thinker whom Comte mentions repeatedly and with all deference in the *Cours de Philosophie positive* as well as in the *Système de Politique positive*. Comte's early work, the *Considérations sur le pouvoir spirituel,* published in 1826, has rightly been called 'a positivistic commentary on Maistre's ideas'.[3] In the calendar of positivism, which divides the year into thirteen months, each month bears the name of a great thinker, and every day of the week serves to call two men to mind whose names the positivistic religion sought to impress on mankind. Thus in the eleventh month, called Descartes, the 26th day is dedicated to the two spokesmen of French traditionalism, Joseph de Maistre and Louis Gabriel de Bonald. And the *Bibliothèque du prolétaire au dix-neuvième siècle,* which Comte later, after his break with the fourth estate, included in the *Système de Politique positive* under the name of *Bibliothèque positive au dix-neuvième siècle,* names 150 volumes in which, divided into the four categories of poetry, science, history and synthesis, the spiritual treasures of mankind are recorded. Among the thirty synthetic works, which include Aristotle's *Politics* and *Ethics,* the Bible, the Koran, Augustine's *City of God,* Descartes' *Discours de la Méthode,* Bacon's *Novum Organon,* Pascal's *Pensées,* as well as works by Bossuet, Bernhard of Clairvaux, Vauvenargues, Condorcet and Corneille's versification of the *Imitation of Christ,* there appears Joseph de Maistre's book *Du Pape.* Comte never wavered in his opinion of de Maistre, who had remained a faithful servant of the king of Sardinia all his life. Comte did emphasize almost regularly, whenever he spoke of Maistre, that the author of the *Considérations sur la France,* the tract on the pope, and the *Soirées de Saint-Petersbourg* propounded a hopelessly retrogressive doctrine which, because it is opposed to the rational progress of human development, is irrevocably condemned to pass into oblivion. But this reservation does not alter the fact that Comte is indebted to the 'minister plenipotentiary' at the imperial court in Petersburg for insights into the structure and functions of society which were of decisive importance.

It is surprising that Comte should have, from the very beginning, thought it possible to appropriate all essential principles of his political philosophy from Maistre's work. How is it possible that the founder of a new religion based on scientific knowledge, which substitutes the idea of *Grand-Être* – that is, of mankind as a unified being encompassing past, present and future – for the Christian concept of God, should consider as one of his most important predecessors the vigorous champion of Christianity and its belief in revelation who attacked the 'philosophism' of the Enlightenment passionately and without quarter and who left no doubt that he considered every basically and exclusively immanent and rationally determined philosophy as 'an essentially disorganizing force'?[4] How can a figure like de Maistre have exerted such decisive influence on

Comte, the founder of a new church that prides itself on being the heir of Catholicism, a man who boldly announces that in his church the high priest, the 'pontiff of humanity', will exercise a degree of spiritual power and independence and thus a uniformity of rule which the Roman papacy, 'always shackled by the sacred college and often at the mercy of councils', never enjoyed?[5] Indeed, to join forces with Joseph de Maistre seemed rather a handicap than an advantage. He had presented a glorification and religious transfiguration of war in the *Soirées de Saint-Petersbourg* which sounded very unpopular to positivist ears in an age that promised industry and peace.[6] He had produced a defense of the institution of the Inquisition in which he raised and answered positively the question whether it would not have been better to have eliminated the originator of the Reformation for the sake of the unity of faith in order to protect the European peoples and states from the bloody and cruel religious wars.[7] To be sure, Maistre had also revealed himself a pugnacious opponent of Gallicanism, which fact would recommend him to the founder of positivism. For this opposition betrayed a tendency toward the idea of a supranational European republic, at the same time providing an apology for the highest spiritual power, which would have been the decisive motive, if Comte had invoked Maistre's book *De l'Eglise gallicane dans son rapport avec le souverain Pontife.* Comte described his position toward Maistre very generally in the *Discours sur l'Ensemble du Positivisme.* 'The vigorous philosophical reaction organized at the beginning of our century by the eminent de Maistre has substantially contributed to the forming of the true theory of progress. In spite of the obviously backward spirit which animated this passing school, its works will always be counted among the necessary antecedents to systematic positivism, although the decisive impulse of the new philosophy has since then swept them away forever by completely incorporating all their essential results.'[8]

The question wherein the permanent contribution of this backward and antiquated school consists can easily be answered in a few words.

What Comte owes to Maistre is the recognition of, and reverence for, the great and lasting importance of the Middle Ages for the political, social, intellectual and religious development of mankind, and the establishment and the laws of 'spiritual power'.[9] In Comte's early work, *Considérations sur le pouvoir spirituel*, a work exceptionally important for understanding Comte, we read: 'The philosophers of the retrograde school, particularly Joseph de Maistre, who today can be considered its head, have, in the course of their defense of the Catholic system, presented some general and very important considerations on spiritual power envisaged in one society or another. But these abstract considerations, although capable of furnishing useful information to those who want seriously to treat of this fundamental question, lack at once the precision and the universality for establishing systematic views. One constantly remarks a radical inconsistency which consists in directly applying to modern societies considerations derived solely from observing the societies of the Middle Ages which were so essentially different. Besides being, as they always are, associated with the project of restoring a system whose destruction, almost complete, is now irrevocable, they still tend, even today, to strengthen the general prejudice against spiritual power instead of rooting it out.'[10] What Comte has in common with Maistre and what separates the two men can most easily be seen if we try to determine the contribution of Condorcet and Maistre to the development of positivism. Condorcet's philosophy of history and Maistre's philosophy of society bore the stamp of the French Revolution and the intellectual and political reaction which followed it. Condorcet undertook the 'fortunate attempt' 'to found politics on history at a time when the anti-historical spirit and sentiment was most prevalent'. His merit rests on his stressing the 'interpretation of the past' at the expense of the 'exploration of the future' in order to create in this way, the only way possible, the basis for a spiritual and political reorganization.[11] But what prevented his achieving lasting success was his 'blind hate' of the past which kept him from seeing the historical continuum and understanding the greatness and importance of the Middle Ages. The *Esquisse d'un Tableau historique des Progrès de l'esprit humain* ends, as Comte put it, with his placing 'a continuous series of retrogressions' before his 'final progress'. Maistre's achievement lies in his making this discrepancy apparent. Having succeeded in appreciating the importance of the Middle Ages, he had been able to make clear the meaning of the distinction between 'temporal power' and 'spiritual power' and also to establish the predominance of the latter over the former.[12] When Comte declares that it was Maistre's intention 'to base the re-establishment of papal supremacy on simple historical and political reasoning', he wants to point out that what is important is not the organization of the Catholic church as such, but rather that the re-establishment of the supremacy of the pope is only an example of the laws governing all political and social bodies, according to which a social order without a spiritual order and an autocratic leadership is simply inconceivable.[13] We owe Maistre's work 'the highly rational analysis of the necessary conditions of all spiritual order'.[14] Comte maintains, in other words, the view that Maistre, in examining the structure and function of the papacy, has accomplished something more vital than the mere analysis of a transitory religious institution, of a church subject to history. Rather, it was reserved for Maistre to make a decisive contribution to the knowledge of the laws of social organizations. For there is no society based on the principle of the division of labor, there is no national community and even less a community of peoples without the indispensable institution of a 'spiritual power' to maintain political and spiritual order – and this holds for the 'occidental republic' which, according to Comte, was gradually to expand into a universal community encompassing all peoples and states on earth. We must not, of course, overlook that Saint-Simon also maintained the distinction between spiritual and political power, and that he was strongly influenced by the political writings of Bonald who was unable to envision a theory of political power which was not closely connected with a theory of religious power. Religious order is prototypal and archetypal for political order;

in other words, the structure of religious order must be reflected in the structure of political order. After the collapse of the traditional spiritual order in the face of the encyclopedists' attack, and after the destruction of the political order of the *ancien régime* represented by the French Revolution, it was no more than natural that men felt not only a longing for, but also a conscious determination to bring about, an encompassing and thorough-going reorganization of the political and spiritual world. Saint-Simon asserted in the *Introduction aux travaux du dix-neuvième siècle* that 'the power of the theologians will pass into the hands of the natural philosophers.'[15]

When Comte wrote, in the *Préface personelle* to the sixth and last volume of the *Cours de Philosophie positive,* that at the age of fourteen he had already felt 'the fundamental need of a universal political and philosophical regeneration', he expressed an attitude which many of his contemporaries unconditionally shared.

For Comte, the revolutionary philosophy was just as justified as the reactionary doctrine, the one because it represented the principle of progress, the other because it was committed to the principle of order. The revolutionary philosophy did not know how to develop a concept of order which corresponded to the course of human development and through which the goal of this development would have become apparent. There was only unordered energy. And the reactionary philosophy did not have the strength to recognize and acknowledge the inner justification and necessity of progress, that is, of the Revolution. It had nothing to offer but the restoration of a static system. The revolutionary school was unable to reconcile the idea of progress with the idea of order because it failed to subject progress to the discipline of order. The reactionary school was unable to combine the idea of order with the idea of progress because it failed to animate order through the assimilation of progress. Whereas revolutionary thinking was dynamic, reactionary thinking was static. This was the situation in the political and intellectual life of Europe at the beginning of the 19th century as seen in terms of the categories of Comte's sociology. The antagonism of revolutionary and reactionary demands led the creator of positivism to speak of the 'great, final crisis'.[16] In this chaotic and critical situation, under the pressure of the hopeless revolutionary and reactionary confusion, the task of positive philosophy crystallized; it was the synthesis of progress and order. The 'great, final crisis', which began with the French Revolution and spread over all of Europe, could, however, not be compared to an unexpected volcanic outbreak. Rather, it was the consequence of modern anarchy in general, which, according to Comte, constituted the essence of the three centuries following the collapse of the theological and political unity in the culture of the Middle Ages. The concept of 'modern anarchy' is a recurrent theme in the three mighty volumes of the *Physique sociale*. But 'modern anarchy', one is led to believe, is also what brought about the formation of positive philosophy in the first place. The very first chapter of the *Cours* makes it unmistakably clear that positive philosophy in general, and sociology in particular, has only one purpose. It consists in overcoming the spiritual and political anarchy of the modern age. This triumph is to result from the scientific knowledge of all the laws which govern the events in the outside world.

If positive philosophy is destined to overcome 'modern anarchy', we are confronted with two questions. The first concerns the real object of 'social physics', or sociology. And the second concerns the causes of anarchy. Or, to put it another way, what is the nature of social and political organization? This question is the crucial one. For since the word anarchy evidently denotes a condition of social reality, it must mean a disorder in society or in any of its constitutive elements. Comte's answer to the questions posed naturally leads to the core of his sociology. In the first chapter of the *Cours de Philosophie positive* we find the crucial sentences. He believes that it is unnecessary to prove to his readers 'that ideas govern and revolutionize the world'. Transposed to social reality, this assumption, formulated in terms of Comte's social philosophy (which it is misleading to call 'social physics') reads: 'Every social mechanism ultimately rests on opinion.'[17] 'The static analysis of our social organism shows that it is of necessity based on a certain system of fundamental opinions.'[18] Comte's doctrine that social institutions are determined by ideas and that the nature of a social body is formed through a complex of opinions has its roots in a tradition of long standing in the history of French thought. One cannot help thinking of the philosophy of history developed by Voltaire in the *Essai sur les Moeurs et l'Esprit des Nations*. Voltaire is concerned with 'the history of the human spirit', and this means that 'the history of opinion must be written'.[19] And not only the static, but also the dynamic analysis of the social organism can come to no other conclusion. Insofar as social organisms are static bodies whose life is regulated by some form of order, and insofar as they are dynamic bodies and thus have a past, present and future, they reveal their basis in ideas and their dependence on opinions. Since the first beginnings of philosophical reflection, Comte declares, man has always seen, with a greater or lesser degree of clarity and distinctness, that the 'history of society [is] mainly dominated by the history of the human spirit'. 'Intellectual evolution' is the 'necessarily preponderant principle in the whole of human evolution'.[20] On the basis of this assertion, which makes the history of society and society itself part of the development of the human spirit, we can understand the importance for Comte of the law of the three stages through which the human spirit must pass. These three stages, the theological, the metaphysical and the positive, which mark the 'unfolding of human intelligence', must have more than merely religious or philosophical significance. For as a 'system of opinion', they constitute the basis of three different forms of political order. Since the 'great, fundamental law' which governs the unfolding of the spirit also determines an order of precedence for the spiritual stages, and since it is the basic law of Comte's sociology that the spiritual order 'is the primary basis of all other true order', it follows that the forms of political order which appear in the course of history must also represent a progression. And, in fact, this political progression also is de-

termined by the principle of increasing rationality. The unfolding of the spirit is synonymous with the development of
reason. 'The attainment of the rational and peaceful state
which alone corresponds to human nature' is the goal of all
'previous evolution'.[21] The history of mankind represents the
'irresistible emancipation of human reason'.[22]

We can now answer the question concerning the cause of anarchy. Anarchy is by nature and in essence spiritual disorder.
'The great political and moral crisis of present societies lies, in
the last analysis, in intellectual anarchy.' Comte continues:
'Our greatest evil, in fact, consists in this profound divergence
which currently exists among all minds with respect to all the
fundamental maxims whose stability is the primary condition
of a true social order. As long as individual minds do not unanimously adhere to a certain number of general ideas capable
of forming a common social doctrine, there is no hiding the
fact that nations will necessarily remain in an essentially revolutionary condition, in spite of all political palliatives which
can be administered, and in fact sanction only provisional
institutions. It is equally certain that if this reunion of minds
in such a communion of principles can one day be attained,
the corresponding institutions will necessarily arise without
giving occasion to any serious disturbances.'[23]

Now that we have found an answer to the question concerning
the cause of modern anarchy, there remains a final problem.
It can be formulated as follows. What is, for Comte, spiritual
anarchy? The answer is, first, the lack of 'spiritual power', the
absence of 'spiritual authority', and second, the failure to distinguish between spiritual and worldly power. This failure to
separate spiritual and worldly power leads irrevocably to despotism. The achievement of positive philosophy culminates,
in its own estimation, in the reintroduction of spiritual authority and the re-establishment of the separation of the two powers.
Or, to go a step further, what else characterizes anarchy other
than its relationship to spiritual disorder? In a social organism,
it is not enough merely to recognize spiritual principles. Rather,
an institution is needed which spreads ideas, fosters their ac-

ceptance, and, most important, interprets and defines them in cases of ambiguity or inconsistency. The problems which arise with the notion of 'spiritual power' as an institution of the social body, and of 'spiritual authority' as the highest organ in it, point to the work of Joseph de Maistre.

Finally, we must point out one last meaning of the concept of anarchy. Comte had already formulated it clearly in the *Cours de Philosophie positive*, and made it central to the *Système de Politique positive* and the *Catéchisme positiviste*. Anarchy also has a moral cause. Although it might appear that Comte was primarily interested in recognizing the laws of the social organism because they revealed the scientifically verifiable static and dynamic aspects of society, we should remember that he tended to emphasize the moral element more and more as time went on. The impression that positivism can properly be summed up in the formula 'know in order foreknow, foreknow in order to provide', in other words, the assumption that the spirit of positivism is content with subordinating thinking to action, is misleading. For positivism does not limit human powers to intellect and action alone; Comte posits, with admirable consistency, a trinity of human functions. 'Sociology ought to treat all real force as simultaneously material, intellectual and moral, that is to say, relative at once to action, speculation and emotion.'[24] But positivism doesn't stop at enumerating the functions of the mind and the soul. Thinking as he does in terms of hierarchy and authority, Comte assigns these forces an order of precedence in which the heart (Gemüt) incontestably assumes the highest place. The religion of positivism is marked by the dominance of the feelings (Herz) over the understanding. 'Positive theory leads to the accurate estimation of human nature by placing in emotions the true center of mental unity.'[25] Only in view of this comprehensive theory of human nature can we understand the insistent claim of positivism to being a program of education which could be trusted 'to preside over the general reorganization of our system of education'.[26] Political abuses may not, as Comte explains in the 47th chapter of the *Cours*, be ascribed to the imperfection of political institutions, but rather must be traced to social ideas and customs. The concept of 'opinion' acquires a broader meaning and encompasses the whole of moral behavior. Comte was always convinced that two characteristics determine the nature of man, and distinguish him from the animals: the intellect and 'sociability',[27] or perhaps better, gregariousness, a word which Comte uses to express man's fundamental dependence on his fellow-man and, simultaneously, to designate all the ethical qualities which are the necessary conditions for living together. Thus Comte, like all of the older sociologists, becomes a moralist. It is in this context that we must understand the statement in his *Discours sur l'Esprit positif* that 'the major social problems of the present time are not essentially of a political, but above all of a moral nature, so that their possible solution depends much more on opinions and customs than on institutions'.[28]

3

Joseph de Maistre's book *Du Pape* (1819) had such a lasting effect on Comte that one is tempted to ascribe to its influence the most essential sections of the philosophy and political thought of positivism, as well as the interpretation of the spiritual and political development of European society from the Reformation to the French Revolution. How strong the impact of Maistre's tract on the pope must have been can be measured by the judgement passed on it by Friedrich Gentz, a Protestant and Kantian, in a letter of the 21st of December, 1820, to his friend and pupil Adam Müller. Gentz, who had in his mature years been very enthusiastic about Burke, writes that he had read the work during his stay in Troppau. 'No writer has moved me so profoundly since I read Burke's *Reflections* thirty years ago. I declare it to be the first book of our century. There are three or four minor flaws in it; but they disappear in the brightness of such sunlight.'[29] In the same period, Maistre and Bonald had published their first polemical writings against the French Revolution and the philosophy of the 18th century. Bonald's *Théorie du Pouvoir politique et religieux dans la société civile démontrée par le Raisonnement et l'Histoire* appeared in Constance in 1796; it was a work whose title alone betrays the highly interesting synthesis of natural and rational right with ideas clearly bearing the imprint of historical considerations. And in Basel, in 1797, Maistre followed with the *Considérations sur la France.* Both works are far more than political polemics. They formulate, each in its own way, a political theory of theocracy, and both present a political, philosophical and religious justification of the restoration movement.[30] We cannot here be concerned with recapitulating the political philosophy of the counter-revolution and the restoration. We must restrict ourselves to pointing out those of Maistre's basic ideas which became important for Comte. Three aspects were decisive: the principle of the spiritual unity of the political community; the principle of authority; and the idea of the unconditional primacy of society over the individual, which stems from a radically anti-individualistic social philosophy. All this is closely tied up with a conviction which gained increasing ground in post-revolutionary France, and which was championed not only by Catholic traditionalism but also, for example, by Benjamin Constant in his liberal constitutionalism. Since all communities are necessarily founded on the idea of sacrifice, and only religion is capable a creating, preserving and confirming a spirit of self-surrender and self-renunciation, it follows that religion must be viewed as the indispensable basis of the community. But whoever recognizes religion as the basis of the state must also, according to Bonald's and Maistre's opinion, affirm and strive for the unity of religion. For only the unity of religion guarantees the unity of the community. But the unity of religion can only be maintained under the condition that an institution exists which is the embodiment and expression of religious unity and, more important, the final authority which determines the content of religion. That means there must be a religious authority. Decisive is not primarily that there is an order which claims to be true or just, but rather that an institution can be appealed to which considers itself, and is recognized as being, infallible. For even the most just order is only a system of general rules which owes its existence and essence to value-judgements. Yet situations necessarily arise all the time in which a conflict of values develops and a personal decision must be made. Furthermore, it is not in man's power to make laws which do not at some time admit of an exception. All this points to the existence of a judging authority, an authority which takes upon itself what cannot be expected of man. So does 'man's weakness and his inability to look ahead', and the nature of things, 'some of which vary to the point of leaving the sphere of the law by virtue of their own motion, others of which, arranged under common genera in imperceptible gradations, cannot be grasped by a general term which would not be false in its shadings'.[31] This authority must meet two correlative requirements: finality and infallibility. There can be no appeal beyond this authority. And this authority must judge 'rightly'. These two things are obviously not the same. A series of court appeals ends in a verdict that cannot be appealed, but never in an infallible decision. Religious authority, however, must be the infallible judge as well as the final one. Maistre is a fanatic of unity. Lack of unity means the dissolution of the community, anarchy, chaos. The unity of faith undoubtedly guarantees the unity of the state. But even more effective is the institution of a hierarchy, that is, the establishment of a highest organ which is expressly entrusted with the responsibility for unity. In the *Lettre à une Dame russe sur la nature et les effets du schisme et sur l'unité catholique*, Maistre wrote in 1810: 'If it were admissable to set up degrees of importance among various divine institutions, I should place the hierarchy above dogma, so indispensable is it for maintaining the faith.'[32] Maistre holds the necessity of a final and infallible authority to be so vitally important that he occasionally seems almost to express the dangerous view that the truth of the faith which sanctions the 'spiritual authority' is not as important as the existence of an authority which guarantees the unity of the doctrine in the community. In December, 1815, he wrote to the archbishop of Ragusa: 'I believe that at this time sensible men of all countries (and even the Protestants) should direct their efforts, each in his particular sphere, toward re-establishing the papal chair in all its legitimate rights. I believe that I myself am in a position to make a society of atheists understand that, on this point, they have the same interests as we do; for since it has been adequately shown by history that a religion is necessary for a people, and that the Sermon on the Mount will always be regarded as a passable code of morality, it is important to maintain the religion which has formulated this code. If its dogmas are fables, there must at least be a *unity of fables*, which will never come to be without a *unity of doctrine* and of authority, which in turn is impossible without the supremacy of a highest pontiff. If, Sir, I were atheist and sovereign, I should declare the pope infallible by public edict for the maintenance and security of my states. There may, indeed, be reasons for quarreling or even risking one's life for the sake of truth, but for the sake of fables, nothing could be more foolish.'[33]

Making the idea of social order, and the idea of the unity of religious doctrine on which order is based, an absolute, conjures up the danger that the inner justification of the doctrine itself is hardly taken into consideration and no longer felt to be an immediate need. Comte, too, called for 'the unity of doctrine'. He, too, enthroned 'spiritual authority'. The accomplishment of philosophical and political positivism consisted in its adopting the structural principles of Maistre's theocracy while robbing it of its original Catholic content. Maistre was preoccupied with two ideas, first, that the inner unity of society and thus its existence could only be guaranteed by a unity of doctrine, and second, that there must be a final spiritual authority; his preoccupation was such that one might be led to believe that his concern with the structural principles of social and political organization was indifferent to the truth and justice of the doctrine.

Maistre gives the impression that Christianity stands and falls with the institution of an infallible authority. 'As soon as there is no infallible authority for all Christians, every question is left to individual judgement.'[34] But 'individual judgement' is, in essence, satanic. 'Protestant vacuity' consists of 'individual judgement' and rebellion against authority.[35] Everything depends essentially and basically on the existence of a highest spiritual authority. 'And thus, without the pope, there is no sovereignty; without sovereignty, no unity; without unity, no authority; without authority, no faith.'[36] In 1814, Maistre wrote Count Blacas: 'Keep this chain of reasoning constantly in mind. There is no public morality or national character without religion; no European religion without Christianity; no Christianity without Catholicism; no Catholicism without a pope, and no pope without the supremacy which is his due.'[37] It is characteristic that Maistre applies his chain of reasoning for religious authority to the realm of politics. When Napoleon returned from his exile on Elba and embarked on his adventure of the hundred-days reign, he declared that the war would begin again and that nothing would succeed if the emperor of Russia were not granted 'a dictatorship based on persuasion and universal conviction. There can be no success without unity, and no unity without this prince'.[38]

In his book *Du Pape* Maistre summarized his doctrine of theocracy and papal supremacy. '*De l'Eglise gallicane dans son rapport avec le souverain Pontife* is the fifth chapter of *Du Pape* in independent and expanded form. It contains the same thoughts. Maistre distinguishes, like Bonald, the 'spiritual order' from the 'temporal order'. Both have the same structure. One can, he writes in his *Etude sur la Souveraineté*, conceive neither of 'a human society, a people without a sovereign', nor of 'a swarm of bees and a beehive without a queen'. 'Society and sovereignty are, then, born together.'[39] Every form of government is, by its very definition, absolute. 'The moment one can resist it on the pretext of error or injustice, government no longer exists.'[40] The structure of religious order is like that of worldly order; religious rule corresponds to the terrestial. These two highest powers have certain essential and fundamental rights. Worldly government enjoys sovereignty, religious government infallibility. 'Infallibility in the spiritual order and sovereignty in the temporal order are two perfectly synonymous words.

Both express that great power which dominates everything, from which all others are derived, which governs without being governed, which judges without being judged.'[41] Both the worldly and the religious order require a 'power, which judges without being judged', a power which settles all conflicts that arise, whether of spiritual or political origin and nature, as final authority, 'without appeal', definitely and bindingly. 'Every judgement which cannot be appealed is and ought to be considered just in every human society, under all forms of government imaginable.'[42] If one should forego such final authority, the worldly and religious power to examine and settle all conflicts would be left to the 'individual judgement' of the individual. Real unity could never be achieved in this way. Without it, there can be no hope that the community will endure and flourish; without it, the community is threatened with destruction. The saving institution is spiritual authority, which alone is the origin and guarantor of unity. Maistre monotonously insists on the idea that unity is assured only if a single institution exists which constantly renews and protects, governs and interprets it. He is fascinated by the inexhaustible strength of his truth which promises to redeem man from the satanic nature of the Revolution, and possessed by the belief in the rightness of his assertion which, for him as for Bonald, is constantly being confirmed by reason and history. This authority is the figure of the pope, 'the natural leader, the most powerful initiator, the great demiurge of universal civilization'.[43] 'There can be no human society without government, nor government without sovereignty, nor sovereignty without infallability; and this last right must witness the dissolution of society in those temporal sovereignties in which it does not exist.'[44]

4

In considering Joseph de Maistre's influence on Auguste Comte, we must not underestimate Saint-Simon's importance in forming Comte's early thought. Saint-Simon also distinguished between 'spiritual power' and 'temporal power'. And the idea of restoring and renewing spiritual power seemed to him, too, to be a necessary consequence of the new philosophy of the 19th century which realized that the chaos left by the encyclopedists and the Revolution could only be mastered by a new spiritual and political order.[45] In this, theocrats and traditionalists like Bonald and Maistre were fully agreed with their opponents Saint-Simon and Comte.

What Comte takes over from Maistre are the views concerning the organizational structure of society. The founder of positivism boldly separates Maistre's theocratic considerations into two parts, and rejects the one as unhesitatingly as he unconditionally accepts the other. Comte believed that Maistre's insights into the structure of society contain truths which should not be discarded. The traditional theology and the Aristotelean metaphysics which constitute the spirit of the Christian theocratic system are worthless. Since for Comte Catholicism was a theocracy, his attitude can also be expressed as follows. Comte distinguishes, within Catholicism, between the religious and the political system, between doctrine and organization, between dogma and the structure of the community. The doctrine contradicts the law of the development of the human spirit which begins on the theological level, passes through the metaphysical stage, and culminates in positivism. The dogma must be discarded, but not the organization. Not only can it remain, it must remain, for it is nothing less than the true structure of the social organism. This structure and no other will determine the spiritual and political organization of mankind in the age of positivism. 'What had to perish in Catholicism was the doctrine, and not the organization.'[46] Comte propagates the same idea in praising the Middle Ages as the highest and most noble form of human development up to the present. The culture of the Middle Ages is exemplary in its harmonic system of religious and political order because, in the period from Gregory VII to Boniface VIII, it succeeded in realizing the only true structure of society. The reason for the decline of the Middle Ages cannot, therefore, according to Comte, lie in the social order, but must be sought in the doctrine alone. 'Positivism today, armed with a suitable doctrine and favored by propitious circumstances, is beginning to take a new look at this immense construction (of the Middle Ages) so as to determine decisively the final formation of the true universal church. Although its social domain may be limited to Western peoples and to those descended from them, its faith is real enough and complete enough to suit all the parties of the human planet equally well.'[47] Since the positivist system is conceived as a philosophy and as a doctrine of the political structure of the social organism, and since the Middle Ages had shown that the laws of the social structure could be realized, it is only a matter of combining the known and true structural principles of the body social with the true philosophy. This was the task which Comte set himself. Positivism takes over the structural principles of the Christian Middle Ages and combines them with a new philosophy, positivism, and a new religion, the positivist worship of the *Grand-Être*, mankind. Catholic theocracy is replaced by positivistic sociocracy. 'If theocracy and theolatry rest on theology, sociology clearly constitutes the systematic basis of sociocracy and sociolatry.'[48] The true 'sociocracy' liberates Western culture and European peoples from their two greatest evils and dangers, from 'anarchical democracy' and 'retrograde aristocracy'. The philosophical and political system of positivism is a Catholicism without Christian content. Comte's positivism strives for a spiritual and political order which has all the structural characteristics of a theocracy with the exception of the one essential characteristic. It is a theocracy without God. Just as Charles Maurras, himself a disciple of Comte's anti-democratic, authoritarian and centralistic system, spoke of 'atheistic Catholics', so could Comte's 'universal church' be described as an 'atheistic theocracy'.[49]

In the first edition of the *Cours de Philosophie positive,* the discussion of sociology takes up about 2400 pages. Of these, 1100 are dedicated to the description of the spiritual and political development of Europe from the Middle Ages to the French Revolution. If one takes into account that Comte discusses the structural principles of society in the first chapter of the work and in the forty-sixth, in which he deals with the necessity and usefulness of social physics and demonstrates the claim of sociology to being a science, it becomes clear that considerably more than 1300 pages are employed in presenting the major spiritual and political problem in the modern history of the European states and peoples. But this problem, seen in its systematic perspective, consists in nothing but the proof that, first, every society constructed according to the principles of positive reason acknowledges and insures the separation of the political and temporal power from the spiritual and religious power, and that, second, 'spiritual power' must be equipped with a highest and final spiritual authority. Seen in its historical aspect, however, this major problem presents itself as an account of social disintegration and the unsuccessful attempts if not to remove its causes then at least to delay its progress. This process of disintegration takes the form of abolishing the separation between the two powers, so that social and political formations arise in which political and spiritual power are in the same hands (which for Comte is despotism and thus detestable). Further, it amounts to the absolute destruction, on principle, of the idea of 'spiritual authority' in general. Insofar as the struggles through centuries for political and spiritual order and for the determination of the right relationship between political and spiritual power can be designated as revolution, one can say that Comte's philosophy set itself the task of ending this vast revolution. Positivism sees itself as the philosophy which is capable of preparing and providing everything that not only halts the disintegration of spiritual authortty but leads to its restoration and to its endowment with a new icontent worthy of recognition and allegiance. Positivism is the political and philosophical system which promises the final victory over modern anarchy which resulted from the destruction of the spiritual authority of the Middle Ages.

The scope of this view makes it clear that the major problem of the predominantly historical part of Comte's sociology corresponds precisely to what we encountered in our consideration of Maistre. The central concern of sociology is, on the one hand, the analysis of the function of the human spirit within the social organism, and, on the other, the attempts toward a synthetic reorganization of the 'spiritual order'. It might be advanced that objectivity predominates in the *Cours de Philosophie positive* whereas subjectivity prevails in the *Système de Politique positive,* in other words, that Comte, in the first work, had striven for scientific knowledge of the laws which connect appearances, but, in the second, had established a new religion and a new priesthood. However, this would fail to take into account that the problem of 'spiritual authority' in the spiritual and the political sense is of absolutely fundamental importance to both works. This objection would also fail to bear in mind that it was under the immediate impact of Maistre's tract *Du Pape* that Comte introduced one of the most important, if not *the* most important, sociological thesis into the *Considérations sur le pouvoir spirituel.* In this work and in the other minor works of his youth, Comte expresses ideas to which he remained true all his life. The difference between the *Cours* and the *Système* should not be exaggerated. For both are concerned with bringing mankind to accept a spiritual and political order and the philosophy on which it is based, and with creating or re-establishing the spiritual and political institutions which make possible the acceptance of this order. Comte is always concerned with leading man to the goal set by the law of spiritual development. Comte is fond of the notion of 'governing opinion';[50] his character has dedicated authoritarian and autocratic tendencies. It is no accident that Comte saw in Frederick the Great the predecessor of the positivist 'final regeneration',[51] that he approved of the rule of convention during the French Revolution, and that he heartily welcomed the plebiscitary Caesarism of Louis Napoleon as being the solution of the revolutionary crisis of 1848. The abolition of the 'parliamentary regime' and the establishment of the 'dictatorial republic' appeared to him as the 'twofold preamble of completely true regeneration'.[52] Napoleon I was for him a tyrant only because he had allied himself with a backward theology in order to gain support for his usurpation of power. Thus the autocratic and authoritarian tendencies in his thinking correspond to his predilection toward authoritarian and autocratic personalities in politics. Comte had, indeed, in the fifty-second chapter of his *Physique sociale* termed sociology 'history without the names of men or even peoples', but that did not prevent him from honoring 'individuals in world history', particularly those of Caesarian character.

A 'social philosophy', 'taking real science as its general and indispensable basis, immediately invokes the scientific spirit to regenerate the political world'.[53] For Comte, the clear and forceful presentation of the inner unity within his works was a matter of the greatest importance. When, in 1854, he published six early works in an appendix to the fourth and last volume of the *Système de Politique positive*, he called attention, in the preface, to the three aspects under which he wanted his work to be considered. The scientific philosophy on the one hand and the science of society and the discovery of the law of human development on the other, which are to be found in the *Cours de Philosophie positive*, serve as the indispensable basis of the 'religious construction' contained in the *Catéchisme positiviste* and in the *Système de Politique positive*. During the first half of his life, Comte saw his task 'in the construction, according to scientific results, of a truly positive philosophy, the only possible basis for universal religion'. The second half, then, would have been devoted to the forming of this religion. But it is his avowal of the unity of his work which is decisive. 'From the beginning,' he writes in the same foreword, 'I have attempted to found the new spiritual power which I am today instituting.' It is not enough for the community that the truth be recognized and the laws of appearances understood. The social organism is not only a static but also a dynamic magnitude. Consequently the complex of true propositions must constantly be adapted to the living, moving body of society and its needs. One must meet objections and resistance of all kinds and above all must combat errors and eliminate misunderstandings; this is particularly urgent since the whole social mechanism rests ultimately on ideas and everything depends unconditionally on the 'rightness' of these ideas. That means that one must, at all costs, see to it that the doctrine remains pure and applicable. This leads to the establishment of a 'spiritual authority' in the form of an institution. For this reason Comte speaks of his 'constant tendency to found a new priesthood'.[54] One could not put it less ambiguously than Comte. 'At bottom, the need for planning organs to guide and proclaim opinion always makes itself felt even in the midst of our spiritual anarchy, every time that a real manifestation unexpectedly appears which could not have taken place if no one had taken the initiative or the responsibility.'[55] 'Our mental and moral anarchy cannot, then, keep public opinion from having leaders and interpreters.'[56] Through the institution of a new priesthood, leadership and interpretation becomes a permanent office, a function of the 'spiritual authority'. No wonder that Comte was accused by the 'revolutionary school' of introducing a theocracy, whereas the 'reactionary school' congratulated him because he cherished the principle of order and authority.

If we see the essence of Comte's sociology in the recognition of the laws to which the social organism is subject in its static and dynamic aspects, we must add that the institution of a spiritual authority, which has direct supervision of the spiritual order and indirect control of the political order, belongs to the necessary elements of the constitution of a social organism. A scientific philosophy and a religion founded on it, together with an authority which preserves their purity, combine to constitute the system of positivism which, through this combination, acquires the ability 'not only to determine and prepare for the future, but also to counsel and improve the present, always according to the exact assessment of the past, by adhering to the sound fundamental theory of human development'. 'No other philosophy can deal with the irrevocable problem which the elite of humanity from now on will pose to its spiritual leaders: [the problem of] reorganization, suitably assisted by positivist reason and real action, without God or king, and giving only social sentiment, both private and public, its due weight.' [57]

132

5

The law of the historical development of man is the law of the development of the human spirit. Three stages characterize this development. They are distinguished according to the manner and means of knowing and according to the object of this knowing. In the theological stage, which is marked by a threefold progression from fetishism through polytheism to monotheism, man has the tendency to interpret all appearances in terms of those which he himself produces.[58] In other words, he tries to understand the world in analogy to himself. On the fetishistic level, he endows all the objects of the outer world with a life which is essentially like human life. Polytheism then compresses the endless multiplicity of the animated world into a limited number of personified beings which are ultimately traced back to a single creative power in the monotheistic system. In the metaphysical or abstract stage, man explains the whole world through 'personified abstractions' called essences. In both stages, the theological and the metaphysical, knowledge is directed, under the all-powerful influence of the imagination, toward 'the innermost nature of beings, the origin and destiny of all things'. The only progress made in the transition from the theological to the metaphysical stage consists in substituting for the supernatural intervention of the gods and God the 'play of metaphysical essences' to explain physical and psychic events. Only in the positive stage does man limit knowledge to appearances and waive any investigation of the reasons for, and the essences of, events and things. He begins to subordinate imagination to observation and restricts himself to ascertaining regularly connected events. Through experiments, he answers unequivocally posed questions. And by comparing the observed regularities he succeeds in determining definite relationships which he is justified in calling laws. The recognition of regular relationships between appearances and the forming of theories permits the positive mind to attain the highest and most useful goal that may be reached by science, namely, fore-knowledge, which, however, is not an end in itself but only then becomes meaningful when 'foreknowledge' becomes 'foresight', pro-vision, and which, of course, presupposes the existence of moral convictions and religious rules. Comte makes it very clear that he considers the three stages of spiritual development necessary, and he attaches great importance to the observation that 'the theological spirit was indispensable for a long time in order permanently to bind together moral and political ideas'.[59] Each of these three stages represents a spiritual system corresponding to a political and economic order. The political and economic constitution is established in accordance with the ideas which govern the spiritual system. Spiritual order, then, determines political order. The fact that, for Comte, a development of the spirit underlies the development of mankind as a social organism bears witness to his heritage from Leibniz; indeed, Comte expressly referred to Leibniz in clinging to the idea of the 'spontaneity of our mental dispositions'.[60]

It remains for us, after this brief consideration of the famous, but also infamous, 'great, fundamental law', to return to our specific subject. We have tried to show that the idea of 'spiritual power' and the institution of the 'spiritual authority' are at the center of Comte's sociology, which indisputably is, at the same time, a philosophy of history, morality and religion. We have also mentioned that Comte viewed modern history, after the collapse of the Middle Ages, as one great revolution whose real basis is the struggle for spiritual power and its authority.[61] We must now sketch this struggle in the most general terms. For only such a sketch can make clear the importance which Comte ascribed to those structural principles of society which Joseph de Maistre developed so impressively.

Modern history is the history of the metaphysical stage. It is the history of a constant revolution. The decisive event is the Reformation, since, in it, Luther, Zwingli and Calvin led the 'attack against papal authority'.[62] This attack resulted in the collapse of spiritual power as a force in Europe. The rebellion against spiritual authority is based on the principle of the 'right of inquiry into religious matters', which, as Comte said, was introduced by Luther, 'though at first in a very restrained manner'.[63] But this freedom, once granted, could not fail to expand into the 'dogma of unlimited freedom of conscience'. Comte's dialectical thinking, which he could on occasion handle masterfully, is revealed in his judgement on freedom of conscience. This freedom was, on the one hand, historically necessary, for only freedom of conscience and the unlimited right to individual examination of every traditional idea and new opinion could destroy theology and thus help the human spirit in its progress toward its second, and finally its third stage. On the other hand, freedom of conscience is no right which must unconditionally be acknowledged in every age. Freedom of conscience and thought is constructive when an antiquated, false system of ideas must be destroyed. But it is destructive when it confronts a true intellectual system. In 1822, Comte wrote the astonishing passage which he considered worthy, not without patronizing self-praise, of partially including in the *Cours de Philosophie positive:* 'There is no freedom of conscience in astronomy, in physics, in chemistry, in physiology, in the sense that anyone would find it absurd not to believe confidently in the principles established in the sciences by the most competent men. If it is otherwise in politics, it is because there are no principles whatever in the interval between the collapse of the old principles and the formation of the new. But to make this transitory fact into an absolute and eternal dogma, into a fundamental maxim, obviously means asserting that society must always remain without general doctrines. It must be admitted that such a dogma in fact deserves the reproach of anarchy which was made by the best defenders of the theological system.'[64] Everything that occurs in the spiritual order has a counterpart in the political order. The principle of freedom of conscience and thought corresponds to the dogma of the sovereignty of the people. In this case, too, it is apparent that the idea of popular sovereignty is constructive insofar as it helps to destroy the old political form which is derived from divine law, but that it becomes destructive because it is incapable of furnishing the basis of a new, lasting political order. Thus, we read concerning the principle of freedom of conscience and the dogma of popular sovereignty: 'born to destroy, both are equally unfit to build.'[65] If one wants to express the innovation in concepts borrowed from the theocratic vocabulary, one must say that the infallibility of the highest authority of the church is transferred to the individual and to the peoples. 'Whereas the dogma of the freedom of conscience substitutes individual infallibility for papal infallibility, the dogma of popular sovereignty replaces the judgement of kings with the judgement of peoples or rather with that of individuals.'[66] Through the idea of popular sovereignty, as we read in the fifty-fifth chapter of the sociology, a kind of moral sovereignty is attributed to each individual, with the result that the masses are empowered to create or destroy social institutions at will. Just as freedom of conscience and thought leads to the 'total isolation of minds' and to the annihilation of the idea of spiritual authority, so the sovereignty of the people has two fateful consequences. It initiates the 'general dismembering of the body politic', and it causes the European states and peoples, who had, under the highest spiritual order in the Middle Ages, been subject to a 'regular and permanent organization capable of habitually sustaining among them a certain voluntary order', to revert to a condition of barbarism in which the law of life is the state of war of everyone against everyone.[67] But since a minimum of order is an indispensable condition of all social and political existence, the state sees itself forced to usurp the spiritual power, that is, to subordinate spiritual order to political order and to exercise the function of a 'spiritual authority' itself. 'Of all the revolutionary prejudices engendered during the last three centuries by the decadence of the old social system, the oldest, the most deeply rooted, the most universal, and the basis of all the others, is the principle according to which no spiritual power may exist in society, or, what amounts to the same thing, the view which subordinates this (spiritual) power completely to temporal power.'[68] Deliverance from the condition of anarchy in which the European states find themselves as a result of acknowledging the sovereignty of the people, and from the radical spiritual and psychological isolation of men which necessarily followed from postulating individual infallibility through freedom of conscience and thought, can only be gained by accepting positive philosophy and the establishment of a spiritual authority. The restoration of 'spiritual power' has two beneficial consequences. For one, spiritual power fulfils its original function, 'the governing of opinions'. And second, it brings about 'the reunion of all European peoples and moreover of the largest number of nations possible in a moral communion'.[69]

6

Comte repeatedly and emphatically stressed that 'spiritual authority' must be supported by free consent if its rule is to be generally binding. In fact, he declared that 'the authority of the new spiritual power' which he envisioned for the future would be relative, since positivism is a philosophy of relativity. At this point, the great difficulties arise which one can hardly say Comte had mastered. For if the highest authority in the positivistic system has made some disposition or decision, it must insist unconditionally on the execution of its measures, since otherwise the very thing which Comte expected from the 'spiritual authority' under all circumstances, the inner unity of the social organism and the spiritual harmony of its parts, would not be guaranteed. If one takes Comte at his word, then the system declares that relative, that is, transitory decisions by the spiritual authority are 'absolute' until the same authority considers a new decision to be better or more expedient. How are arbitrary decisions in this new positivistic hierarchy to be eliminated, and how are errors and mistakes to be avoided? Comte, of course, believed that the possibility of defects of all kinds in the positivistic authority would be excluded because this authority was committed to, and bound by, positive philosophy, which is nothing but the totality of scientific and thus verifiable propositions. According to him, it is justified to demand and foster 'the assent given propositions concerning things capable of being verified, propositions unanimously accepted by men who have acquired and tested the ability necessary for judging them'.[70] Assent to verifiable propositions always presupposes scientific knowledge of the given field and a command of the methods of research. That means that only the specialist, the expert, can verify. The rest are bound by the commandment of belief, 'that is to say the disposition to believe spontaneously, without preliminary demonstration, the dogmas proclaimed by competent authority'.[71] Such a belief Comte calls 'the general and indispensable condition of establishing and maintaining the one true intellectual and moral communion'. To all intents and purposes, this system amounts to an authoritarian bureaucracy of experts.

In his description of spiritual authority in the Middle Ages, Comte had shown that the spiritual order could only be maintained as long as 'the right to immediate supernatural inspiration' was limited to exceptional cases and restricted more and more to a select few. Ultimately, all divine communication was reserved as a matter of principle to the highest ecclesiastical authority. Comte must obviously claim this same function for the spiritual authority of positivism. Otherwise the despised principle of the freedom of conscience and thought would be reintroduced into the social organism and would make illusory the blessings promised by the positivistic autocracy. Comte was forced to limit all spiritual progress and all increase in knowledge to the initiated, to the learned and competent, and thus he became a proponent of an exclusive rule of technical experts and engineers, of bankers and priests, in other words of the intelligentsia of positivism whom he entrusted with the spiritual and political organization of the conditions of human life in the age of global industrialism. If it is true that the spirit of positivism unfolds hierarchically in the trinity of 'knowledge', 'foreknowledge' and 'foresight', that is, if foresight is the highest purpose and organizing factor of the whole system, then positivist political thought must center its attention on this foresight which must lie, in consequence of its rational nature, exclusively in the hands of an educated and provident leadership.

All this doesn't alter the fact that Comte involves himself in a contradiction by making the relative absolute. Positivism becomes a dictatorship of groups that have monopolized the economy, a dictatorship of spiritual authority which controls the life of the mind. That spiritual power will take precedence over worldly power follows from the fact that only the unity of the spirit guarantees the unity of society and that 'the whole social mechanism rests ultimately on opinions'. Positivism, whose intention it was to free man, turns into the opposite, the enslavement of man, because, strangely enough, it rejects man's co-operation in this work of liberation. Man is to be transplanted into an earthly paradise in spite of himself by having all his relationships and activities regulated from above. Comte declared in the *Cours de Philosophie positive* that real existence is an attribute not of individual man but of mankind. 'Under both the static and the dynamic aspect, individual man, properly speaking, exists only as a pure abstraction; only mankind is real, above all in the intellectual and moral order.'[72] Since man's development is dependent on society, only mankind has real existence.[73] But what would mankind be without man? No matter how highly we esteem what man has handed down in the way of ideas and abilities from the past, it cannot be denied that it was men who accumulated the treasure of insights and capabilities which mankind has at its disposal. Comte's failure to recognize the basic dialectic relationship between man and mankind is one of the fateful errors which led him to desire mankind's salvation without considering the salvation of individual man.

Obviously, Comte, too, was faced with two questions in connection with the problem of re-establishing a spiritual authority: first, in which way the spiritual authority could be protected from the interference and encroachment of political power and of the masses, and second, how it must be constituted in order to command respect. These questions are unavoidable because Comte was fully aware 'that man is not less inclined to revolution than to submission',[74] and that the 'love of domination which surely is indestructible in man' is part of his nature.[75] Comte also did not believe in the power of human reason in the sense of the Enlightenment. He speaks of 'pitiful reason' which finds itself confronted with an unbelievably complicated universe,[76] and he admits that 'the feeble influence of reason on our imperfect nature' does not permit the new positivistic priesthood to make the dignity of the true social theory apparent.[77] Such insights must be kept in mind if we are to evaluate the tension which threatens the system of positivism from within. On the one hand, Comte points out the imperfection of man's reason, on the other, he assumes that the spiritual and political groups and their leaders, who, since they order and guide everything, must also know everything, possess a measure of rational prudence which is hardly compatible with 'pitiful reason'. On the one hand man is told that his *libido dominandi* is indestructible, on the other, that he is expected to submit to a system in which the 'preponderance of the heart over the mind' is to be the law of existence.[78] Where are the forces to be found on which spiritual authority may rely for support? This problem is particularly difficult to solve because Comte rejects all direct participation of the people in political rule. 'All direct participation of the people in political government, in the ultimate decision on social measures, can only lead, in our times, to a revolutionary situation.' If one were to apply this 'direct participation of the people in government' to the final stage of society, the positivistic age, this participation would be 'necessarily anarchic'.[79] But Comte also rejects the principle of election in establishing a spiritual power. 'Every choice of superiors by their inferiors is profoundly anarchical.'[80] The spiritual hierarchy, which is responsible for the control of ideas, is directly subordinate to 'the motive force of the High Priest of Humanity who names, replaces and even recalls all its members at his discretion and on his sole responsibility'.[81] The highest spiritual authority in the positivistic 'universal church' determines its successor itself in accordance with free choice.[82] The leading political groups fill their ranks by co-optation. But the question concerning the forces on which spiritual authority is based still remains unanswered. Comte believed in a pre-established harmony between the new philosophy and the proletariat. 'Our proletarians alone are suited to become the decisive helpers of the new philosophers.'[83] 'After the establishment of a general doctrine, the principle condition for constituting the empire of public opinion consists in the existence of a social environment capable of ensuring that fundamental principles will permanently prevail. That is what is mainly lacking in Catholic spiritualism, whose failure was thus inevitable, even if the beliefs had been less fragile. I have already indicated now the modern proletariat, in contrast, offers very strong support for the new spirituality.'[84] Comte expressed this belief in the inner harmony between positivism and the proletariat in the *Discours sur l'Ensemble du Positivisme* which appeared in the year of the revolution, 1848. But serious vacillations appeared very soon thereafter. For in 1855, Comte expressed the opinion that 'the mass of conservatives or retrogrades are the true milieu of positivism' because they alone defended order against the insurrections of communists and socialists.[85] Comte nursed another hope. It will always be held to his credit that in the historical part of his sociology he defended the Middle Ages against the calumny of the 18th century. The fact that he sometimes overdid his praise, in which he was not even surpassed by the romantics, is consistent with his doctrine of the structure of society, the eternally valid prototype of which was, for him, the Middle Ages with its spiritual and political hierarchy. Comte counted on the rise of a new knighthood. The young and particularly perceptive representatives of the leading classes should develop into an additional support for the new priesthood through universal positivistic education – 'a kind of new chivalry'.[86] Stamped by the spirit of positivism, filled with the political mission of science, they would enter the service of spiritual authority and thus foster the salvation of mankind.

But all these answers cannot hide the fact that the 'spiritual authority' stands on shaky ground and is not proof against misuse. In the last analysis, in terms of actual consequences, Comte is the champion of a political and spiritual dictatorship. He erects 'a well-organized system to suppress completely all independent thought', a fact which John Stuart Mill, is his well-balanced appreciation of the *Cours de Philosophie positive* had not failed to notice. Mill writes: 'When we consider that the complete dominion of every nation of mankind is thus handed over to only four men – for the Spiritual Power is to be under the absolute and undivided control of a single Pontiff for the whole human race – one is appalled at the picture of entire subjugation and slavery, which is recommended to us as the last and highest result of the evolution of Humanity.'[87] Since Comte had not even considered the possibility that his system of philosophy could ever be questioned, he sacrificed freedom of thought. Thus he became guilty of an offense against the paradoxical statement of his early years: 'Everything is relative, that is the only absolute principle.' Like all systems which make a totalitarian claim, Comte's assumes that if only everyone uses the powers of his mind correctly and thinks clearly he must necessarily arrive at his, Comte's, conclusions.

His de-Christianized theocratic system, which subordinates spiritual and political life to the alleged science of positivism, made Comte the forerunner of the totalitarian systems in our day.[88] Even Joseph de Maistre's political philosophy must arouse the strong suspicion that the absoluteness and necessity of a highest, final authority, guaranteeing religious and thus political unity, was determined to too great an extent by essentially political considerations.

This technical apparatus for insuring the unity of belief had very little to do with the Christian religion, or the truth of any religion for that matter. Comte believed that by adopting the mere structure of the theocratic constitution, he had salvaged the only part of theocratic doctrine which could assure the unity of positive philosophy and religion. But what remained was rather an imperfect construction; it was the machinery for instituting an order in a social organism which would wipe out the last remnant of freedom. Neither Maistre nor Comte had anything even faintly resembling a satisfactory attitude toward the problem of freedom of conscience. Both were excessively interested in the spiritual unity of the community, and expected to secure this unity through religious institutions. Both feared spiritual anarchy and, in the desire to avoid this, the worst of all evils, fell victim to the idea of an order which can hardly be distinguished from despotism. Their evaluation of the Reformation lacks the degree of discrimination which even a contemporary Catholic interpretation of history might have demanded. It is ironic that, in the great conversation through the ages, Joseph de Maistre, who passionately revered the Jesuit order, should be subjected, on the part of one of its members, to the criticism that his 'traditional' philosophy, which was a source of Comte's ideas, was 'absolutely heterodox in several of its fundamental theses'.[89] And Georges Sorel is surely right in saying: 'Comte had fabricated a caricature of Catholicism in which he perserved only the administrative, executive and hierarchical rubbish of this church.'[90] He was wrong only about the far-reaching consequences of this caricature.

CHAPTER SIX

THE IDEA OF SANCTION:
JEREMY BENTHAM AND PIERRE-JOSEPH
PROUDHON

I

The question what a sanction is presents itself, oddly enough, because the political, legal and ethical philosophy of the last hundred years has been little concerned with this problem. Here, too, the exceptions prove the rules. Our essay will remain fragmentary. Much that might be useful cannot be taken into consideration. The field of psychology, for example, would be rewarding, for it could be shown that the works of both Sigmund Freud and Carl Gustav Jung include, implicitly or explicitly, a doctrine of sanction in the form of a pathology of the soul. Ethnologists like Westermarck, Marett or Malinowski have, on various occasions, directed their attention to the same question. Konstantin von Monakow's concept of the biological conscience, the syneidesis, expressly places the problem of sanctions on a biological basis, so that physical and psychic illness is seen as a sanction which follows an arbitrary disturbance of the biological process. The history of religion in all ages cannot do without the concept of sanction. The conception of the karma is nothing but the realization of the idea of requital, and the Old Testament is a grandiose illustration of the idea of sanction in which a God makes a covenant with His chosen people and immediately punishes its frequent transgressions. In the image of the Last Judgement, of the human and individual eschatology, is embodied, among other things, the idea of sanction based on the belief in the immortality of the soul and in the resurrection of the body; such a belief is an essential presupposition of any religious sanction. The theories of natural and rational right, which would have the

144

state founded on a contract, were forced to deal with the problem of sanction, a fact which leaves its mark on Rousseau as well as on his notable contemporary opponent Burke. For whenever a contract is made, a sanction punishing a breach of the agreement must be included. Nietzsche's doctrine of the revaluation of all values and Gobineau's *Essai sur l'Inégalité des Races humaines* are systems of cultural philosophy which, although the word itself is rarely used, constantly avail themselves of the concept of sanction. Since there are philosophers who prefer legal metaphors in their use of language because they see the problems of epistemology, ethics and history in the light of jurisprudence, one might here, too, expect to gain insights into the problem of sanctions. Kant and Hegel are famous examples for this. And, finally, aren't many great tragedies of all ages concerned with the breach and restoration of some order? For our purposes it is irrelevant whether the atonement and the restoration of order is brought about by internal or external pressures.

The word sanction and its meaning is well-known to us from everyday legal terminology. It is not difficult to distinguish two aspects under which a sanction must be considered: its objective structure and its subjective effect. The sanction which is appended by the lawgiver to the law itself sets up a penalty which anyone who breaks the law must expect to pay. Sanctions are established for the eventuality of a breach of law. They are the lawgiver's inevitable answer to the violation of the reciprocity which characterizes law. And finally, they are by their very nature dependent on those measures of force which must be at the disposal of the legislator for punishing infringements of the law. Thus, the classical definition of sanction in the second book of Justinian's Institutes reads: we call sanctions those parts of a law by which punishments are fixed for those who violate the law. A sanction is the protection of communal order by means of force as applied by the state. A sanction extends as far as the power which enforces its observance. That means that sanction and power are necessarily and inextricably bound together. For only force makes the realization of a sanction possible. Without the protection of force, a sanction loses its meaning: it ceases to be a sanction. This relationship of sanction and force misleads one to identify sanction with force, for example in the statement that force is the specific characteristic of a sanction.

But the consideration of the objective structure of the sanction must be supplemented by the analysis of its subjective effect. This effect consists in the fact that the members of the community allow their concrete behavior to be determined by the threat of punishment contained in the sanction. In other words, a sanction is effective because of the threatened reprisal against a breach of law which is included in the complex of motives directed toward the attainment of a given goal. Sanctions are motives for human action. Whether or not they have a preventive effect depends essentially on the degree of insight and on the moral character of the individuals who are united by a sanctioned order into a community. Thus, a subjective readiness to accept sanctions as a determining factor of behavior is required to make them effective; this in turn presupposes that one recognizes and accepts as justified the force which carries out the sanction. One cannot will and accept a communal order which is protected by sanctions without at the same time willing and accepting the force which effectuates this protection. Sanctions are applied to protect those things which, for ethical and religious reasons, the community considers worthy of establishing and maintaining by force.

Of course, law is not the only form of order at work within the community. Since socially organized life is subject to other kinds of order, the possibility of other systems of sanctions must be taken into account. To be sure, the modern state has a monopoly on the use of force and thus a monopoly on those sanctions requiring its application. But every constitution contains various regulations which are of the greatest importance for a community and which require extra-legal sanctions if they are to command respect. We must therefore try to understand what constitutes a non-legal system of sanctions.

All social relationships between men and all social structures

146

have a definite function. They serve a purpose; they realize some meaning. In order to achieve regularity and dependability, man creates an order. The proper functioning of the social structure or of social relationships is contingent upon the respect afforded a certain number of basic rules. These rules, consolidated to form an order, become effective in that the order itself becomes a motive of action in those concrete cases in which it or its function is challenged. Man must orient his behavior in accordance with the meaning of this function. In this way he not only satisfies the demands of the order but also fulfils the requirements of the social structure. But an order can expect to determine behavior only if it can counteract or punish intentional or unintentional offenses. Social order requires protection, for it does not have the character of a system of natural and inevitable laws. Rather it only exists by, and derives its validity from, being made law and thus being raised to the level of a probable motive for action. This does, of course, not mean that it is exposed to the arbitrary will of individuals, but that its maintenance must be the object of common concern. The protection of order is the result of the readiness on the part of the members of a community to punish any violation of the order. This protection is also called a sanction. It consists in a more or less forceful and unequivocal approval or disapproval of the offender on the part of the community. Usage, conventional morality, customs and public opinion are forms of sanction, which admittedly change in permanence and scope from place to place and in various ages. Sanction is everything which serves to determine the behavior of men as members of a family, a profession, a class, a nationality or of mankind as a whole, as expressed in the form of a reaction on the part of their fellow man. The system of values and its hierarchical order to which a community considers itself committed in its economic, political, moral and intellectual organization finds expression in usage, morality, custom and public opinion just as in law.

This analysis does not exhaust the concept of sanction. We must consider one last dimension of its nature which becomes clear if we recall the original meaning of the word sanction. The last great French moralist and first critic of the French Revolution, Rivarol, writes in the eighth part of his *Tableaux de la Révolution française :* 'All legistators have added to the bonds of law the chains of religion.' The meaning of the word sanction becomes apparent in this statement. Legal order derives its claim to recognition from religious sources. Legal order is not only an order based on force; it is also a sanctified and therefore an inviolable order. Legal order is not just subject to man's discretion. It is not only a function of the political, social and economic power-factors present in the community. Rather, it is an order which is valid and has a claim to being accepted because it rests, in the last analysis, upon conformity with divine will and divine reason. The verb *sancio*, which is related to *sacer* (holy), means to sanctify, to make inviolable through religious consecration. Through religious sanction, an order achieves a distinction of the greatest importance; religious sanction lends the political and social struggle an absolute quality. Through religious sanction, an historically changeable, essentially transitory structure is consecrated and thus removed from the realm of debate. Those things which are by their nature unstable and precarious, like human systems of order, whose functioning depends on the insight and will of men, tend, due to their weakness, to establish themselves more firmly by appealing to religious sanction. And institutionalized religion was always prepared to assume this function, which permitted it to exert varying degrees of influence on the administration of political power and enabled it to use the power of the state to realize religious sanction. From the tenth book of Plato's *Laws* to the eighth chapter of the fourth book of Rousseau's *Contrat social,* non-believers and heterodox individuals are cited before the court which punishes offenses against the religion sanctioned by the state with exile, prison or death. The heretic trials of the Christian churches constitute their precise counterpart. Religious sanction is problematical inasmuch as it bestows the dignity of a divine nature on a real, historical order which is tailored to suit certain economic and social conditions and is based on an historical system of values. Religious sanction is problematical in another way. Whereas law and custom are content, at least to a certain extent, with behavior which externally corresponds to their expectations, religious sanction is concerned with conviction and conscience. The imagination understood as the possibility of envisaging something which is not given by the senses, the imagination understood as the possibility, as Kant emphatically says, of undertaking 'the considered expectation of what is to come', and the belief in the substantiality of the soul constitute the power of sanction. When the belief in the immortality of the soul dwindles, heaven and hell lose their meaning, unless one can convert the expectation of punishment and reward in the next world into inner meaning, that is, into psychological facts which appear in the form of consequences in the successful or unsuccessful process of psychic individuation. But the real difficulty of religious sanction consists in the objection which has always been, and must always be, raised from the standpoint of ethics, namely that the expectation of reward and punishment fundamentally endangers true moral action – the doing of good for its own sake. Finally, there is one more possibility of conflict. What authority has the right to determine a sanction, and how can the inner law be recognized which is to be protected and validated by this sanction? This question includes the problem of religion. Whatever the answer may be, it must admittedly by given by men who then insist that their decision is in agreement with the will and reason of God. But this assertion means admitting the possibility of error and misuse of religious sanction, a possibility which appears precisely when historical forms of life and systems of order are pronounced sacred. Who would seriously assert human infallibility? And who would be presumptuous enough to declare that man's potentialities are not subject to misuse?

2

If we are not mistaken, it was Jeremy Bentham who first tried to understand the idea of sanction in its importance for the community and to classify its various forms. His work on moral and legal theory had a fruitful and lasting influence on the development of English judicial practice at the end of the 18th and the beginning of the 19th centuries.[1] His writings were still being praised, for example by Leslie Stephen, in the second half of the last century as an 'armory for legal reformers'. And John Stuart Mill, in a well-balanced, just and truly sympathetic essay on Bentham, said that it was his true calling to carry the war against errors in theory into the realm of practice. In his book, *An Introduction to the Principles of Morals and Legislation,* which appeared in the year of the outbreak of the French Revolution, 1789, Bentham distinguishes four sanctions: physical, moral, political and religious. Physical sanction consists in the pleasure or pain which, given certain conditions, always follow from man's behavior. If, in this life, pleasure or pain set in or may be expected on the basis of the regular course of nature (whereby this course may not be altered through the human will or through supernatural intervention), one can say that they belong to the realm of physical sanction. If, within a political structure, a person or group of persons are responsible for administering the community in accordance with the will of the sovereign or of the ruling power, then it must be assumed that this administrative authority is founded on political sanction. If man's behavior is influenced by the expression of approval and disapproval on the part of his fellow-man without appeal to an unambiguous or unchanging criterion of judgement, then one may see in this a manifestation of moral sanctions. And finally, if a higher, invisible being exerts an influence on man's behavior in this or the next life, this influence is based on religious sanction.

According to Bentham, 'the forces and the only forces by which the human will is influenced are motives'.[2] Therefore, if sanctions are to be conceived of as effective forces, that is, forces which determine man's concrete behavior, they must be motives. A sanction is for Bentham a motive which exerts a binding and ordering influence. Sanctions are motives for actions. The source of power consists in the pleasure or pain resulting from the motives by which man lets himself be guided. 'Nature has placed mankind under the government of two sovereign masters: pain and pleasure.' They are the regulative principles of human life. It is natural for man to seek happiness and avoid pain. Everything that secures pleasure and good, and brings happiness and advantage, and everything that eliminates pain and evil, and helps to prevent misfortune and harm, is useful. The principle of happiness is identical with the principle of utility. Bentham furthermore believed in the identity of the principles of individual and collective utility. According to him, one is an adherent of the 'principle of utility' if his standard for approving or disapproving of human action and communal affairs is determined by the expectation of an increase or decrease of the happiness of the community. Subjective, individual happiness is just as dependent on the prosperity of the community as collective happiness is on the well-being of individuals. Conformity with the 'dictates of utility' guarantees the increase of happiness, lack of conformity with them results in a decrease of happiness. By reason of the 'natural constitution of the human frame' man acts in accordance with the principle of utility. Even if he does not always succeed in bringing his behavior into harmony with this principle, at least he attempts to order his actions accordingly. Bentham had no doubt that the only reliable, effective and ultimately ethical and legally justified sanction was the physical one. Political sanction, that is, the connection established by law between behavior and reward or punishment, moral sanction, that is, the law of public opinion as expressed in morals and customs, and religious sanction, that is, the complex of religious and ecclesiastical regulations and provisions, do not have the clarity and inevitability of physical sanction. Rather, they are exposed to error and misuse. The possibility of misunderstanding or misusing sanctions is given in the fact of human freedom. Political, moral and religious sanctions direct their appeal to a being endowed with free will and understanding, whereas physical sanctions remain in a realm in which the course of events cannot be affected by freedom or understanding. 'Of the four sources from whence pain and pleasure may be said to take their rise, there are three which are under the influence of intelligent voluntary agents, namely the political, the moral and the religious sanction.' According to Bentham, only the fourth sanction, the physical, enjoys the inestimable advantage of being so constituted that it functions clearly and surely without being subject to error and misuse. But if men could appeal to such a natural principle and orient their indispensable systems of sanctions accordingly, it can hardly be understood why Bentham, on the basis of Helvétius' utilitarian principles, should have been the first to feel called upon to explain the law, founded on man's constitution, which governs his moral and social behavior, and to instruct him concerning his true advantage. Although the principle of utility and of happiness is, for Bentham, self-evident, he is forced to admit that this self-evident and therefore incontestable principle is capable of being misapplied and misinterpreted. This amounts to admitting that one cannot rely on its functioning naturally and regularly. Bentham fell victim to the very difficulty he hoped to avoid by establishing the utilitarian principle. For what does the principle of utility or happiness mean? The establishment of this principle is nothing less than the establishment of a criterion for good and evil. In a note to the second edition of his *Introduction* of 1823, Bentham writes with admirable clarity that the 'greatest happiness principle or greatest felicity principle' is that principle 'which states the greatest happiness of all those whose interest is in question, as being the right and proper, and only right and proper and universally desirable, end of human action: of human action in every situation and in particular in that of a functionary or set of functionaries exercising the powers of government'. It is, then, a matter of finding the 'standard of right and wrong', 'by which alone the propriety of human conduct, in every situation, can with propriety be tried'. One can raise various objections to Bentham's work, but not on the score of having failed to look within traditional moral philosophy for a valid principle of moral and

political behavior. However, the search was to no avail. Philosophy had proved inadequate to the very task on which maximum interest had always been focused: the knowledge of what, in a concrete case, is right or wrong for all times and places. Moral philosophy seemed incapable of satisfying this most urgent desire. For, whether it is asserted that man has an inborn and unerring moral sense, or that he possesses a 'common sense' capable of distinguishing between good and evil, whether the measure of good and evil is considered given in the law of nature or the law of reason, in the idea of natural justice or fairness, or finally, whether an appeal is made to divine inspiration or selection in the sense that good and evil are understood as conformity or non-conformity with the revealed divine will, it could not be denied, according to Bentham, that all these definitions prove to be incapable of providing a 'standard of right and wrong' which stands the test of all individual cases. All these theories amount to declaring a subjective state to be a generally valid standard, and to proclaiming an institution or an inspiration, an immanently or transcendentally founded law, to be the foundation of a universal order. The unavoidable subjectivity and relativity of the moral and legal criterion of good and evil bore within it, according to Bentham, a consequence which was as dangerous for the individual as it was fateful for the community. 'The mischief common to all these ways of thinking... [that is, these attempts to determine valid standards for good and evil] is their serving as a cloke, and pretence, and aliment, to despotism: if not a despotism in practice, a despotism however in disposition: which is but too apt, when pretence and power offer, to show itself in practice. The consequence is, that with intentions very commonly of the purest kind, a man becomes a torment either to himself or his fellow-creatures. If he be of the melancholy cast, he sits in silent grief, bewailing their blindness and depravity: if of the irascible, he declaims with fury and virulence against all who differ from him; blowing up the coals of fanaticism, and branding with the charge of corruption and insincerity, every man who does not think, or profess to think, as he does.'

It is easy to see what Bentham wanted to do. He sought an ethical and legal formula which would meet two requirements: it should be incontestable, that is, self-evident, and it should be incapable of being misused. He thought he had found it in the principle of utility or, as he preferred to call it, the greatest happiness principle. The principle of utility, which is identical with the principle of individual happiness and communal welfare, appeared to meet both requirements. For men naturally, necessarily and as a matter of course strive for happiness. And misuse is impossible because the self-evidence of the principle does not permit of subjective interpretation and thus makes universal agreement possible. But Bentham was mistaken on both counts. The illusion could have been avoided if he had taken into account that pleasure and pain are not only quantitatively but also qualitatively different. Therefore it is impossible to find a universally valid criterion for determining happiness. And this insight is of the greatest importance for a doctrine of sanctions. For the three higher forms of sanction cannot be reduced to the physical one, since the sanctions have no common denominator. Moreover, physical sanction can only be understood in the context of the other three sanctions. Physical sanction is by no means as independent of the other sanctions as Bentham seemed to believe. To the contrary, it is decisively influenced by moral, political and religious sanction. However, one would do Bentham an injustice if one were to refute him only on the basis of an analysis of the pleasure principle. For, if one takes the essential motivation of his work into consideration, it becomes evident that he wanted to exclude subjectivity from the interpretation and application of moral and political principles in order to preclude despotism and arbitrary rule.[3]

However, one cannot help admitting that Bentham's doctrine of sanction is inadequate. His investigation does not penetrate deeply enough; it fails to describe the structure and significance of religious sanction, and neglects to offer a discussion of the *forum internum*, the conscience, without which the concept of sanction is inconceivable. Jeremy Bentham thought he was exempt from solving these problems for two reasons, first, because he asserted that all four forms of sanction could be reduced to one principle, the principle of pleasure, and second, because he assumed that the higher forms of sanction should be eliminated since they are subject to error and misuse. Bentham thus closed his eyes to a fact of historical life which cannot be denied fundamental importance. Granted that physical sanction is by no means unambiguous and reliable, granted that it, too, is dependent on a being endowed with free will and understanding, and that it is therefore decisively influenced by the nature of the remaining sanctions, it must be admitted, in view of the intellectual and psychological history of mankind, that history itself can be understood as an evolution of systems of sanctions. In fact, one could say that history is a struggle between such systems. In the course of history, systems of sanctions compete for the dignity of being considered the ultimately valid and determining forces of life. We shall attempt to demonstrate this with an example.

3

It is a striking fact that the political and legal philosophy of the last hundred years has almost entirely ignored the problem of religious sanction. This peculiarity is probably connected with the fact that the age of positivism tended to indentify right with might and to equate law with coercion. This identification made it impossible to understand the original relationship of legal order to religion. It fails to take into account that the validity of legal order is not contingent merely upon the possibility of the enforcement of sanctions which the state by definition has at its disposal. It also overlooked the fact that political sanction, in the last analysis, points to, and strives to justify itself in, moral and religious sanction. The thinker we believe to be relevant in this connection is Pierre-Joseph Proudhon. Proudhon, who was unjustly scorned by Marx, is the author of the *Système des Contradictions économiques ou Philosophie de la Misère*: he completed his significant and unusually powerful work *De la Justice dans la*

Révolution et dans l'Eglise (1858) with a *Douzième Etude* entitled *De la Sanction morale*. Proudhon's philosophy of history and of society culminates in a philosophy of sanction; he sees the misfortune of his time in the destruction of a force capable of administering sanction. The dissolution of the traditional systems of sanctions appears to Proudhon as an evil fate which had befallen not only France but all other European states. Proudhon, in his capacity as the advocate of the ideas of the French Revolution and as the reformer of the political and social order of his age, sees his task in the establishment of a new system of sanctions. As in the case of Barthold Niebuhr, Adalbert Stifter and Jakob Burckhardt, the central element of his moral and political diagnosis is the comparison of 19th century conditions with those of the declining Roman empire. 'As in Caesar's times, society is menaced by dissolution, and as in Caesar's times, the church believes that it alone has the strength to regenerate it.' For the third time in the history of the West, mankind is experiencing what Greece and Rome had experienced earlier; universal doubt, having destroyed religion and politics, is laying waste to ethics. 'It is this which constitutes modern dissolution.'[4] 'No thought of justice, no regard for liberty, no solidarity among the citizens. Not one institution which is respected, not one principle which is not denied . . . No more authority, spiritual or temporal: everywhere souls are thrown back upon themselves, without support, without light.' The present age is characterized by the same decadence which befell Greece and Rome, and expresses itself in the dissolution of standards of value and of the principles of political life and of social order. 'There is nothing more which holds: the rout is complete.' Nothing demonstrates modern decadence as clearly as the loss of sanction. Proudhon, then, sees the problem of modern society not only as an economic problem. Contrary to Marx, the problem of modern society is, for Proudhon, an eminently moral one. When the Christian churches and the Western religions were no longer capable of providing the sanctions necessary for all social and political life, the need for sanction became clearly and ominously apparent. Nothing

weighs more heavily on modern society, Proudhon says, than the recognition that its ideas of right and duty lack sanction. The problem of sanction is of the utmost importance for Proudhon because it always presents itself in the form of an alternative. For the existence and integrity of sanction on the one hand, and the collapse and ultimate destruction of sanction on the other, means 'certainty or doubt, knowledge or ignorance, liberty or servitude, civilization or barbarism, virtue or crime, wealth or misery, order or anarchy, progress or decadence, life or death'.[5] Moral law, robbed of sanction, is incomplete, 'whether it is the content of the law which lacks the character of authenticity and certainty demanded by conscience, or whether it is the rewards and punishments attached to the law which prove to be questionable or insufficient'.[6] The most important characteristic of the 'authenticity' and 'certainty' of sanction consists in its representing the universal conscience of mankind. If the idea of sanction assumes such surpassing importance in a system of political and social philosophy as it does for Proudhon, it is not surprising that, within such a system, the history of mankind is understood as the history of revolutions brought about by changes in the systems of sanctions which support and justify political and social order. For it is the moral conscience of mankind which, for Proudhon, manifests itself in religious and political revolutions; *it* is the real content of 'moral sanction'. In the course of history, one system of sanctions is superceded by the next. Through his philosophy of justice, Proudhon wanted to establish that system of sanctions which he held to be the last possible one. This last system of sanctions represents the original and true substance of the Revolution. Proudhon distinguishes three systems of sanctions in the history of Western man: the collectivist system of Greek and Roman antiquity, which was characterized by the unconditional political and religious subordination of the individual to the social body; the Christian ecclesiastical system of the Middle Ages, which was based on a dualism between a kingdom of absolute value in the next world and a kingdom devoid of all value in this world; and finally the sys-

tem which had found its adequate expression in the 'philosophy of the Revolution'. The 'substance of the Revolution' is
the idea of justice; the third and final system of sanctions is
based on the idea of a universal harmony including both nature
and history because both are subject to the single, rational law
of justice. The systems of sanctions are threatened with collapse
the moment moral certainty dwindles and inner truth disin-
tegrates. A system of sanctions then suffers from the lack of
'absolute authenticity'. If a traditional system of sanctions loses
its convincing, ordering and authoritative force, if, as Proudhon puts it, the 'official stimulation' has become impotent,
then the conscience of a people seeks a new way which promises it a new 'absolute authenticity'. This happens in various
ways: 'now by a change of gods and a renewal of cults;...
now by mystical associations... or by religious purification
such as the Gnostics, the Albigensians, the Hussites and the
reformers attempted; now by political revolutions or restora-
tions like those of Lycurgus, Zerubbabel, Solon, Brutus and
finally, like the French Revolution. Each of these great movements is a reaction of the universal conscience against its corruption, a true manifestation of moral sanction: thus remorse
arises in the soul of the peoples'.[7] The French Revolution
brought with it the last possible kind of sanction. Church and
state as the proprietors of the systems of sanctions in this and
the next world are replaced by an order characterized solely
by the law of inner sanction. This form of sanction must be the
last because there is no going beyond the recognition of the
autonomy of reason. Only this sanction, which is exercised by
the human conscience, can guarantee the autonomy of reason;
it alone frees man from the external sanctions which until then
were represented and applied by the state and the church.
'The exultation of the universal conscience is the signature and
seal by which the authenticity of the moral law is recognized,
the joy and remorse of the soul are its penal sanctions. Everything in this world takes place within it. But will that suffice
to assure outer order? Christianity did not believe so. As for us,
the generation of '89 and '93, long may it live, it is our entire

guarantee, our entire hope, and we want no advantage from it. The felicity of justice, the calamity of crime, such are, in the last analysis, the clearest and purest of the goods which the social Republic promises its elect, the unique prize which it offers the man of honor, the only barrier which it erects against the guilty: this is the whole substance of the Revolution.'[8]

Clearly, Proudhon did not eliminate the problem which he accuses the traditional systems of sanctions of having failed to solve. As soon as one attempts to clarify the question, how the universal conscience, whose standard of judgement is the idea of justice, is to be concretely realized in an historical context, one sees oneself confronted with the same difficulties which Bentham thought he could overcome by asserting the primacy of physical sanction. For universal conscience, as Proudhon's own sketch of history shows, requires concrete historical realization. But Proudhon's conception of the universality of conscience remains, because it anticipates a new kind of human order. So does his insistence on the idea of inner sanction, although, strictly speaking, it is no longer a sanction, since it merges with the ethical commandment to do good for its own sake. We should like to close with a story about a monk told by Jean-Marie Guyau, in his *Esquisse d'une Morale sans Obligation ni Sanction* of 1884. One day, so Sire de Joinville relates, Brother Yves saw an old woman in Damascus, who was carrying a bowl of fire in her right hand and a phial of water in her left. Yves asked her what she planned to do with these things. She answered that she wanted to burn paradise with the fire and quench hell with the water. Yves asked, 'and why do you want to do that?' The woman replied, 'because I do not wish that anyone do good in order to gain the reward of paradise, nor for fear of hell, but simply for the love of God.'

CHAPTER SEVEN

HISTORICAL AND NATURAL RIGHT
AND THE IDEA OF ORDER
AS A PROBLEM OF POLITICAL PHILOSOPHY

I

The current discussion of political and legal philosophy hinges on the notion of natural right. No wonder; our age is marked by a shattering of the sense of right almost unparalleled in more recent history. Two world wars and the critical, portentous interval between them have made the political state of emergency into a kind of permanent and normal condition of society and have led to an increase and centralization of state power which appears to make the distinction between the private and the public sphere illusory. The law of political self-preservation caused governments everywhere to disregard and violate their constitutions. The revolt against constitutionality was significantly intensified by the latent condition of civil war which spread and deepened steadily in the period between the wars. It was the necessary consequence of totalitarian and imperialistic ideologies, which aspired to a new hegemony and to a reorganization of peoples and states in Europe and in the whole world through a revolutionary overthrow of the existing order. It was also the consequence of the fact that, in all nations, political parties developed which received directives from abroad and thus were potentially prepared to commit treason in decisive moments. The Second World War, like the French wars against Europe in the age of the great Revolution, was waged ideologically and propagandistically as a civil war. The state's measures for self-protection necessarily curtail the constitutionally guaranteed rights of the citizens. The modern totalitarian state, which has at its disposal the technical apparatus for influencing men optically and acoustically for its own

purposes, makes uncertainty in the realm of law a principle of its action. In order to preserve itself, it would like to do nothing more than to turn men into a formless, malleable mass. The cunning scientific methods for creating terror and the deliberate, medical alteration of personality represent the ultimate extreme of deliverance into the hands of a radical irrationalism which makes all action subject to 'punishment' and thus no action 'safe'. These methods serve a planned increase of uncertainty in the realm of law, the purpose of which is to make man a pliant instrument or passive object of arbitrary power.

After the Second World War, under the frightening impression of the 'legal' crimes perpetrated under national socialism, a wave of new interest in the principles of natural right and in the idea of the right of resistance against the power of the state swept through Germany.[1] Both tendencies sought and found a context in the Western natural-rights tradition which, since Hegel and the triumphal progress of the historical school on the one hand, and the predominance of positivism on the other, had been forced into the defensive. The verdict pronounced on the ideology and practice of the totalitarian state, and on the radical racial doctrine of law, applied as well to those intellectual trends which were guilty of having helped to pave their way. Legal positivism was forced to undergo most severe criticism. In fact, as Gustav Radbruch wrote in an appendix to the fourth edition of his *Rechtsphilosophie* (1950), it had, 'with its conviction that "law is law," made the German legal profession powerless against laws of arbitrary and criminal content'. For consistent legal positivism, every state appears as a 'rule of law' (Rechtsstaat) 'insofar as we understand by the term rule of law a state which has a legal order' – thus Hans Kelsen in his *Reine Rechtslehre* of 1934. The identification of right and state rests on the conception that both are nothing more than the regulation of human conduct by force without any evaluation of its moral justification. The expression 'rule of law', Kelsen declared in his work *Der Soziologische und der juristische Staatsbegriff* (1922), is a redundancy. 'The rule that force be exercised only when and how a despot commands that it be exercised is just as legitimate as that force be exercised when and how a popular parliament decides to do so.' It is of no consequence which hypothesis concerning the origin of political power one prefers. For both cases merely express a radically subjective ideological prejudice which cannot be generally binding or valid.

Nor can historicism escape severe criticism. For the philosophical consequences of historicism, originally intended as a counter-movement against the abstract and universal doctrine of rational right in the 18th century, appeared to be epistemological and moral relativism. For if it is true that man's nature is essentially historical, then all knowledge is necessarily transitory. It is characteristic of historicism that it sees the totality of what a man accomplishes as the expression of his soul. Thus it can effect a momentous and ominous transformation; the process of understanding is no longer to be understood as directed toward the object, but becomes the manifestation of an individual, temporally and spatially conditioned mind. It is no longer correspondence to the facts but rather the adequate or inadequate expression of inner, psychological factors which is the measure of knowledge. The so-called irrefutable truths and eternal insights, says Oswald Spengler in the *Untergang des Abendlandes,* are only true for him who created them and only eternal in terms of that subjective view of the world to which they owe their existence. 'General validity is always a false inference from oneself to others.'

Radical historicism reached the same conclusions as consistent positivism. If moral insights change according to place and time, if they are only the manifestation of a complex of individualized drives or of a single mind, then no general norms can be set up, and the enforcability, through convention or sanction, of a specific mode of conduct becomes the criterion of justice. This means that might and right are identical. This identification necessarily follows from the rejection of the possibility of separating norm and fact. Of course, it is impossible to separate completely norm from fact in the realm of intellectual and social reality; the two are interdependent and constantly interacting. The use of force always presupposes the readiness to exercise it. In practice, this means that functionaries are willing to perform the missions assigned to them, whether for personal reasons ranging from the sincere conviction that the use of force is justified to considerations of prestige or expediency, or for religious, pseudo-religious or ideological reasons. What we are trying to say is that factuality (or 'positivity', to use Hegel's word in the sense of his early writings) cannot exist without reference to norm. Every form of order claims to be an order founded on principles. This very phenomenon betrays the mutual interdependence of the normative and factual realms.

It is understandable that the rejection of the idea of natural right as we find it in both historicism and positivism should be labeled nihilism, as in Leo Strauss' book *Natural Right and History* (1953). There can be no doubt that behind the notion of natural right lies man's longing for a criterion which permits him to evaluate critically the changing spiritual and political scene. The rebirth of natural right is the result of the disintegration of the sense for legality, the reaction to positivistic and historical relativism. Man appeals to natural right when he is stifled by the positive and the factual, or when he is seized by despair in the face of the overwhelming might of the centralized state. Natural right comes into its own whenever man finds himself at the mercy of the laws of society which he not only cannot master but cannot even influence any longer, whenever man has lost control over those things which should be the stuff to try, prove and fulfil his own destiny, whenever man rebels against the power of omnipotent collectivity for the sake of his economic and spiritual independence. It is the rebellion against facts which have absorbed norms, and against norms which lend the aura of justice to mere factual power, which constitutes the return to a right of nature. Natural right apparently can do all this because, by its very nature and origin, it is an idea above and beyond time and place. The idea of natural right embodies the standard of value by which the factual and the positive are measured. Only the just order of society revealed by the idea of natural right can prove a worthy goal and fulfilment of life. Natural right becomes the 'conscience of positive law', the 'guarantee that positive law satisfies the idea of right and achieves the immediate goal of protection by law while keeping in mind the ultimate goal of justice'. In his Berlin lecture *Über das Naturrecht* in 1948, Heinrich Mitteis took a stand which marked the high point in the struggle against historicism and positivism. 'Natural right is truly valid right... Natural right breaks positive right.' There would be no objection to this definition and its unquestionably revolutionary implications if there were clear and undisputed agreement on the question of what is to be accepted as natural right. The attempt to discover natural norms remains unavailing. Anyone expecting a natural rights code containing commandments and prohibitions for the various realms of social life will be disappointed. Man's nature is extremely reserved when questioned about the laws governing it. Whenever we try to grasp the fundamental constitution of man in order to discover the principles which a natural-rights code would have to include, his nature seems to elude us. In its place, we discover some one historical form of man's existence. Wherever and whenever we think we are dealing with man's nature pure and simple, we discover instead some formed and stylized nature. If, following the old rule, we summarize natural right in the commandment that one must live in accordance with nature, we meet with the fundamental difficulty that one is never able to encounter this 'nature'. One is tempted to hold the concept of nature to be a mere construction of human longing. The legend of natural man who lived in an original and just paradise turns out to be a myth created by civilized man who is weary of his artificial life dependent on manifold technological skills and permeated with instruments and devices, and who now dreams of a condition which has never had, and will never have, anything to do with reality. It seems as though we are dealing with a dream in which we create a nature corresponding to our desires, a nature which includes those things we consider worthy of having. Could it be that man's nature lies precisely in his

creating and maintaining a culture? Could it be that man's nature consists in what Hegel called 'mediation' (Vermitt-lung)? In other words, must we accomplish those things which nature denies us on the natural, instinctive level, through our own planning based on gradually increasing knowledge of nature's laws and on our 'considered expectation of the future', as Kant once put it? This would mean that natural functions operate in a medium of will and intent, imagination and aes-thetic creativity. But it would also mean that the natural func-tions represent a task which man, on the basis of his capacity 'to choose his own way of life and not, like the animals, be tied to one particular one', must accomplish in freedom and by reason. Man, as the being which has been released from the tutelage of nature, and has entered into the condition of free-dom, stands, 'as it were, at the edge of an abyss', to quote Kant once more; he must choose his life and he must lead his life. In other words, life is man's task and responsibility. Now, if these assumptions are right, what can 'natural' mean for a being capable, with the help of reason and imagination, of misusing his natural biological functions, of alienating them from their original purpose, and of subjecting them to a process of refine-ment? What can 'natural' mean for a being capable, as man is, of self-estrangement, so that his existence seems fo find its fulfilment in his social rôle or atrophies in some function within an economy based on the division of labor? What can man's nature be if, lacking instinct but endowed with imagination and reason, he is meant to determine his own destiny? How can a catalogue of rights be derived from human nature, if this nature consists in mediation, self-estrangement, culture and civilization? (By culture we mean everything having to do with *cultura animi*, by civilization everything connected with the establishment and organization of society.) Even if we admit that cultures and civilizations can be seen to degenerate and deteriorate, this by no means justifies the concept of a 'natural' culture or 'natural' civilization. Philosophies of history and politics are concerned, almost without exception, with what they consider their most important and pressing task: finding the reasons for the rise and fall of cultures and states. They regularly and unanimously place their main emphasis on moral and spiritual factors, such as selfishness, which clouds the view for the whole of society, or the lack of a capacity for sacrifice. That means that history and the state are considered man's work, and that he is made responsible for them.

In the last analysis, there are only two principles which can properly claim to represent the essence of natural right: 'Do what is just, and abstain from what is unjust', and the time-honored rule, 'To each his own.'[2] Custom has it that like is to be treated like, and unlike unlike. But the determination of likeness and unlikeness presupposes a scale of values. This scale of values, however, by no means guarantees that like remains like, and unlike unlike. For isn't there a dangerous ambiguity in the concept of likeness? Likeness can be affirmed or denied according to the selecting perspective which is applied. Things can be alike in some ways, unlike in others. What happens when two parties with differing interests each demands action conforming to their perspective? In both cases, one would have treated like like, and unlike unlike; natural right would not have been violated. And yet it is evident that natural right cannot offer a clear solution in the case of a typical conflict.

It is no accident that in contemporary philosophy a strong and well planned attack is being leveled against historicism.[3] The struggle against the historization of man has begun. Thus the idea of natural right is winning support from those philosophical movements which oppose natural man to historical man. The philosophy of our day is striving to re-establish the nature of man. To oppose natural man to historical man means to expect to be able to deduce a complex of norms from a constant nature of man which is beyond historical change and serves as a point of orientation. The appeal to man's nature is intended to guarantee an order independent of spatial and temporal circumstances. It is evident that everything depends on a single question: what is the nature of man? There can be no doubt that two complex and ambiguous concepts are combined in the notion of natural right. Neither the concept of

nature nor the idea of right are independent of man's philosophical and religious understanding of himself. Both the history of
natural right and the history of man's self-interpretation are as
rich and varied as they are full of mutually contradictory elements. Can the Christian interpretation of man as a being
depraved through his own guilt, dependent on grace for undeserved salvation, and challenged by God, be reconciled with,
say, the Ciceronian hymn in the first book of the *Laws?* There
we find man depicted as a clever and discerning being, capable
of foresight and endowed with memory; created by the highest
being, he is gifted with the power of reason and the capacity
for reflection, so that, of everything on earth and in heaven,
man alone is *particeps rationis*. And since there is nothing higher
than this reason common to both God and man, he finds in the
societas rationis the primary relationship between himself and
God. Or can the view of Thomas Hobbes, who declares with ma-
nificient terseness that a 'perpetual and restless desire of power
after power that ceaseth only in death' is the 'general inclina-
tion of all mankind', be equated with that of Carl Gustav Carus,
according to whom, following Plato and Plotinus, each human
personality is determined by 'the innate peculiarity and uniqueness of its idea', by 'the peculiar inner godliness of its particular
nature'? It might be objected that these examples have been
selected for the sole purpose of emphasizing the differences between these views on the nature of man. But since it is impossible even for the various theological systems of the Christian
churches and sects to find a common formulation of natural
right, it should not be surprising that no such formulation can
be found for the entire Western natural-rights tradition beginning with Plato and Aristotle on the one hand and the sophists
on the other. Even if one were ready to reduce this tradition to
two sources, the one voluntaristic, the other rationalistic, the
differences would remain great enough; one can hardly reconcile
idealist-rationalistic natural right with existentialist-volunta-
ristic natural right. If man's nature lies in his reason, he has a
rational social constitution from which, with the aid of the
understanding, a just and eternally valid order can be deduced.

But if man's nature lies in a pre-rational or perhaps even anti-rational will to self-assertion or procreation, or in unconscious desires and drives, then right and order become a function of specific decisions and situations determined by the momentary distribution of power among the individuals involved.[4]

In view of the manifold contradictions which arise in trying to define the concept of the *natura hominis,* it is extremely difficult, if not impossible, to determine the basis for a code of nature. But even if we recall the many, mutually exclusive principles of law which have claimed to satisfy the demands of justice, this does not mean that the idea of natural right does not correspond to a profound and indestructible human need, and that it is not justified by the very constitution of man. The justification of natural right lies in the ideas of standard and justice. The idea of natural right springs from the need for opposing positive order with an order that should be. Natural right is man's designation for true order. It includes what man believes to be his inalienable property and his indisputable rights. But it does not guarantee either that he can effect his rights or that he can formulate what it is that he possesses in such a way that it is valid for all times and in all places. For it is part of the nature of ideas that they are incapable of being adequately realized.

2

There could hardly be a more instructive and complete statement of the contrast between a theory of law and state which justifies its methodology and criteria through history, and such a theory which derives method and criteria from nature, than the famous article announcing the founding of the historical school. Friedrich Carl von Savigny's book *Vom Beruf unserer Zeit für Gesetzgebung und Rechtswissenschaft,* published in 1814, was an answer to Anton Friedrich Justus Thibaut, who, in a work *Über die Notwendigkeit eines allgemeinen bürgerlichen Rechts für Deutschland,* of the same year, had argued the advantages of a pan-Germanic code of law. Thibaut was considered a champion of natural right. He was thus the descendent of a move-

ment in the 18th century in which, as Savigny put it, 'an utterly unenlightened desire for knowledge had stirred throughout Europe'. Instead of a 'sense and feeling for the greatness and uniqueness of other ages, as well as for the natural development of peoples and constitutions', they cultivated 'unlimited expectations of the present time' which they believed destined to be nothing less 'than the true representation of absolute perfection'. Turning now to Thibaut's doctrines, we are struck by two pecularities. Quite contrary to the other champions of natural right who defend a cosmopolitical universalism, Thibaut is a decided advocate of the small state. 'Large states,' he said, 'are always in an unnatural state of tension and exhaustion!' A large state must practice the 'suppression of individuality and variety for the sake of unity', and there is 'no really intimate connection between the regent and the subjects'. With their 'wealth of variety, the Germans will always maintain a distinguished position among the peoples of the world, whereas, if the powerful hand of a single individual were to succeed in bringing full political unity to the German peoples, everything could easily be reduced to dullness and monotony'. And second, Thibaut displays a strongly developed sense for the intellectual and psychic peculiarities of peoples and states. Since, as he points out, 'our whole native legal system' is 'incomplete and empty', 'at least ninety out of a hundred legal cases' must 'be decided on the basis of adopted foreign legal codes, canon law and Roman law'. The last and major source of law remains Roman law, 'that is, the work of a nation very foreign to us, from its most decadent period, which bears the traces of its decay on every page'. Only someone emotionally biased could consider the Germans fortunate 'in having accepted this ill-conceived work' and seriously urge that it be retained. The Germans do not understand those ideas of the Roman people, 'which necessarily made an infinite number of things easily understandable for the Romans which for us are a puzzle'. Roman law corresponds 'to the spirit of the Romans' but not to that of the Germans. One cannot, therefore, accuse Thibaut of not having had a concept of national character (Volksgeist) or of trying to subject the German peoples to a universal, rational world-law. Rather, he envisioned a code which, born of the German spirit, would clearly and unequivocally express its views on law. 'Therefore grant the citizen the priceless good fortune of letting him live under the protection of strong, unaffected laws, free, safe and defiant of his neighbor, and enjoy his rights as head of a family, property-owner and businessman without anxiety or fear of his fellows. This will revive the true German spirit, furnish the state with vigorous defenders, and free us of the numerous excrescences which have until now tended to foist all the French affectations and distortions upon our people.' Whoever strives for 'a German national code' as 'the result of national strength' can hardly be accused of lacking a sense of 'law corresponding to a people and its tradition'. Admittedly, a strain of natural-rights doctrine is undeniably present in Thibaut's thinking; he considers civil law to be 'founded, on the whole, only on the human heart, understanding and reason'. All too often, Thibaut feels, 'the sanctity of tradition' conceals prejudices conditioned by place and time. And he is aware that a doctrine of law which orients right according to the specific spirit of a people, according to the time and place or circumstance, is open to the serious objection that, by taking historical facts into consideration, one ends up by 'finally declaring everything thinkable to be right or at least not wrong, because even the maddest notions have had their adherents here and there'. Whoever adapts right to time, place and the spirit of a people is guilty of 'confusing the usual consequences of a given phenomenon with what, according to reason, can and should be'. The orientation of right according to historical facts manifests a 'lack of any profound sense of right'. That is the natural-rights philosophy at the center of Thibaut's legal thought.

Now what does Savigny bring forward against this? The natural-rights theory is found wanting in that it seeks systems of laws which 'avoid all historical peculiarities and, being purely abstract, are equally applicable to all peoples and ages'. Savigny opposed the idea of a practicable natural or rational right, which promised to be 'valid as an ideal code of law for all times and situations', primarily with the doctrine of national character (Volksgeister), according to which civil law and constitutions, customs and languages have a certain character peculiar to the peoples in question. And secondly, inquiring into the origin and development of law, he concludes that it arises involuntarily out of the common consciousness of the people, and does not owe its existence to legislation, which has *ex definitione* the character of intention and rational reflection. The legislator acts 'freely and at his own discretion', 'according to his measure of insight and strength'; the proper way, however, for a people to create law is, according to Savigny, entirely different. Custom and national belief bring forth law. Everywhere, 'silent, inner forces', not the discretion of the lawgiver, are at work. Law is originally unwritten law. The metaphors which Savigny uses to describe the origin of law are borrowed from nature; just as a people represents an organism, so is the development of law a process of growth. Laws and constitutions, customs and beliefs are brought forth 'by the higher nature of the people as a constantly growing and developing whole'. This 'higher nature' can only be understood as a nature determined by mind and soul. The 'material of law' necessarily proceeds 'from the innermost nature of the nation itself and of its history'. 'Every age should strive to penetrate, rejuvenate and preserve this material.'[5] Such is the confession of faith of the historical school.

But the doctrine of historical right was faced with an enormous difficulty. It did provide an arsenal of intellectual weapons suited to a conservative or even reactionary political philosophy, which was capable of resisting the idea of an abstract, rational world-law. But precisely the development of German jurisprudence, in its adoption of Roman law, (that 'fateful event' lamented by Georg Beseler) confronted it with a case which could only be considered a serious aberration, in fact, a terrible mistake. The organic development of the idea of right on the part of a people thus admitted of deviations. But that meant that the silent, inner forces of the people's spirit clearly did not show themselves strong enough effectively to withstand foreign influences. Georg Beseler, in his famous book *Volksrecht und Juristenrecht* (1843), spoke of 'describing a completely normal, organic development of law without any particular disturbances'. But there are also phenomena which disturb any normal development, such as despotism and violence, by which a people can be forced out of the course of its natural development. At this point, the entire system of organic metaphors has become very problematical. Two things become evident: first, the conception of a people as a 'natural whole' and a 'living organism' is questionable; an explanation must be sought for the fact that a foreign notion of right can influence a nation's own peculiar sense of right. And second, the nature of a people's spirit assumes a normative function; it becomes a measure for determining whether a legal maxim conforms to the character of a people or not.

If we now try to formulate the result of the comparison between Savigny's historical conception of law and Thibaut's natural conception, we notice a strange merging of the two positions. Both schools are founded on the idea of standard. And both are faced with the necessity of explaining why there are deviations from this standard. The historical school contrasts the normal, undisturbed development of a people's idea of right with the possibility of deforming this idea of right. It makes use of the idea of a true right, in other words, of natural right, in the sense of the standard, correct right, the right proper to an individual people. And the natural school – Savigny called it the unhistorical school – believes that it is in possession of rational right and must consequently be able to explain why the rational is not always realized. It finds itself forced to explain this fact be reference to historical circumstances. The historical view of right would lead to an unconditional surrender of norms to facts if it did not repeatedly refer to the idea of a standard which is always called upon when normal development is compared to abnormal development. And the natural view of right would lead to a total separation of rational right from reality if it did not constantly try to adapt reason to historical facts, which also means trying to raise facts to the level of reason. The failure to realize natural right must be explained historically. And historical right must refer to the idea of natural right, because the concept of standard is founded on trans-historical validity.[6]

3

The central concept of political philosophy appears to us to be the concept of order.[7] There can be hardly any doubt that all social structures, large and small, permanent or transitory, have, from the very beginning, some kind of order. Wherever life has meaning, a society is founded among men. The realization and fulfilment of meaning exceeds purely subjective and personal limits; it affects and involves one's fellow man. And since it is a socially constructive force, it necessarily institutes an order. A family has an order just as a friendship does. All public and private associations, regardless of the purpose for which they may have been established, find an order suitable to their interests and intentions. All peoples have a mental and psychic constitution which they preserve through many generations despite favorable and unfavorable circumstances and fortunes. We are accustomed, wrongly, to be sure, to abstract the concept of order as such from the structures we call states. In an age in which a universal, rational technology has decreased the distance between continents and made the mutual economic, political and ideological interdependence of all peoples a law of all human action, it is necessary to re-examine the idea of order. In doing so, we must not overlook the tendency of religion, in protecting the unity and purity of the faith, to strive for an order as soon as the content of faith and revelation is formulated into dogma, and to develop a cult for the worship of the highest being and the attainment of salvation. It cannot be denied that the Western Christian churches and sects created a system of order which was exemplary because it bore in it the essential elements of order as such.

We want to clarify whether what we call order does not have a definite structure. We emphatically do not want to assert that

173

in all realms of life – in the family, in friendship, in private and public associations, within classes, among peoples, in churches and states, or for all of mankind – the concept of order can be used without any differentiation of meaning. The decisive question for us is whether a valid order, that is, an order which determines men's actions through its meaning and purpose, itself has a specific structure. We believe that we can answer the question in the affirmative. We are of the opinion that, if an order is to prevail, certain conditions must be fulfilled. And we are furthermore of the opinion that an order, to be effective, must possess certain indispensable characteristics. The concept of order includes certain institutions without which the authority of the order itself would become questionable. If order is to accomplish its task, it must be provided with the necessary means to do so. There is, one might say, a logic of order. It includes the institutional tools which make possible the realization of order.

Wherever there is order, a multitude of people is united into a single body. We know of no social structure that does not have an order. Order is vulnerable; the attempt will always be made to violate it or to evade it. Order is not arbitrary, and yet it depends on the human will; for whether or not it is valid depends on man who acknowledges it by abiding by it. Order is never something which has its way, by some natural necessity, against the will of man. There is, in this sense, no inevitable order. Order arises from the nature of things, but it is up to man to discover what this nature of things is. Where there is to be order, the order itself, or at least the meaning and purpose expressed in it and determining it, must be made the motive force of human action. Herein, in the final analysis, lies the validity of order. Whoever seeks the fulfilment of life's meaning makes the meaning of order the law of his actions. He submits to the order, which follows from the recognition of meaning with a kind of inner necessity. If it is true that the validity of order consists in the acceptance of order, it follows that order is mediated, that is, that it is something which is realized in the medium of intention and consideration, of planning and expectation. Order is always the work of man; he is responsible for it, even if it results from 'natural' demands and if it objectifies basic physical needs and drives. Ultimately, therefore, it is, as is all of social existence, a necessary factor of ethical action and moral behavior.

In speaking of order in society, we must consider the factor of time. For a given order fulfils its meaning and purpose in time; this is the case even when, as in religion, we are dealing with eternity. Therefore, the concept of order is not, or at least not primarily, a static but rather a dynamic one. It consolidates the three temporal dimensions of past, present and future, which determine its structure and content. Order extends between memory and expectation; these are the poles which determine life within an order. Precisely because the realization of meaning in societies is dependent on time, we must bear in mind the temporal structure of order. This is what Burke did in his powerful formulation of the relationship between order and time. 'Society,' he says in the *Reflections on the Revolution in France,* 'is not a partnership in things subservient only to the gross animal existence of a temporary and perishable nature. It is a partnership in all science; a partnership in all art; a partnership in every virtue, and in all perfection. As the ends of such a partnership cannot be obtained in many generations, it becomes a partnership not only between those who are living, but between those who are living, those who are dead, and those who are to be born.'[8]

Since society exists in time, it must count on the unexpected, just as it can rely on the traditional. It must always be in a position to realize the sense and purpose for which it exists. Under the most favorable conditions, this happens only through a creative reinterpretation of the meaning of the order. Under less favorable conditions, this takes place by routine adaptation to changed inner and outer circumstances. All this means that an ordered social structure must be capable of action. It must be able to plan, to foresee possible action and reaction on the part of the outside world, in short, it must be able to act suitably at all times. Furthermore, it must be able to resolve conflicts within the social body and solve new problems on the basis of the spirit of the order itself.

The concept of order is determined by the interrelation of three elements, which together represent the logic of order. Order presupposes spiritual unity. That means that consensus and loyalty are the conditions necessary for order. This raises two problems which every order must solve. Together, they constitute the structure we believe to be peculiar to every form of order. The first problem is, how can order arrive at the unity and consensus which are its conditions? The answer is, through a system of education and a complex of sanctions. The second problem is, what is required to make the social structures capable of action? The answer appears to be, the establishment of an institution of authority.

These definitions, of course, do not do full justice to social reality. For it is clearly characteristic of this reality that man lives simultaneously on several levels of order, which fact naturally raises the question how these orders are related to one another. For it cannot simply be assumed that the various kinds of order are linked with one another through a generally accepted, hierarchically graduated system of values. Rather, we must assume that the coexistence of a number of systems of order occasions friction and conflict, and that the meaning and purpose of the individual systems of order are anything but in harmony with one another. In other words, the question of the order of orders arises. Since every form of order is self-sufficient, that is, since every order unfolds its own laws and develops its own will to live in relationship to those who live within it, it follows that the various social groups encounter one another in an atmosphere of rivalry and competition. A conflict situation is unavoidable; it brings with it the necessity for finding the means of resolving it. That means, first, making a decision, and second, making the decision effective, so that the parties accept it and submit to it. The situation can be put still another way. Every order has an authority which makes society capable of action. Now, if various orders collide, this means that various authorities come into conflict. The question necessarily arises, how are the various authorities related to each other? Is there a hierarchy of authorities? Is there a final authority? What are its powers? And on what does it base its claim to recognition?

Let us now turn to an examination of the elements of order. Consensus is assent.[9] Assent to the meaning of an order has many aspects. They range from emotional consent, trust or belief, and determination in which the nature and forces of the heart (Gemüt) find expression, to the conscious acceptance of the technical means for guaranteeing the realization of a rational goal. Greater difficulties arise when we try to describe the concept of loyalty. Loyalty is an imponderable which seems to defy conceptual limitation. Loyalty is not resentful submission to a decision on the part of society, with a feeling of having suffered injustice. It is also not an expression of triumph at having had one's way. Let me suggest an analogy. One cannot define democracy as the rule of the majority, but rather as the readiness to accept a decision which might be reached against one's own will, and as the possibility of continuing to voice one's views and convictions because the factual majority may not, by legal means, prevent the formation of a movement directed against its will. Similarly, one can say of loyalty that it is an emotional and spiritual membership in a social structure, in its meaning and order, which does not change even if one's own interpretation of this order is different from that which appears to the other members of the society to be desirable. The test of loyalty is the acceptance of a decision without threatening to destroy the order or to withdraw from the community. Loyalty has something to do with trust, and with the belief that possibly the other side is not entirely wrong, with the knowledge that it, too, wants the best. Conduct is loyal even if it expresses an opinion opposed to the orthodox one; in other words, the loyal citizen needs not maintain silence which might give the impression that he is in agreement. Loyalty takes into account the unavoidable tensions which always appear within the social structure. For the members of a society are never entirely in agreement. Loyalty is whatever serves to balance these tensions. But loyalty undoubtedly has a limit, which is reached when assent must be withheld on the grounds of one's knowledge and conscience. What does sanction mean? We are accustomed to its classical definition in the second book of Justinian's *Institutes* of the *corpus civilis* as those parts of a law which determine punishments for those who violate the law. Sanction is the quintessence of legal consequences which follow the violation of law; it means the protection afforded the order of a society by means of force on the part of the state. Sanction and force are inseparably joined. But this conception of sanction is much too narrow to capture the real essence of sanction. It is very odd that the philosophy of law has so flagrantly neglected the concept of sanction. We are accustomed to understand by the term sanction the totality of deterrent measures which are capable of influencing the social behavior of man. Sanctions represent the protection of order. They consist of a more or less forceful and clear expression of approval or disapproval on the part of society toward anyone who violates the order. Custom and conventional morality, usage and public opinion are forms of sanction, although they change in scope and consistency from place to place and age to age. Sanction includes everything which, in the form of a reaction of his fellow man, serves or can serve to make predictable the attitude and behavior of man as a member of a family, a profession, a class, a people or mankind as a whole. In sanctions, everything is consolidated which is considered right and desirable, proper and useful by all the various social groups.

But we have not yet exhausted the full implications of the concept of sanction. We find sanctions wherever we encounter the innermost motives of human action. The concept of self-determination includes both the concept of freedom and the idea of being determined by the self. This being determined by the self expresses itself through conscience. Of course, conscience assimilates the norms valid in the immediate and general vicinity in order to insure their observance. Admittedly, it can be shaped by proven tradition and convention determined by interest. But its real and essential task is to denounce offenses against oneself. Conscience exercises the function of an authority.

But we must take one more step without which we cannot hope to discover the true source of sanction. The order of a community is not only the order based on force. Nor is it merely the order which is protected by custom and usage, conventional morality and public opinion. Order has a religious foundation. It deduces its validity from its conformity with a divine will and a divine reason. The order of this world appears as an image or an emanation of the order of the next. The verb *sancio* means to sanctify, to make inviolable by religious consecration. Religious sanction lends order a distinction, the consequences of which are of profound significance: religious sanction introduces the aspect of the absolute into the political and social struggle. Through religious sanction, an historically changing structure, conditioned by manifold material interests, is consecrated and thus removed from the realm of intellectual debate. Whatever is by nature unstable and precarious, such as human order which depends on the perception and will of man, will easily succumb to the temptation of consolidating its position by appealing to religious sanction. Institutionalized religion has always been ready to assume this function which promised it considerable influence over the use of political power. From the tenth book of Plato's *Laws* to the eigth chapter of the fourth book of Rousseau's *Social Contract,* the non-believers and unorthodox are cited before a court which punished lapses with banishment, imprisonment and death.

It remains for us to characterize the third and last element which appears to be essential to the concept of order. What does the institution of authority mean? Order, we have remarked, rests on consensus and loyalty. Its protection consists in a system of sanctions which guarantee the predictability of social behavior. Every order is a vital unity, but one which is composed of willing and thinking beings. Such a unity must be capable of action, that is, it must, outwardly and inwardly, represent the whole. This means that it must be provided with an authority which assumes the function of representation in such a way that its decisions demand recognition and acceptance. Authority is a unifying force. But that is only one side of its function. The other side, no less important, consists in resolving those social conflicts which necessarily arise. Wherever and whenever a common will, that is, a system of commandments and prohibitions emerges, it becomes apparent that there is no complex of rules capable of satisfying all the demands made upon it by life in society. Rules are derived from experience. But social experience refers essentially to the past and the present. The future remains a book with seven seals even if imminent problems can be anticipated and a solution for them successfully prepared on the basis of latent social, political and spiritual tendencies within the society. In spite of the uncertainty of the future, humanity is responsible for coming generations. Every system of rules is, *ex definitione,* incomplete. Therefore, there must be some authority to fill these gaps. Every system of rules is, of necessity, abstractly formulated, and thus cannot be justly applied in a large number of specific instances. There must, therefore, be an authority which makes the order applicable by interpreting the spirit where the letter is silent or inadequate. Obviously, such an authority must take on human form. It is one of the undisputed insights of legal and political philosophy that the good society is characterized by the rule of law.[10] Aristotle says in the *Politics* (1287a), that whoever demands the rule of reason seems to demand the rule of God and law, for the law is impassionate reason. Championing the rule of man means introducing the animal part of his nature. But the idolatry of law fails to recognize that the inevitable shortcomings of law and even of impassionate reason make it imperative that man not be ignored, for it is he who must make law, reason and order practicable by interpreting and supplementing them. Plato expressed this aptly in the *Statesman* (294a). Because of the inability of law to encompass what would be most just and proper for everyone and thus to require what would really be best, and because of the great variety and inconsistency of individual people and individual actions, no art of any kind can simply institute something which will last for all times. The inference to be drawn from this fact is that not the laws, but the man endowed with truly royal wisdom (ὁ ἀνὴρ μετὰ φρονήσεως βασιλικός) should have power.

In the 248th of his *Paradoxes*, Sebastian Franck bears witness to the immortality of this recognition. He says, 'No law is ever so good and just that love or distress could not induce it to make an exception.' And Franck goes on to say that one may not imprison reason, the source of all human rights, in the letter of the law, for there are many cases 'in which the letter cannot reach the right decision', so that one must act in accordance with free reason as though there were no code.

The function of authority can only be exercised by man. When a law is applied, an abstract commandment of reason interpreted, or an order made practicable, it becomes a question of selecting the individual who is to carry out these tasks. Reference to general definitions of reason, law and order are of little or no use; the *who* alone is of the utmost importance. At this point, we must consider the last two problems raised by the concept of order. Since man is *de facto* subject to the demands of various kinds of order, competition and conflict must necessarily arise among the various systems of sanctions. Montesquieu once expressed this idea very clearly in the *Cahiers*: 'There are three tribunals which are almost never in agreement, that of the law, that of honor, and that of religion.' Wherever there is competition and conflict, an appeal to authority becomes necessary. But which authority? We do not avoid answering this question when we refer to a hierarchy of authorities such as the judiciary system of courts of appeal. The possibility of appealing a verdict to a higher authority only means that we arrive at the concept of a final authority beyond which no appeal is conceivable. Who, then, is to be the final authority in cases of conflict between systems of order and their sanctions? The second problem is this: if it is true that the authority must be a living individual, someone of flesh and blood, then obviously we must count on his being subject to error and delusion, prone to misusing and misunderstanding his office, and governed by his own subjectivity and the law of his own individual self. We simply cannot avoid having to be prepared for the dangers to which man is exposed even when, or perhaps only when, he tries to determine justice and recognize truth. Although we tend to believe that the final authority coincides with the just decision commanded by reason, and is therefore inherently incontestable and irreproachable, we cannot disregard the fact that every human authority, even the final one, is prey to error, delusion and subjectivity. The necessity of having a final authority in the social structure does not guarantee the rightness of its decisions. This leads to the question of the *de facto* primacy of the possibly fallible final authority. To put it differently, if even the final authority is not exempt from error and delusion, how is the relationship between authorities to be regulated? What rights can a lesser authority, right or wrong, claim with respect to the final authority, right or wrong? These questions are unavoidable. For the decisive conflicts within a society are those among the authorities of the various kinds of orders existing together in a society. Political philosophy, then, is a doctrine of conflicts among orders and authorities.

With this, we have apparently exhausted the questions raised by the logic of order. Before we try to find any answers, let us glance at the realm of the state, which is most likely to cast light on these questions. But first, we must consider some of the consequences of our way of looking at the history and logical structure of political and legal philosophy.

Accepting our threefold structure of the concept of order would obviously not mean that one would then know all about the complex of sanctions and the institution of the final authority. Nor would a decision for or against any given form of the state have been made. For the moment, we only want to point out the laws governing all social structures. The object of our study is not the monarchical, aristocratic or democratic constitution, or the mixture of these three classical forms of the state which Polybius held to be truly prototypal. Nor are we concerned with the modern forms of the state, such as plebiscitary Caesarism or the one-party state with charismatic and later institutionalized and dictatorial leadership (which latter, to be sure, is exposed to repeated struggles for power on the part of rival exponents of various positions). For it is our assertion that all states, without exception, have to deal with problems of the structure of order. All states must come to terms, in some way, with the logic of order. It is wrong to believe that one could neglect one or the other element in favor of the third. To put it another way, political philosophy must always be prepared to encounter the threefold structure of order when dealing with the state. Recognizing the logic of order is not a matter of considering the forms of the state, but of seeing that every form of the state represents a specific encounter with the logic of order; the unavoidable conclusion is that the problem of consensus, the problem of sanction and the problem of authority are dialectically related to one another. If we consider the history of Western political philosophy from the point of view of the structure of order as determined by the three elements of consensus, sanction and authority, we can, without difficulty and without doing violence to historical fact, demonstrate that not every political philosophy has dealt with the totality of these problems in the same way. We could, in fact, employ this tripartition of the structure of order as a principle for categorizing political philosophies, and show that the exclusive concentration on one of the three problems has always had most serious consequences. For it would seem evident that only by taking the totality of these problems into account can we expect to find a solution which does justice to political and spiritual reality. There have been political thinkers whose concern with the problem of consensus has been dangerously one-sided, as, for example, Jean-Jacques Rousseau, to mention the most famous and influential figure of recent times. Jeremy Bentham and Pierre-Joseph Proudhon strongly emphasize the problem of sanction. And for Thomas Hobbes, Joseph de Maistre and Louis Gabriel de Bonald, the problem of a final authority is of such unconditional priority that one might think it the only really crucial problem of political philosophy.

We must inquire into the meaning of this peculiar partiality. The preference shown one problem tends to make the solution of the others dependent on the mastery of the first. Could it be the promise of overcoming the difficulties connected with the other problems which leads to this concession of priority to the first? This sounds very abstract; let us suggest some examples. Hobbes is extremely distrustful of man's voluntary capacity for consensus and loyalty which are, of course, conditions for establishing and, even more, for preserving the community. Man is, to be sure, endowed with reason, but his passions, the will to power and the fear of violent death, impair the unifying function of reason to such a degree that decisions concerning good and evil, justice and injustice, cannot be entrusted to individual reason. The extent of Hobbes' distrust of man, and the contempt in which he held the power of reason in man's psychological economy is evidenced by the admission he makes in the eleventh chapter of the *Leviathan:* 'For I doubt not, but if it had been a thing contrary to any mans right of dominion, or to the interest of men that have dominion, *That the three Angles of a Triangle, should be equall to two Angles of a Square;* that doctrine should have been, if not disputed, yet by the burning of all books of Geometry, suppressed, as farre as he whom it concerned was able.' Thus Hobbes' whole philosophical interest shifts to the final authority, to the political sovereign who alone is invested with the power of ordering the community. But the strange thing is this: how can one consider the individual man capable of suppressing a Euclidian theorem if it were to his advantage to do so, and at the same time believe that the omnipotent sovereign would not commit this offense in as far as it would be to the interest of his 'right of governing'? Hobbes understood very well the importance of spiritual unity for the political community. For this reason he did everything in his power to strengthen the unifying and preserving factors, indeed, to make them the real basis of unity. He did so by making the final authority absolute, hoping that it would submit to the law of reason. There was no guarantee that this would be the case. For who would be able to restrain the 'perpetual and restless desire of power after power' on the part of the sovereign and force him to make reason the law of his actions? Thus, we read in the twenty-sixth chapter of the *Leviathan*: 'That Law can never be against Reason, our Lawyers are agreed; and that not the Letter, (that is, every construction of it,) but that which is according to the Intention of the Legislator, is the Law. And it is true: but the doubt is, of whose Reason it is, that shall be received for Law. It is not meant of any private Reason; for then there would be as much contradictions as the Lawes, as there is in the Schooles; nor yet... An *Artificiall perfection of Reason, gotten by long study, observation, and experience*... and therefore it is not that *Juris prudentia,* or wisedome of subordinate Judges; but the Reason of this our Artificiall Man the Commonwealth, and his Command, that maketh Law.' The rule, *auctoritas, non veritas facit legem,* does not, of course, mean that the sovereign, the final authority, should or could make falsehood and irrationality law; it means that only sovereign sanction can make truth and rationality the binding law in the community. Since Hobbes sought nothing so much as unity in the state, he had to examine the reasons for dissension and discord. Thus Hobbes wrote in *De Cive* (chapter 12, § I): 'Of the doctrines which lead to dissension, the first is that every individual has the right to judge what is good and evil.' For this reason, the citizen of the state may not constitute an authority. For the sake of unity, the sovereign is also entrusted with determining the articles of religion which must be believed or, more precisely, at least outwardly recognized in the community. Something is good or evil, just or unjust, religiously true or religiously false when, and only when, the state, 'Gods vicegerent on earth', declares it to be so. Maistre, Bonald and Comte argued along the same lines. Political philosophy is reduced to a single problem, that of determining the final authority which alone is assumed to be able to safeguard the spiritual unity of the body politic.

For Rousseau, the situation is quite different. Oddly enough, he neglects to deal with precisely this problem of authority. Rousseau is interested in seeking and defining the spiritual unity which alone gives the state the right to exercise physical and moral force. This unity is the general will, which is not only the quintessence of justice but also the embodiment of the general welfare. In fact, it is the concretion of objective reason. Since the general will fulfils these three functions admirably, it must be the fundamental and binding law of the community. The general will presupposes that every citizen, when he reflects deeply enough, without inner reservations and without being influenced by the opinions of his fellow citizens, must, by nature of his reason, recognize the general will as that which he himself really wants and is forced to admit to be useful and right. Objective and subjective reason become identical in the general will. For Rousseau, therefore, virtue is the 'conformity of the particular will to the general will'. One could also say that, in so far as man truly wills, he wills the objectively reasonable. When men join together in a state, they cannot rationally will other than in accordance with the general will. But Rousseau distinguishes between the general will and the will of all. What does he mean by this? In addition to an objective will, man has a subjective will. It is the will conforming to the conditions of the moment, the will expressing the bias caused by the concrete situation, by temporally and spatially conditioned interests. It is reason dimmed by passion and interest which is at work here, not objective reason. This subjective will is the basis of the will of all. For Rousseau, it is not only possible, but quite probable that a conflict must arise in the state between these two wills. Then the state has the right to force the citizen to give up the subjective will in favor of the objective will and to adjust subjective reason to objective reason. That means that the state forces the citizen to be himself. Force on the part of the state means the restoration of objective reason and the objective will in the individual man who has fallen away from both. Force is justified by the fact that it is used only to enforce those things which every citizen really must will, once he has recognized what he truly willed when he made the social contract. If the general will and the will of all are opposed, who can be trusted to know what the general will really is? Assuming that the majority of a people, under the influence of subjective considerations, were to will something which contradicts the general will, who is to be the champion of the general will – the minority, which was unable to get its way? What would happen if someone were to declare himself to be the incarnation of the general will and thus conclude that he is in possession of the truth, as opposed to those who merely express the will of all? It becomes apparent that Rousseau's doctrine cannot answer this question, which, after all, determines whether or not a usurper can come forward in the name of the true will of the people and justify the use of force on the grounds that he only wants to lead the people back to what they are, that is, what they really want.

All modern totalitarian states are founded on the conception that a party and its leader represent the true will of the people. Rousseau's original intention, of course, had been to reconcile the general will as embodied in reason, justice and the general welfare, with the will of all as determined by selfish, changeable, but powerful particular interests. But the process which in fact took place led to the disappearance of the distinction between what is justly and therefore legitimately willed and what merely holds itself to be justly willed; this resulted in the identification of the general will with the will of all. It cannot be denied that this fateful identification determined the development of European political and legal thought and therefore the actual history of Europe.[11] Jacobinism in the age of the French Revolution, plebiscitary Caesarism and the totalitarian state of the 20th century are the result of the fiction of the identity between the general will and the will of all. The true will and the just will have been absorbed by the actual will. Right and might have become one and the same.[12]

In connection with Rousseau, it is well to recall Fichte. In his lectures on *Die Staatslehre oder das Verhältnis des Urstaates zum Vernunftreiche* (1813), Fichte, in Robespierre-like exaggeration, taught that everyone having the knowledge and power to do so had not only the right but the holy duty of 'subjugating [men] to justice by force'.[13] Fichte employs the concept of the tyrant who, since he is also an educator, has the right to force his subjects to knowledge and freedom. He assumes '[an] educator of mankind installed by God Himself in accordance with the law of morality', an educator 'of divine right', whose use of force may extend to knowledge. For 'force is the condition for producing knowledge and acquiring culture'.[14] Obviously, Fichte must consider the question who may be the 'despot (Zwingherr) according to justice' at any given time. Every political being has its rights. And right requires force. 'Anyone can be a despot who has the necessary knowledge and capacity; he does not thereby infringe on the outer or inner freedom of anyone as long as he demonstrates that it is the right which he enforces, and prepares the people to understand the right by educating them. The condition for this is that the concept of right be so clear and offer such strong evidence of its objective validity that its author can, in good conscience, be convinced that education will lead all other men to the same insight.' Force, in short, can only be justified if it is used to bring about what is right. This right may not be based on subjectivity or opinion, but must prove to be true, to be the just right. Whoever is or strives to be a 'tyrant for the right' must demonstrate 'that his judgement concerning the right is accepted as identical with objective right'. The question, then, who has the right to be the sovereign, must receive the answer: 'the highest understanding, and, since this does not exist in time, the best human mind of a time and people'. When this best mind has been found, declares Fichte triumphantly, 'everything is elevated'. But how is it to be found? How can one determine whether a subjective, individual judgement concerning the right coincides with the objective and general judgement concerning the right? The true despot is whoever proves capable of persuading others of objective knowledge. 'But how does he prove that it is not merely his own individuality which he holds to be objective knowledge? Answer: If he succeeds in convincing several persons, in fact, everyone he approaches.' It is the teacher, that is, the philosopher, who is capable of carrying out this process. 'If it is possible for a people to have a rightful sovereign, then this people must have teachers from among whom the sovereign can be chosen or appointed. We have a class at our disposal which does not create itself but develops through the grace of God. (The only thing which truly exists through the grace of God is the common, scientific understanding, and the only outward appearance of this grace is the act of real life, crowned with success.) The selection of the sovereign is left once more to the inscrutable will of God, where it properly belongs, beyond the human will, and this in accordance with the understanding, that is, in the recognition that the limits of the understanding have been reached, and the realm of the absolute, factual and given begins.' Fichte unjustly accuses Rousseau of having used a concept of right in the *Social Contract* which is not *a priori* and founded on reason, but empirical, arbitrary and fictive. For Fichte is, of course, equally incapable of preventing the knowledge of rational right from being dependent on the inner and outer conditions of any given time. Therefore, this knowledge can never be absolute but must always be relative. Fichte accordingly takes refuge in the concept of the best mind of a time and a people. The best mind is that mind 'which best understands the eternal law of freedom in terms of its time and its people'. We are faced with the monstrous fact that a best relative mind may exercise absolute rule over freedom and knowledge. And who is to guarantee that the best relative mind of a time and a people really does manage the affairs of state?

It has become apparent that Fichte is concerned with the elements of the same problems with which we have been dealing, although we are by no means willing to accept his conclusions. For how can the best mind of a time and a people be recognized? And what would happen if there were two or more pretenders to this title? These questions are all the more justified since Fichte admits that that which is right cannot be determined once and for all, because right is conditioned by historical situations which change according to place and time. If it is true, as Fichte asserts, that any given measure can 'never [be] the best one possible', 'but only the best for the time', and if it is true that the conditions of man's social life change in the course of time, then it unavoidably follows that the possibility of a redetermination of just right must remain open. But this redetermination is both a philosophical and a political problem – philosophical because it is part of the nature of philosophy to reflect on justice, political because the mastery of the philosophical task depends on a political order which permits this process of redetermination. Whenever, therefore, the attempt is to be made to determine justice anew, we are dealing not only with a purely theoretical but also with an eminently practical problem. For the old order which once was just and is still considered partially just is protected by power; it is an order which, if it were to lose its justification in the idea of justice, would also lose its right to exercise force founded on this justification. And every new order has the tendency to require observance of its laws as quickly as possible by means of force. Therefore philosophy is dependent on a political order which permits it to do what it knows it should do.

The attempt to give priority in political philosophy to the problem of authority is based on the notion that the final authority is the absolute foundation and guarantee of unity, first, because a single active authority in the community assures the unity of all decisions, and second, because the final authority controls the political instruments of power. But the control over the political instruments of power is, in fact, assured only as long as the individuals entrusted with these instruments can be counted on to carry out the orders and decisions of the final authority because of their acceptance of all the factors functioning as sanctions. This means that the highest authority is dependent on a complex of sanctions, by which, of course, we do not mean only a system of punishments, but all the other kinds of sanctions as well. All religious and moral conceptions contained in the complex of sanctions must be believed; they must be the determining motives of conduct and action. Only then can the final authority succeed in realizing its intention. But all sanctions rely on those factors of the heart (Gemüt) and the will, the mind and the reason which

determine and characterize the realm of consensus and loyalty. Fear of a lack of consensus has always led to the attempt
to conceptualize the principle promising unity as clearly as
possible in material and spiritual symbols. This was done by
making the spirits of peoples into entelechies and substances,
as for example in the works of Montesquieu, Herder and the
historical school of the romantic period. Man was conceived as
having a predominantly physical, psychic or spiritual nature,
the structure of which is objectively definable and measurable.
A criterion was sought from which the community could permit no deviation. But deviations from a rational criterion pre-
suppose something like freedom and self-determination, like
flexibility and instability. And further, it is a fundamental and
essential part of the idea of criterion that it is always subject to
the conditions of being realized. In other words, the idea of a
standard is always realized in a medium, in an intermediate,
that is, through and in man who lives as an individual self under
historical conditions.

We are approaching the end of our study. We began by maintaining that order is a basic concept in political philosophy.
We asserted that three elements of order could be distinguished:
spiritual unity, which is determined by the meaning and purpose of order and expresses itself in consensus and loyalty; the
complex of sanctions, which is entrusted with the protection
and maintenance of order; and authority, which makes society
capable of decision and action. And finally we pointed out that
the state is itself an order which includes within it a multitude
of other forms of order. The last question with which we must
deal is that of the relationship of the state, with its claim to final
authority, to the other kinds of order with the same claim. In
other words, is there a law governing the order among forms
of order which is binding once and for all? There is no such law.
There can be no such law because man is a being subject to
error, delusion and guilt. Man may never assert that he has
recognized justice itself or knows *the* truth,[15] even if he claims,
indeed, must claim final authority for himself, since decisions
must be made if conflicts are to be resolved. The necessity of a

final authority guarantees neither the rightness nor the justice of a final decision. One may find this fact distressing, but it cannot be avoided and cannot be undone. Whoever concludes that a final authority is always just because it is necessary, denies man's self-determination. He establishes a monopoly of the final authority which can only be bought at the price of renouncing the rights of conscience. It does not help to ascribe to man an *a priori* function of reason and to believe that, although this reason is occasionally lacking in the individual man, the reason of the final authority is infallible. The history of political philosophy and its present state speak a clear and unmistakable language. The absoluteness of the final authority was asserted and demanded not so much because the head of the state was believed to be factually infallible, but rather because he seemed to be the best guarantor of the unity of the community. Unassailability is demanded of the final authority because it cancels out the conceivably differing decisions of individual human minds. But one cannot limit individual reason simply because it is capable of both true and false perception, quite apart from the fact that there is no guarantee that Hobbes' all-powerful sovereign, Fichte's despot for freedom, or indeed the modern dictator protected by praetorians and secret police can do no wrong.

What are the consequences? Does the logic of order leave us without counsel? No. The facts we have described lead to necessary, politically definable consequences; the order of the community must be such that its members have, at all times, the inviolable right to redetermine justice through critical analysis of the existing order, and through reflection on what is desirable. That means that, whenever this process is monopolized by a party and its leadership who proclaim themselves the advocates of the true interests of the community, this analysis necessarily ceases, forcing man to give up his right to self-determination; he ceases to be an independent authority. The dividing line can be clearly drawn. For whenever the attempt is made to deny a part of a people the right to decide on spiritual, political and economic matters, and to rob majorities or minorities of the means of expressing their just desires, there can and may be no compromise. But the existence of such an order, which permits justice to be sought in freedom and re-determined in responsibility toward society, is, in view of our study, dependent not on the order itself, but on men who are prepared to create and defend such an order. Order exists because men make its meaning a determining factor of action. Therefore all order is no more than a piece of paper unless it is supported by courage, loyalty, devotion and wisdom. Conflicts, truly tragic conflicts, cannot be avoided. But one can and should attempt to resolve these conflicts with a minimum of human sacrifice and a maximum of respect for the individual conscience.

POSTSCRIPT

This volume combines published and unpublished studies. Since they turn on only a few problems of political philosophy, the author hopes that their inner unity will become apparent. Admittedly, the first and last efforts more closely resemble a sketch than a complete and final statement; that does not necessarily mean that they do not contain a definite and definable point of view. However, there clearly remains much to be done for a political philosophy. Some repetition was unavoidable, since the individual contributions were to be kept in their original form.

The discussions of Burke, Rivarol, Lamennais, Comte and Joseph de Maistre appeared in 1945, 1954, 1948 and 1956 in the *Schweizer Beiträge zur allgemeinen Geschichte,* published by Werner Näf and Ernst Walder. We should like to express our thanks for their kind permission to republish the articles in this volume. The introductory lecture was printed, slightly abridged, in the *Neue Zürcher Zeitung* in 1947. The last two chapters, also lectures, were held in Zurich and at the Freie Universität in Berlin, in 1952 and 1956, and are published here for the first time.

NOTES

I

PHILOSOPHY AND POLITICS

1. *Grundlinien der Philosophie des Rechts,* § 340. Hegel expressed similar views in the *Encyklopädie der philosophischen Wissenschaften im Grundrisse,* Heidelberg, 1817, § 450.
2. *The Writings and Speeches of Oliver Cromwell* by Wilbur Cortez Abbot, Cambridge, 1937, Volume I, pp. 696-699, and *Oliver Cromwell, Briefe und Reden,* translated from the English by Max Stähelin, with an introduction and commentary by Paul Wernle, Basel, 1911.

II

EDMUND BURKE AND
GERMAN POLITICAL PHILOSOPHY IN THE AGE
OF ROMANTICISM

1. Concerning political philosophy of the romantic period in general and Burke's influence in particular, cf. Wilhelm Metzger, *Gesellschaft, Recht und Staat in der Ethik des deutschen Idealismus,* Heidelberg, 1917, pp. 221-223, 234; Paul Kluckhohn, *Persönlichkeit und Gemeinschaft. Studien zur Staatsauffassung der deutschen Romantik,* Halle a. d. Saale, 1925, on Burke, pp. 32-36; Carl Schmitt, *Politische Romantik,* Munich and Leipzig, 1925 (second edition). Also Siegbert Elkuß, *Zur Beurteilung der Romantik und zur Kritik ihrer Erforschung,* Historische Bibliothek, volume 39, 1918, pp. 88, 91-92. – Metzger's and Elkuß's works are not free of error. It must be kept in mind that the German image of Burke is based almost entirely on the *Reflections.* This limitation is hardly permissable even if one restricts oneself to the romantic period, for the *Reflections* were not the only work with which Gentz and Adam Müller were familiar; it is entirely inadmissible if one wants to understand Burke's political doctrine. German intellectual history is still under the spell of the passionate and gigantic portrait which the romantics painted of him. One must examine historically whether this portrait is accurate. This can only be done by taking into consideration all the writings and speeches of Burke in which his social philosophy finds expression. One must also not overlook the fact that the political philosophers of romanticism, like Burke himself, who was a politician, had clear political aims in evaluating historical and social reality. They did, of course, strive for knowledge, but nonetheless had specific political aspirations. Georg von Below therefore called Burke the 'father of political romanticism' in *Die deutsche Geschichtsschreibung von den Befreiungskriegen bis zu unseren Tagen,* Munich and Leipzig, 1924 (second edition), p. 185 (cf. p. 17). –

The entire problem has been dealt with in Werner Näf, *Staat und Politik im Zeitalter der Romantik*, in *Staat und Staatsgedanke*, Bern, 1935, pp. 159-162, where it is also demonstrated that 'romantic realist politics' is an impossibility, p. 165. – Further, Karl Mannheim, *Das konservative Denken, Soziologische Beiträge zum Werden des politisch-historischen Denkens in Deutschland*, Archiv für Sozialwissenschaft und Sozialpolitik, volume 57, 1927, who, insofar as he speaks of Burke (pp. 129-130) fails to recognize that Burke's conservatism is something different from that of his German adherents. – Concerning Burke's knowledge of French conditions and his relationship to French politicians, cf. Stephan Skalweit, *Edmund Burke und Frankreich*, Arbeitsgemeinschaft für Forschung des Landen Nordrhein-Westfalen, Geisteswissenschaften, Heft 60, Cologne-Opladen (no date, appeared 1956). Further, A.M. Osborn, *Rousseau and Burke: A Study of the Idea of Liberty in Eighteenth Century Political Thought*, New York, 1940.

2. The *Reflections on the Revolution in France* are quoted from Burke, *Selected Works*, edited by E. J. Payne, Oxford, 1875, II, p. 185.

3. Novalis, *Blütenstaub*, Aphorism 104. *Works*, edited by Paul Kluckhohn, Leipzig (no date), II, p. 34.

4. Frieda Braune, *Burke in Deutschland*, Heidelberger Abhandlungen zur mittleren und neueren Geschichte, Heft 50, Heidelberg, 1917, deals with Burke's reception in German periodicals and on the part of Brandes, Rehberg, Gentz and Adam Müller. She does not consider Stein, Niebuhr and Novalis, among others. Cf. further Friedrich Meinecke, *Weltbürgertum und Nationalstaat*, Munich and Berlin, 1928 (7th edition), pp. 136 ff.

5. Cf. Erich Botzenhart, *Die Staats- und Reformideen des Freiherrn von Stein*, Tübingen, 1927, pp. 202-225. Further, Gerhard Ritter, *Stein. Eine politische Biographie*, Stuttgart-Berlin, 1931, I, pp. 156ff. 'Stein,' Ritter writes, 'will assume a highly peculiar position between epochs. He had outgrown the tradition of political rationalism of the old style, but never became a romantic or even a disciple of the semi-romantic "historical school". He always remained a son of the 18th century, for whom moral principles and moral improvement were a thousand times more important than the principles of an aestheticizing view of history. He was a practical rationalist who appealed to the "laws of reason and nature" in the same breath with, and with the same emphasis as, he did the "earnest lessons of history" in justifying his policies, and whom no veneration of the unconscious creative forces of a fictive "spirit of the people" could prevent from believing firmly and actively in the "calling" of his own time and person to legislation.' (p. 159). This excellent characterization of Stein's position in the history of ideas can be applied, *mutatis mutandis*, to Burke. The partially quietistic tendency of the organic theory of the state and of the historical school was foreign to him. For that, he was too much of a statesman, who could not accept organic growth in practice. Cf. also Max Lehmann, *Freiherr von Stein*, Göttingen, 1923 (3rd edition), who rather summarily considers the relationship to Burke (pp. 383-384, 407).

6. Freiherr von Stein, *Briefwechsel, Denkschriften, Aufzeichnungen*. Edited at

the request of the German and Prussian Governments and Municipal Councils by Erich Botzenhart, Berlin, 1931 ff., III, p. 617. This volume contains the historical and theoretical works of Stein to which we refer.

7. Niebuhr, *Geschichte des Zeitalters der Revolution*, Hamburg, 1845, I, p. 92. The principles of political philosophy which Niebuhr acquired in the course of his studies of the French Revolution and the ideas which prepared it, are to be found mainly on pp. 207, 211, 214 and 216.

8. Niebuhr, *Kleine historische und philologische Schriften*, Erste Sammlung, Bonn, 1828, p. 97.

9. Thus Georg Kuentzel, *Niebuhrs Römische Geschichte und ihr zeitgenössischer politischer Gehalt*, Festgabe für Friedrich Clemens Ebrard, Frankfurt a.M., 1920, p. 184.

10. Gunnar Rexius, *Studien zur Staatslehre der historischen Schule*, Historische Zeitschrift, volume 107, 1911, on Burke, Rehberg and Savigny, pp. 518-520, 523. Heinrich Ahrens, *Naturrecht oder Philosophie des Rechts und des Staates*, Vienna, 1870 (sixth edition), I, pp. 168-169, depicts Burke as a co-founder of the historical school.

11. Cf. Savigny, *Vermischte Schriften*, Berlin, 1850, I, p. 110.

12. *Reflections*, II, p. 112.

13. This thesis has also strongly affected the social philosophy of Franz von Baader. His treatise *Über das durch die Französische Revolution herbeigeführte Bedürfnis einer neuen und innigeren Verbindung der Religion mit der Politik* (1815) takes up ideas which are not foreign to the *Reflections*. The form which Burke gave to the social contract – the partnership of the living, the dead and the unborn – Baader considered to be particularly fruitful. See Baader, *Sämtliche Werke*, edited by Franz Hoffmann, Leipzig, 1851-1860, VI, p. 70; further, the *Vorlesung über spekulative Dogmatik*, VIII, p. 219. Baader's treatise *Elementarbegriffe über die Zeit als Einleitung zur Philosophie der Societät, Werke*, XIV, pp. 29ff. is deeply indebted to Burke. The corresponding passage is in the *Reflections*, II pp. 113-115.

14. *Reflections*, II, p. 39.

15. Fichte launches an attack on Rehberg's *Untersuchungen* in the *Beiträge zur Berichtigung der Urtheile des Publicums über die französische Revolution* (1793), in the course of which he must have encountered the name and ideas of Burke which Rehberg presents in detail. – In spite of his remarkable agreement with Burke's social philosophy, one cannot speak of a direct influence of Burke on Hegel. Cf. Theodor Haering, *Hegel*, Leipzig and Berlin, 1938, II, pp 335-337.

16. Concerning Humboldt and Burke, see S. A. Kaehler, *Wilhelm von Humboldt und der Staat*, Munich and Berlin, 1927, pp. 148-149. It should also be mentioned that Friedrich Ancillon, the fruitful political writer and teacher of Friedrich Wilhelm IV, and from 1832 on, following Bernstorff's resignation, the foreign minister of Prussia, held political and ethical views which recall Burke. Particularly instructive: *Zur Vermittlung der Extreme in den Meinungen*, 2 volumes, 1828-1831, and *Essais de Philosophie, de Politique et de Littérature*, 4 volumes, 1831-1832, containing a direct reference to Burke, III, p. 223. – Concerning Metternich and Burke's *Reflections*, cf. Heinrich von Srbik, *Metternich*.

Der Staatsmann und der Mensch, Munich, 1925, I, pp. 94-95, 333; of a more recent date is Hans Lang, *Politische Geschichtsbilder zu Anfang des 19. Jahrhunderts (Metternich-Friedrich Gentz- Adam Müller).* Berner Untersuchungen zur Allgemeinen Geschichte, edited by Werner Näf, Heft 14, Aarau, 1944, p. 13. – Of particular interest is Srbik's positive judgement of Ancillon, who was, 'as a Prussian minister, a loyal follower of Metternich', I, pp. 330-331. The *Allgemeine Deutsche Biographie* (I, pp. 420ff.) makes short work of Ancillon.

17. Josef Breuer, *Die politische Wirksamkeit des Kriminalisten Anselm von Feuerbach. Ein Beitrag zur Geschichte der Entwicklung des politischen Denkens in Deutschland,* Halle a. d. Saale, 1905, p. 39.

18. Stahl refers to Burke, in his *Philosophie des Rechts,* Heidelberg, 1856, (3rd edition), I, p. 553, as the 'most powerful and thorough writer of the counter-revolution', and as 'one of the most outstanding political writers of all times' whom we owe an 'immortal book on the French Revolution' (p. 555).

19. Stahl's judgement is close to that of J. C. Bluntschli in the *Geschichte der neueren Staatswissenschaft,* Munich and Leipzig, 1881 (3rd edition), pp. 484 and 487. But Bluntschli rediscovered Burke's 'liberal nature', which the romantics had not seen or had not wanted to see, since they were, in fact, much less interested in Burke's love of freedom than in his inclusion of man in the social structure and in historical context. But one must give both aspects of Burke's thinking their due. The romantics also had little understanding for Burke's anticipation of a liberal colonial policy, magnificently expressed in the powerful speech *On conciliation with the colonies,* out of which the ideas of a federalistic commonwealth were to develop. They saw Burke from an excessively one-sided, continental point of view.

20. Cf. Richard Samuel, *Die poetische Staats- und Geschichtsauffassung Friedrich von Hardenbergs,* Frankfurt a.M., 1925, who discusses extensively the importance of Burke for Novalis' views on the state (pp. 78ff.).

21. *The Letters of B. G. Niebuhr,* edited by Dietrich Gerhard and Wilhelm Norwin, volume II: *1809-1816,* Berlin, 1929, p. 337. This judgement on Müller in the letter to Dore Hensler of October 31, 1812, is not to be found in the *Lebensnachrichten über B. G. Niebuhr,* Hamburg, 1838-1839.

22. Wilhelm Grimm's opinion and Savigny's verdict are expressed in Savigny's letter to Jakob Grimm of October 1, 1810: Adolf Stoll, *Friedrich Karl v. Savigny. Ein Bild seines Lebens mit einer Sammlung seiner Briefe,* Berlin, 1929, II, pp. 56-57.

23. Adam Müller, *Vorlesungen über die deutsche Wissenschaft und Literatur,* Dresden, 1807 (2nd edition), pp. 149-150.

24. This is the interpretation of Franz Schnabel in his *Deutsche Geschichte im neunzehnten Jahrhundert,* Freiburg im Breisgau, 1937 (2nd edition), I, p. 192, who also remarks that Burke's concept of the state is reminiscent of the Aristotelian and Thomistic doctrine of the state.

25. *The Works of the Right Honourable Edmund Burke,* London, 1854-1856, II, p. 79.

26. *Reflections,* II, p. 233.

27. *Reflections*, II, p. 91.
28. *Reflections*, II, p. 92. Charles Parkin, *The moral Basis of Burke's Political Thought*, Cambridge, 1956.
29. Karl Hillebrand, *England im 18. Jahrhundert*, in *Zeiten, Völker und Menschen*, Berlin, 1881, V, p. 55.
30. Heinrich von Sybel, *Burke und Irland*, in *Kleine historische Schriften*, 1869 (2nd edition), II, p. 456.
31. *Reflections*, II, p. 39. The assertion which Robert von Mohl makes in *Die Geschichte und die Literatur der Staatswissenschaften*, Erlangen, 1855, I, p. 256, must be considered one-sided and misleading. Burke is included, along with Carl Ludwig Haller, in the group which 'opposes the state based on law by propounding the inner justification of the *de facto* state'. But this amounts to a failure to recognize the religious and 'natural-rights' basis of the state which characterizes Burke's thinking, by imputing to it the Juvenalian principle of *Hoc volo sic jubeo, sit pro ratione voluntas*. The foundation and justification of the state in and through its factual power may (at least partially) apply to Haller, whose naturalistic theory of power Heinrich Leo calls 'a caricature of Burke's, a translation of Burke's brilliant doctrine into something graspable, wooden and therefore once more untrue'. Quoted from Kurt Guggisberg, *C. L. von Haller, Die Schweiz im Deutschen Geistesleben*, volume 87, Frauenfeld, (no date, appeared 1938), p. 125. – A highly impressive, brilliant description of the nature and reception 'of one of the most curious books ever to be written', of Burke's work on the French Revolution, appears in Georg Forster's *Geschichte der Englischen Literatur 1788-1791*, reprinted in *Georg Forsters sämtliche Schriften* edited by his daughter, with a biographical sketch by G. G. Gervinus, Leipzig, 1843, volume VI (Kleine Schriften, Part 3), above all pp. 77-81. Forster's just appraisal is all the more significant in view of the fact that Forster did not share Burke's negative stand on the Revolution in France. Forster called attention to Burke's idealized interpretation of the exemplary English constitution.
32. *Reflections*, II, p. 109.
33. Friedrich Meinecke, *Die Entstehung des Historismus*, Munich and Berlin, 1936, I, pp. 288ff.
34. This judgement on Burke is to be found in Daniel J. Boorstin, *The Genius of American Politics*, Chicago, 1953, p. 72. Quoted by Hans Kohn, *American Nationalism. An interpretative Essay*, New York, 1957, p. 231. Cf. also Russel Kirk, *The conservative Mind. From Burke to Santayana*, Chicago, 1953. Further, the excellent introduction to the anthology *The Conservative Tradition*, edited by R. J. White, which appeared as volume IV of *The British political Tradition*, edited by Alan Bullok and F. W. Deakin, London, 1950. – Another American work on Burke worthy of mention is Irving Babbitt, *Burke and the moral imagination*, in *Democracy and Leadership*, Boston, 1924. – Henry Thomas Buckle's brilliant portrait of Burke in the *History of Civilization in England*, Leipzig, 1865, II, pp. 154-175, in spite of its admiration for 'the most eminent political philosopher England has ever possessed', turns on the untenable distinction of a pre- and post-revolutionary Burke. This view

depends on the evaluation of the Revolution and its consequences for all of Europe, which Burke considered predominantly under the aspect of war. If one believes that the Revolution clearly represents progress, as Buckle does, and above all hardly considers its messianic and nationalistic desire for expansion, and its establishment of an absolutistic autocracy in the Napoleonic age or treats it as an unessential accessory, then Buckle's thesis becomes at least understandable. – A kind of counterpart to Buckle is the image of Burke which Hippolyte Taine sketches with great eloquence in the *Histoire de la Littérature anglaise*, Paris, 1873 (3rd edition), III, pp. 335-344. Burke appears as the 'champion of a principle', and the identity of the pre- and post-revolutionary Burke is clearly established. 'He has fought nobly for noble causes – against the outrages of power in England, of the people in France, and of individuals in India.'

35. Novalis, *Fragmente und Studien,* edited by Kluckhohn, II, p. 195, and III, p. 244.

36. Adam Müller, *Die Elemente der Staatskunst,* Berlin, 1809, I, p. 51.

37. Savigny, *Vom Beruf unserer Zeit für Gesetzgebung und Rechtswissenschaft,* Heidelberg, 1840 (3rd edition), 14, p. 11.

38. Niebuhr, *Geschichte des Zeitalters der Revolution,* I, p. 214.

39. That this discrepancy was clearly felt in German political philosophy is proved by Joseph Görres' powerful tract *Deutschland und die Revolution,* (1819), in which he says that the 'forming Proteus' has become 'a mechanicus' 'who builds political planeteria'. Since every age should act in accordance with its spirit, 'so he (the mechanicus) should not be confused by stubborn contradiction'. Görres saw the signs of the times more clearly than Adam Müller, who published his treatise *Von der Notwendigkeit einer theologischen Grundlage der gesamten Staatswissenschaften und der Staatswirtschaft insbesondere* in 1819. Görres writes, in the above-mentioned work: 'Religion, which has, for the most part, withdrawn itself into the hearts of men, has, for the moment, ceased to be an important architechtonic principle.' See Görres, *Gesammelte Schriften,* edited by Wilhelm Schellberg and others, Cologne, 1928 ff., XIII, pp. 133 and 135. In this work, Görres had reserved a religious rebirth for a later age. Of course, Görres, too, knew Burke, as shown, for example, by the *Rheinische Merkur* and *Europa und die Revolution* (1822).

40. *Works,* V, p. 153.

41. *Reflections,* II, p. 109.

42. *Works,* III, p. 82. – Alfred Cobban, in *Edmund Burke and the Revolution against the eighteenth Century,* London, 1929, points out that Burke rejected the analogy between the state and the animal organism (pp. 89-91).

43. *Works,* III, p. 86. – Cf. also Eugenio Garin, *Introduzione alla dottrina politica di Burke,* Florence, no date.

44. Burke uses the concept 'artificial' in the same sense as, say, Hobbes in *De Cive,* where he makes the distinction, in the fifth chapter, between the animal 'states' and the states of men. The agreement among men, which leads to the state, Hobbes calls 'artificial' because it is the product of the will and reason.

45. Compare the same idea in Hume's *Essay of the first Principles of Government. The Philosophical Works of David Hume,* edited by T. H. Green and T. H. Grose, London, 1907, III, pp. 109-110.
46. *Works,* III, p. 79.
47. *Reflections,* II, p. 122.

III

RIVAROL AND THE FRENCH REVOLUTION

1. For Rivarol's biography, the reader is referred to the indispensable and excellent work, *Rivarol. Sa Vie, ses Idées, son Talent d'après des Documents nouveaux* by André Le Breton, Paris, 1895. Le Breton is also the first to have utilized Rivarol's notebooks fully.
2. The *Oeuvres complètes de Rivarol* appeared in five volumes in Paris, in 1808. This edition includes writings erroneously attributed to Rivarol.
3. Sulpice de la Platière, *Vie philosophique, politique et littéraire de Rivarol,* Paris, 1802. Quoted by Mathurin François de Lescure, *Rivarol et la Société française pendant la Révolution et l'Emigration,* Paris, 1883, p. 368.
4. H. de la Porte, *Notice sur Rivarol,* Paris, 1829. Quoted by Lescure, op. cit., p. 369.
5. *Correspondence of The Right Honourable Edmund Burke,* edited by Charles William Fitzwilliam and Richard Bourke, London, 1844, III, p. 207.
6. *Pensées inédites de Rivarol,* Paris, 1836, p. 82. The *Maximes et Pensées* of Rivarol included in the various selections of his works are, for the most part, a collection of aphorisms taken from his works. During his life he never published such a collection, and it was not included in the first edition of his writings in 1808.
7. Cf. particularly Mathurin François de Lescure, op. cit., pp. 473ff.
8. Paul Bourget, *Etudes et Portraits,* Paris, 1889, pp. 39-40.
9. Jacques Mallet du Pan, *Über die Französische Revolution und die Ursachen ihrer Dauer.* Translated, with a preface and notes by Friedrich Gentz, Berlin, 1794, p. 5.
10. Mallet du Pan, op. cit., pp. 105-106.
11. Cf. Burke's excerpts and his commentary to Vattel's international law in *The Works of Edmund Burke,* Boston, 1839, IV, pp. 132ff.
12. *Oeuvres choisies de Rivarol,* edited by Mathurin de Lescure, Paris, 1880, II, p. 205.
13. *Mémoires et Correspondence de Mallet du Pan pour servir à l'Histoire de la Révolution française,* collected by André Sayous, Paris, 1851, I, p. 395.
14. *Oeuvres,* I, p. 163.
15. *Oeuvres,* II, p. 108.
16. *Works,* IV, p. 10.
17. Mallet du Pan, op. cit., II, p. 134.
18. *Works,* III, p. 135.
19. *Works,* IV, p. 344; the reference to Islam, IV, p. 434. In our day, it has become the controversial fashion to refer to totalitarian movements as 'Islamism'. Cf., for example, Jules Monnerot, *Sociologie du Communisme,* Paris, 1949.
20. Mallet du Pan, op. cit., II, p. 135.

21. Mallet du Pan, op. cit., I, pp. 179-180.
22. Helvétius, *De l'Homme*, 1773, II, p. 332.
23. Condorcet, *Esquisse d'un Tableau historique des Progrès de l'Esprit humain*, Paris, 1822, p. 205.
24. Condorcet, op. cit , p. 206.
25. Idem., p. 214.
26. Idem., p. 216.
27. Idem., p. 217.
28. Idem., p. 262.
29. Idem., p. 262.
30. Idem., p. 263.
31. Idem., p. 215.
32. Idem., pp. 247-248.
33. *Works,* II, p. 183.
34. *Works,* IV, p. 422.
35. *Works,* IV, pp. 344-345.
36. *Oeuvres de M. de Bonald,* Paris, 1858, III, p. 29.
37. *Oeuvres du Comte Joseph de Maistre,* Lyon, 1857, I, p. 74.
38. *Discours préliminaire,* p. 212.
39. Le Breton, op. cit., p. 249.
40. *Oeuvres du Comte Joseph de Maistre,* Lyon, 1857, I, p. 5.
41. Le Breton, op. cit., pp. 179-180. Rivarol included this criticism of Sieyès, without mentioning the name, in the discourse *De la Souveraineté du Peuple,* published posthumously. Cf. *Pensées inédites,* p. 230.
42. *Discours préliminaire du Nouveau Dictionnaire de la Langue Française,* Paris, 1797, p. 39. We quote this first edition, because the *Discours* usually appears much abridged in the modern selections.
43. *Discours préliminaire,* p. 237.
44. *Pensées inédites,* p. 220.
45. *Oeuvres choisies,* II, p. 122.
46. *Oeuvres choisies,* II, p. 125.
47. Alexis de Tocqueville, *L'Ancien Régime et la Révolution, Oeuvres complètes,* Paris, 1952, II/1, p. 33.
48. *Pensées inédites,* pp. 95-96.
49. *Oeuvres choisies,* II, pp. 127-128.
50. Cf. Burke, *Appeal from the New to the Old Whigs, Works,* III, pp. 424-425, and de Maistre, *Considérations sur la France, Oeuvres,* I, p. 162.
51. *Oeuvres choisies,* II, p. 183.
52. *Oeuvres choisies,* II, p. 184.
53. *Oeuvres choisies,* II, p. 185.
54. *Pensées inédites,* p. 229.
55. *Pensées inédites,* p. 229.
56. *Pensées inédites,* p. 128.
57. *Oeuvres choisies,* II, pp. 186, 182, 185.
58. *Oeuvres choisies,* II, pp. 80-81, 40.
59. *Oeuvres choisies,* II, pp. 72, 83, 138. Also of importance: *Discours préliminaire,* p. 197.
60. *Oeuvres choisies,* II, p. 73; *Pensées inédites,* pp. 100-101, further 71-72, 74-75, 81, 159.

61. *Pensées inédites*, p. 112.
62. *Oeuvres choisies*, II, p. 233.
63. *Discours préliminaire*, p. 188.
64. *Discours préliminaire*, p. 189.
65. *Discours*, p. 191.
66. *Discours*, pp. 195-196.
67. *Discours*, p. 195.
68. *Discours*, p. 199.
69. Sainte-Beuve, *Causeries du Lundi*, Paris, 1852, V, p. 66.
70. *Discours*, pp. 235-237.
71. *Oeuvres de Maximilien Robespierre avec une notice historique, des notes et des commentaires par Laponneray*, Paris, 1840, III, p. 550.
72. *Discours*, p. 192.
73. *Discours*, p. 231.
74. *Discours*, p. 224.
75. *Discours*, p. 225.
76. *Discours*, p. 215. Cf. the *Dialogue entre roi et un fondateur de Religion*, first published by Le Breton, pp. 258-259.
77. *Pensées inédites*, p. 100.

IV

LAMENNAIS' POLITICAL PHILOSOPHY

1. Cf. F. Duine, *La Mennais. Sa vie, ses idées, ses ouvrages d'après les sources imprimées et les documents inédits*, Paris, 1922. This book includes a bibliography. – Waldemar Gurian's *Die politischen und sozialen Ideen des französischen Katholizismus, 1789-1914*, Mönchen-Gladbach, 1929, presents a good analysis. Among the older works, Ernest Renan's brilliantly written appreciation of his Breton compatriot deserves mention, although it is based on the hardly tenable position that Lamennais is of importance only as a man and a stylist. Cf. *Oeuvres complètes d'Ernest Renan*. Edition définitivement établie par Henriette Psichari, Paris, 1948, II, pp. 109ff.
2. It is strange that Lorenz Stein, in his *Geschichte der sozialen Bewegung in Frankreich* (Leipzig, 1850, II, pp. 409ff.), includes Lamennais among the religious communists. Cf. also Charles Gide and Charles Rist, *Histoire des Doctrines économiques*, seventh edition, Paris, 1947, II, p. 602; further Georges Hoog, *Histoire du catholicisme social en France*, Paris, 1942. A comparison between Karl Marx and Lamennais, whom Marx once referred to as a 'catholicizing, politicizing dreamer', would be very instructive. Vid. Marx-Engels, *Historisch-kritische Gesamtausgabe*, Berlin, 1932, VI, p. 10.

V

AUGUSTE COMTE AND JOSEPH DE MAISTRE

1. See R. G. Collingwood's *An Autobiography*, Oxford, 1951. – By the same author: *The Idea of History*, Oxford, 1946.
2. *Catéchisme positiviste ou Sommaire Exposition de la Religion universelle*, Nouvelle Edition, P. F. Pécaut, Paris, 1909, pp. 5-6.

3. Henri Gouhier, *La Jeunesse d'Auguste Comte et la Formation du Positivisme*, volume III: *Auguste Comte et Saint-Simon*, Paris, 1941, p. 333 (note 42). Gouhier also establishes, in his indispensable work, that Comte mentions Maistre's name for the first time in 1824. See also Maxime Leroy's *Histoire des Idées sociales en France*, volume II: *De Babeuf à Tocqueville*, Paris, 1950, pp. 235ff., and volume III: *D'Auguste Comte à P.-J. Proudhon*, Paris, 1954, pp. 84ff.

4. *Considérations sur la France*, Oeuvres du Comte Joseph de Maistre, Lyon, 1857, I, p. 67.

5. *Système de Politique positive ou Traité de Sociologie, instituant la Religion universelle*, Paris, 1851-1854, IV, p. 257.

6. *Soirées de Saint-Pétersbourg*, Septième Entretien.

7. *Lettres à un Gentilhomme russe sur l'Inquisition espagnole*, Oeuvres II, pp. 59-60, 96-99. – But Maistre cannot be accused of inconsistency. He expresses the view that Bossuet should have died after holding his *Sermon sur l'Unité de l'Eglise* in 1681. In 1682, Bossuet had written the *Quattor propositiones cleri Gallicani*, with which, according to Maistre, he made himself guilty 'of incontestable wrongs'. Bossuet 'should have died after giving his sermon on unity, just as Scipio Africanus should have died after the battle of Zama: there are, in the life of *certain* great men, *certain* moments after which they have nothing more to do in this world'. *Lettres et Opuscules inédits du Comte Joseph de Maistre*, Lyon, 1883 (eighth edition), I, p. 380. Bossuet died in 1704.

8. *Politique positive*, I, p. 64.

9. It should be remembered in this connection that Maistre knew Vico. Cf. Elio Gianturco, *Joseph de Maistre and Giambattista Vico. Italian Roots of the Maistre's Political Culture*, Columbia University, 1937.

10. *Appendice général du Système de Politique positive contenant tous les Opuscules primitifs de l'Auteur sur la Philosophie sociale*, Paris, 1854, p. 197.

11. *Politique positive*, III, p. 614.

12. *Politique positive*, III, p. 615.

13. *Philosophie positive*, Paris, 1830-1842, IV, pp. 25-26.

14. *Philosophie positive*, IV, p. 180. Concerning Maistre, also pp. 34, 78, 184.

15. Quoted by Henri Gouhier, *La Jeunesse d'Auguste Comte et la Formation du Positivisme*, volume II: *Saint-Simon jusqu'à la Restauration*, Paris, 1936, p. 309; see also pp. 303, 307-308.

16. *Discours sur l'Esprit positif*, Paris, 1844, § 39.

17. *Philosophie positive*, I, p. 48.

18. *Philosophie positive*, IV, p. 649.

19. Voltaire, *Oeuvres complètes*, 1785, XXI, pp. 264-265.

20. *Philosophie positive*, IV, p. 648.

21. *Politique positive*, I, p. 401.

22. *Philosophie positive*, V, p. 490.

23. *Philosophie positive*, I, pp. 48-49.

24. *Politique positive*, II, p. 267.

25. *Politique positive*, II, p. 272.

26. *Philosophie positive*, I, p. 41.

27. *Discours sur l'Esprit positif*, § 44.

28. *Discours sur l'Esprit positif*, § 45.

29. *Briefwechsel zwischen Friedrich Gentz und Adam Müller*, Stuttgart, 1857, pp. 336-337.
30. Concerning the relationship of the two theocrats to one another, that is, in fact, concerning the almost entire absence of such a relationship, cf. Fernand Baldensperger, *Le Mouvement des Idées dans l'Emigration française (1789-1815)*, Paris, 1924, II, pp. 146-147.
31. *Du Pape, Oeuvres du Comte Joseph de Maistre*, Lyon, 1857, III, p. 163.
32. *Lettres et Opuscules inédits du Comte Joseph de Maistre*, Lyon, 1883 (eighth edition), II, pp. 267-268.
33. *Lettres et Opuscules*, I, pp. 378-379. The emphases are the writer's own.
34. *Lettres et Opuscules*, II, pp. 276-277.
35. *Lettres et Opuscules*, I, p. 322.
36. *Lettres et Opuscules*, II, pp. 277-278.
37. *Joseph de Maistre et Blacas. Leur Correspondance inédite de l'Histoire de leur Amité 1804-1820*. Introduction, Notes et Commentaires par Ernest Daudet, Paris, 1908.
38. *Lettres et Opuscules*, I, p. 323.
39. Francis Bayle, *Les Idées politiques de Joseph de Maistre*, Paris, 1945, pp. 43-44.
40. *Du Pape*, p. 18.
41. *Du Pape*, pp. 17-18.
42. *Du Pape*, pp. 21-22.
43. *Du Pape*, p. 298.
44. *Du Pape*, p. 147. Concerning Maistre's work in general, cf. the spirited, somewhat uncritical work of Constantin Ostrogorsky, *Joseph de Maistre und seine Lehre von der höchsten Macht und ihren Trägern*, Helsingfors, 1932, which gives a good survey of the 19th and 20th centuries' estimation of Maistre. Adolfo Omodeo, *Un reazionario: il conte Joseph de Maistre*, Bari, 1939.
45. Cf. the excellent discussion by Henri Gouhier, *La Jeunesse d'Auguste Comte et la Formation du Positivisme*, volume II: *Saint-Simon jusqu'à la Restauration*, Paris, 1936, pp. 303ff., 307ff., 338, in which he points out the esteem in which Saint-Simon held Bonald. I was unable to obtain Jean Lacroix's book, *Vocation personelle et tradition nationale*, 1942.
46. *Philosophie positive*, V, p. 490.
47. *Politique positive*, II, p. 305.
48. *Politique positive*, I, p. 403.
49. Cf. Charles Maurras, *Auguste Comte*, in: *Romantisme et Révolution*, Versaille, 1928, and Maurras, *La Démocratie religieuse*, Paris, 1921. See also the excellent chapter on Comte in Henri de Lubac's *Le Drame de l'Humanisme athée*, Paris, 1950 (fourth edition). The Jesuit Lubac clearly sees the grave danger of Maurras' position.
50. *Politique positive*, IV, p. 257.
51. *Catéchisme*, p. 376.
52. *Catéchisme*, p. 10.
53. *Philosophie positive*, IV, p. 211.
54. *Appendice général du Système de Politique positive, Préface*, p. 111.
55. *Politique positive*, I, p. 148.
56. *Politique positive*, I, p. 149.

THE IDEA OF ORDER

57. *Politique positive*, I, pp. 126-127.
58. *Discours sur l'Esprit positif*, § 3.
59. *Discours sur l'Esprit positif*, § 8.
60. *Catéchisme positiviste*, p. 79.
61. *Appendice*, p. 180. 'The entire course of this period (the 16th, 17th and 18th centuries) one can justly call revolutionary.'
62. *Appendice*, p. 10.
63. *Appendice*, p. 16. – Charles Maurras, the resolute follower of Comte and blind zealot for the monarchical restoration, for whom the Reformation and the Revolution constitute an inner unity and who sees the Revolution as a necessary consequence of the Reformation, credits Comte with being 'the first critic of the reform movement after Bossuet'. Vid. *L'Ordre et le Désordre. Les 'Idées positives' et la Révolution*, Paris, 1948, p. 32.
64. *Appendice*, p. 53; further, *Philosophie positive*, IV, pp. 49-50. The same argument: *Catéchisme*, pp. 371-372, 375.
65. *Appendice*, p. 54.
66. *Appendice*, p. 54.
67. *Appendice*, p. 184.
68. *Appendice*, p. 182.
69. *Appendice*, p. 196.
70. *Appendice*, p. 41.
71. *Appendice*, p. 207.
72. *Philosophie positive*, VI, p. 692. 'There is, at bottom, nothing real but humanity.' *Politique positive*, I, p. 334.
73. *Discours sur l'Esprit positif*, § 56.
74. *Politique positive*, II, p. 272.
75. *Appendice*, p. 288.
76. *Appendice*, p. 28.
77. *Politique positive*, I, p. 327.
78. Comte also speaks of the 'subordination of intelligence to sociability'. *Politique positive*, I, p. 5. Cf. also Paul Arbousse-Bastide, *La Doctrine de l'Education universelle dans la Philosophie d'Auguste Comte*: volume I, *De la Foi à l'Amour*; volume II, *De l'Amour à la Foi*, Paris, 1957.
79. *Politique positive*, I, p. 134.
80. *Catéchisme*, p. 311.
81. *Politique positive*, IV, p. 225.
82. *Politique positive*, IV, p. 256.
83. *Politique positive*, I, p. 129.
84. *Politique positive*, I, p. 144.
85. Henri de Lubac S.J., *Le Drame de l'Humanisme athée*, p. 265.
86. *Politique positive*, I, p. 327.
87. John Stuart Mill, *Auguste Comte and Positivism*, London, 1882 (3rd edition). Walter Bagehot writes in a similar vein in his famous book, *Physics and Politics or on the Application of the Principle of 'Natural Selection and Inheritance' to Political Society* (1867), when he says that Comte and his followers 'want to organize society, to erect a despot who will do what they like, and work out their ideas; but any despot will do what he himself likes, and will root out new ideas ninetynine times for once

that he introduces them'. Comte recommends the 'rule of a hierarchy – a combination of savants orthodox in science'. 'Yet who can doubt that Comte would have been hanged by his own hierarchy?' Boston, 1956, p. 43.

88. In this connection, cf. the chapter *La Cité des Savants* in Etienne Gilson's *La Métamorphose de la Cité de Dieu*, Paris, 1952; further, F. A. Hayek, *The Counter-Revolution of Science. Studies in the Abuse of Reason*, Glencoe (Illinois), 1952, who analyses Saint-Simon, Comte and their disciples in view of contemporary developments.

89. Henri de Lubac S. J., *Le Drame de l'Humanisme athée*, p. 275. See also the chapter on Comte and Taine in Ernst Cassirer, *Das Erkenntnisproblem in der Philosophie und Wissenschaft der neueren Zeit. Von Hegels Tod bis zur Gegenwart (1832-1932)*, Stuttgart, (no date, appeared 1957), pp. 250ff.

90. Georges Sorel, *Reflexions sur la Violence*, Paris, 1930 (seventh edition), p. 209. – Vilfredo Pareto's *Les Systèmes socialistes*, Paris, 1903, volume II, pp. 205ff., also attacks the ecclesiastical absolutism of Comte's system.

VI

THE IDEA OF SANCTION: BENTHAM AND PROUDHON

1. Vid. David Baumgardt's monograph, *Bentham and the Ethics of Today*, Princeton, New Jersey, 1952.

2. Jeremy Bentham, *The Limits of Jurisprudence defined. Being Part Two of An Introduction of the Principles of Morals and Legislation.* Now first printed from the Author's Manuscript with an Introduction by Charles Warren Everett, New York, 1945, p. 152.

3. Bentham's *Handbook of Political Fallacies*. Revised, Edited and with a Preface by Harold A. Larrabee, Baltimore, 1952, is a welcome supplement to our knowledge of this English social reformer. The first edition appeared in 1824.

4. *De la Justice dans la Révolution et dans l'Eglise*, Paris, 1858, volume I, p. 3.

5. *De la Justice dans la Révolution*, volume III, p. 500.

6. Op. cit., III, p. 495.

7. Op. cit., III, pp. 511-512.

8. Op. cit., III, p. 513.

VII

THE IDEA OF ORDER
AS A PROBLEM OF POLITICAL PHILOSOPHY

1. Cf. Heinrich Weinkauff's lecture *Über das Widerstandsrecht*, Juristische Studiengesellschaft Karlsruhe, Heft 20, Karlsruhe, 1956.

2. Heinrich Rommen, *Die ewige Wiederkehr des Naturrechts*, Leipzig, 1936, pp. 229-230. Further, Hans Nef, *Gleichheit und Gerechtigkeit*, Zurich, 1941; Gallus M. Manser O.P., *Das Naturrecht in thomistischer Beleuchtung*, Freiburg in der Schweiz, 1944; Hans Ryffel, *Das Naturrecht*, Bern,

1944; Helmut Coing, *Die obersten Grundsätze des Rechts. Ein Versuch zur Neubegründung des Naturrechts,* Heidelberg, 1947; Carl J. Friedrich, *Die Philosophie des Rechts in historischer Perspektive,* Berlin-Göttingen-Heidelberg, 1955, pp. 110ff. For a recent critique of natural right, see Hans Kelsen, *Was ist Gerechtigkeit,* Vienna, 1953. This is, of course, by no means an exhaustive list of references.

3. Karl Löwith, *Die Dynamik der Geschichte und der Historismus,* Eranos-Jahrbuch, volume XXI, Zurich, 1953; Karl R. Popper, *Misère de l'Historicisme,* Paris, 1956, as opposed to Theodor Litt, *Die Wiedererweckung des geschichtlichen Bewusstseins,* Heidelberg, 1956. Further, Carlo Antoni, *Il Storicismo,* 1957.

4. Cf. Hans Welzel, *Naturrecht und materiale Gerechtigkeit,* Göttingen, 1951.

5. *Über den Zweck der Zeitschrift für geschichtliche Rechtswissenschaft,* 1815. Reprinted in *Vermischte Schriften von Friedrich Carl von Savigny,* Berlin, 1850, volume I, p. 113.

6. It is very characteristic that Otto Gierke, in his well-known lecture on *Die historische Rechtsschule und die Germanisten,* Berlin, 1903, completely fails to do justice to Thibaut's position.

7. In our context, cf. the fundamental works of Rudolf Smend, *Verfassung und Verfassungsrecht,* Munich and Leipzig, 1928; Dietrich Schindler, *Verfassung und soziale Struktur,* Zurich, 1932; R. G. Collingwood, *The new Leviathan or Man, Society, Civilization and Barbarism,* Oxford, 1942; Ernest Barker, *Principles of Social and Political Theory,* Oxford, 1951. For a discussion of the broader context in terms of the history of ideas, see Frederic Watkins, *The political Tradition of the West. A Study in the Development of Modern Liberalism,* Cambridge (Mass.), 1948; further, Walter Lippmann, *The Public Philosophy,* London, 1955; Alfred von Martin, *Ordnung und Freiheit. Materialien und Reflexionen zu Grundfragen des Soziallebens,* Frankfurt a.M., (no date, appeared 1956), particularly pp. 29ff. Werner Maihofer, in his work, *Vom Sinn menschlicher Ordnung,* Frankfurt a.M., 1956, approaches these questions in another way.

8. Franz von Baader, under the influence of Burke, understood the relationship between time and society. Cf. *Elementarbegriffe über die Zeit als Einleitung zur Philosophie der Societät und der Geschichte. Franz von Baaders Sämtliche Werke,* edited by Franz Hoffmann, Leipzig, 1851, volume XIV, pp. 29ff. See also Gerhart Husserl, *Recht und Zeit,* Frankfurt a.M., 1955.

9. Guglielmo Ferrero, *Pouvoir. Les Génies invisibles de la Cité,* New York, 1942, p. 155. Also German: *Macht,* Bern, 1944.

10. For example, compare the antithetical works of F. A. Hayek, *The political Ideal of the Rule of Law,* Cairo, 1955, and Georg Cohn, *Existenzialismus und Rechtswissenschaft,* Basel, 1955. For a general discussion of the entire complex of problems, cf. also Josef Esser, *Grundsatz und Norm in der richterlichen Fortbildung des Privatrechts,* Tübingen, 1956.

11. Cf. Lord Eustace Percy of Newcastle, *The Heresy of Democracy. A Study in the History of Government,* London, 1954.

12. Concerning Rousseau, compare the antithetical discussions of J. L. Talmon, *The Origins of Totalitarian Democracy,* London, 1952, and

Friedrich Glum, *Jean-Jacques Rousseau: Religion und Staat. Grundlegung einer demokratischen Staatslehre*, Stuttgart, 1956.

13. *Johann Gottlieb Fichtes sämtliche Werke*, edited by J. H. Fichte, Berlin, 1845, volume IV, p. 436.
14. Op. cit., p. 440.
15. See also Fritz Medicus, *Das Mythologische in der Religion*, Erlenbach-Zurich, (no date, appeared 1944); Henri Miéville, *Tolérance et Vérité*, Boudry-Neuchâtel, 1949, and Gustav Mensching, *Toleranz und Wahrheit in der Religion*, Heidelberg, 1955. Further, Ernst Gerhard Rüsch, *Toleranz. Eine Theologische Untersuchung und eine aktuelle Auseinandersetzung*, Zollikon-Zurich, 1955.